MA HAIDE The Saga of American Doctor
George Hatem in China

MA HAIDE The Saga of American Doctor George Hatem in China

Sidney Shapiro

Cypress Press
San Francisco

First Edition   1993

Published by Cypress Press
3450 Third Street, Unit 4 B,
San Francisco, CA 94124
USA
ISBN 0-934643-01-6

Printed in Singapore

CONTENTS

CONTENTS

ACKNOWLEDGEMENTS

Many persons contributed to the making of this book. I express gratitude to a few very busy friends who took the time to read the manuscript and offer editorial advice:

Huang Hua, former Chinese Ambassador to Canada, China's Chief of Mission at the UN, and later Chinese Minister of Foreign Affairs. He was a young interpreter in 1936 when he met George Hatem, who had not yet acquired the name Ma Haide.

Zhang Wenjin, who later became China's ambassador to the United States, knew Ma Haide since 1947 in Yanan.

Wu Weiran, Chief Surgeon of the Beijing Hospital, became both his doctor and intimate friend in the seventies.

Israel Epstein, presently Chief Editor of *China Today*, was a war correspondent representing the *New York Times* when he met Ma Haide in Yanan in 1944.

Ruth Weiss, Viennese-Chinese and linguist extraordinary, knew George Hatem since 1933 in Shanghai....

I thank also his numerous colleagues and friends, from East and West, who submitted to interviews and assisted generously.

I am particularly indebted to Zhou Sufei (pronounced "Sue" "Fay"), George's wife and loyal companion during forty-eight years of marriage, who provided not only the framework for the book but invaluable details and insights.

Needless to say, none of the above can be deemed to endorse my views or bear any responsibility for my errors.

PROLOGUE

Membership in the Chinese Communist Party is not the sort of thing one would have predicted for the American son of immigrant Maronite Catholics from Lebanon. But the metamorphosis was, in a way, inevitable. Travelling to Shanghai in 1933 as a young doctor fresh out of medical school, he intended only a short stay picking up experience in the tropical and venereal diseases with which the port city was rife. The sufferings of the people and the horrors he saw soon drove him into the arms of the resistance, first as a sympathetic helper, then as a full participant.

He was sent to Yanan—"cradle of the revolution"—deep in the hinterlands of the beleagured Liberated Areas. The first foreign doctor to arrive, he treated peasants and soldiers and members of the top leadership, dressing wounds at battle fronts and setting up a medical network. In Yanan he married a beautiful actress, acquired the Chinese name "Ma Haide", and joined the Communist Party. Unofficial greeter and volunteer guide to the "liberated areas", he helped foreign visitors—from journalists to the US Military Observers Group irreverently labelled the "Dixie Mission"—better comprehend China's amazing new social experiment.

After the People's Republic was established in 1949, Ma Haide was appointed Advisor to the Institute of Dermatology and Venereology in Beijing. His talents as doctor and medical administrator flourished while China moved from one shattering development to the next—Land Reform, the Korean War, the anti-Rightist campaign, the Great Leap Forward, the Communes, the Cultural Revolution—events in which he was deeply involved. An entry in the forties in his Communist person-

1

nel record by the fanatic head of Party Security smearing him as a "suspected foreign agent" severely limited his political activites and affected his professional status.

But he never lost faith in China's future, and pushed on with his pioneering medical reforms. His achievements in leprosy, venereal diseases and public health were internationally hailed as unique, as comparing in importance with the eradication of yellow fever and the bubonic plague!

"Dr. Ma" lived and worked with a gusto, a brio, that charmed Chinese and Westerners alike. He knew more about New China than any living foreigner. Journalists, medical specialists, international figures, sought him out in China and lionized him when he went abroad. A superb "diplomat without portfolio", he created reservoirs of good will at a time when China was being harried and boycotted by the West.

Ma Haide, George Hatem, was an integral part of China's crucial half-century from the thirties to the eighties. He participated in the unprecedented changes from feudalism to a closed Soviet-type socialism to an era of reform and opening to the outside world called "socialism, Chinese style". His personal story, fascinating in its own right, is at the same time an inside view of the revitalized great Asian Dragon, reflecting the triumphs of New China and probing the causes of its failures. For this reason famous writers and film makers begged to be allowed to record Ma Haide for posterity. But he was always "too busy" with matters he considered much more important—world health and harmony.

We were close friends for the last forty years of his life, and I knew him better that most. Although he seldom spoke about his past, from what he himself told me, from what others recollected, and from what I personally witnessed, after his death I was gradually able to piece it together. I have put it all down in this biography—the remarkable saga of a remarkable man, Ma Haide, George Hatem, and the milieu in which he lived.

NEW AMERICA, OLD CHINA

His father, Nahoum Hatem, came to America from Beirut in 1896 at the age of 14 with a group of other Maronite Catholic Arab teen-agers. They had been indentured by a Lebanese contractor to work for five years, first slicing sugar beets, then in a woollen mill, in Lawrence, Massachusetts, until the cost of their passage was paid off. After completing his stint in the mill, Nahoum enlisted for five years in the Army and obtained U.S. citizenship. Then, in 1908, silver dollars from his discharge bonus jingling in his pocket, he returned to Lebanon.

He rode slowly on a spirited horse through the streets of Hammana, his home town, looking for a bride to bring back to America. Peering over the low courtyard walls lining the road, finally he found her. Fair-complected, with lusterous black hair and dark eyes, she was charming as she sat quietly embroidering in the garden. He tossed a silver dollar into her lap. She glanced up and saw a dashing fellow with a fine mustache and curly hair, boldly staring at her, and she blushed.

From then on, events moved quickly. Her name was Thamam Joseph. Nahoum called on her parents, who came originally from the neighboring village of Bahannes. Like Nahoum, they too were Maronite Catholic Arabs. He begged for their daughter's hand in marriage. Since the young man was a "well-to-do American" of good character, consent was soon granted. The happy couple were wed in a Maronite church, and sailed off for Lawrence, Massachusetts.

After a brief period in Lawrence, they moved to Buffalo, New York where, on September 26, 1910, George was born. His parents spoke Arabic to each other, and at home they called

3

him Shafik. Sister Shafia was born in 1912, Freda in 1914, and Joseph in 1915.

That same year, 1910, Nahoum's brother—another George —arrived in America from Lebanon and married Ma Haide's mother's sister Zmurad, then also living in Buffalo.

"It was kind of funny," Dr. Hatem recalled. "George was my uncle because he was my father's brother, but also because he was married to my mother's sister. And Zmurad was my aunt because she was my mother's sister and also because she was married to my uncle George. They produced four children —Theresa, Martha, Amelia and Ernie, who were, in a sense, doubly my cousins. Our two families, maybe because we were so closely interwoven, were always very devoted."

Things went fairly well for a while. Little George's parents —whom he called Mom and Dad, were a handsome pair. Thamam's soft beauty, Nahoum's bold good looks, his wax-tipped mustache, were a joy to behold. They were a loving family. The children were kissed and hugged a lot. The warm, emotional atmosphere of George's childhood permanently shaped his temperament. He felt deeply, though he covered it with an insouciant air.

By the twenties, times were hard in Buffalo. Nahoum, unemployed for several years, took whatever short-term jobs he could find—from brass foundryman to carpenter. The Hatems sank deeper into poverty. The children were under-nourished. Thamam fed them with batches of round flat breads she baked once a week in a home-made oven, filling the breads with white beans, and sometimes olives — when she could get them. Because she needed coal for the baking, George would go with the other poor kids and pick clinkers near the railway station until the yard detectives chased them away.

"It was a little scary," he said, "but I liked the excitement."

His illiterate parents, like so many other immigrants, were determined to give their children an education. George started primary school in 1916 at the age of six. Run by Maronite Catholic priests, nuns and brothers, it was called St. John Maron's School, and discipline was very strict. The teaching was in English, but George also learned to read and write a little Arabic. He still remembered a few phrases in later years.

"Each morning I set out in a cut-down old suit of Dad's and a pair of second-hand shoes," George said. "They were girl's shoes, which he had bought because they were the cheapest he could find. I refused, in horror and indignation, to wear them. I knew the other boys would tease the life out of me, but Mom and Dad insisted. I didn't want to hurt their feelings, so I would leave the house with the shoes on. But the moment I was out of sight I would hide them beneath the platform of a nearby warehouse and put on my old tattered pair which I had concealed in my schoolbag. I would reverse the process on the way home. Dad often complimented me on having kept the girl's shoes in such excellent condition."

Although the Hatems had to watch their pennies, George was inherently cheerful and optimistic. The boys he played with were children of other immigrants living in the same neighborhood. They fought and wrestled, Blacks and whites, Christians and Jews, quite unconscious of the racial and religious prejudices bedevilling their parents.

"I don't remember being particularly depressed by our poverty," George said. "All my schoolmates were just as poor, and kids can ususally find ways to create their own pleasures. A few of us agreed to sweep out the local movie theatre every day after school in exchange for being allowed to watch the next performance. I fell in love with Alma, the young lady who played the piano accompaniment to the silent films. I thought she was beautiful—slim and blue-eyed and blonde, like the Good Fairy I read about in my storybooks."

The boys found a silver dollar someone had dropped beneath a seat, and squabbled over who should have it. The noise brought the manager out. He settled the argument by announcing the coin was his and coolly walking off with it. George was furious at this injustice. He laughed when he told me about it, and said Marx or Mao would probably have called it his "first encounter with the perfidy of the monied class"! At the time to George it was yet another proof of the unreasonableness of the adult world.

Nahoum got a job in the Lackawanna plant of the Bethleham Steel Mill, and they moved to Lackawanna, New York. George transferred to P.S.3, subsequently named Roosevelt Primary. His father gradually worked himself up to the position of foreman, but the plant went on strike and he was fired. Once again the Hatems were broke.

During the 1918 epidemic the whole family came down with influenza. They lived on food brought by local charities and neighbors. But there was a positive side to this disaster. An old family practitioner attended all the immigrant families in their area. Very poor himself, he never asked for money. People repaid him with a little of whatever they had in the house. He gave the children candy, nuts and the like, and saw the unemployed through all kinds of illnesses and injuries. He remained George's lifelong hero. The boy decided some day to be a doctor like him.

"Though I must admit," George recalled with a grin, "at the age of eight that was not the only reason I had for wanting to practise medicine."

The flu had given him emphysema from a chest infection. In the charity hospital the overworked interns were quick and crude. After freezing his skin with ethyl chloride, which didn't really kill pain, they would poke in a drain very roughly and leave it there.

"Maybe if I become a doctor I can do the same thing to them!" George thought darkly.

Lackawanna was a grimy smoke-filled milltown. Thamam's plump face was becoming care-worn. Although Nahoum managed to retain a dapper appearance in spite of his threadbare clothes, illness, poverty and worry were making him irritable. They lived upstairs in a dilapidated wooden frame house which swayed a little in the wind. There seemed no end of petty squabbles.

George was bored by P.S.3's dull teaching methods. His quick mind was generally far ahead of the lectures, and he couldn't be bothered to do his home work regularly, or make an effort on the tests. This, plus the unhappy family atmosphere, brought out an obstreperous streak. He was disobedient, he got poor marks in school. Beatings with a strap on the backside, and even on the soles of the feet, Arab style, did nothing to improve his disposition. Weeping, he would bury his face in Thamam's soft bosom.

"We love you, Shafik." she would whisper in Arabic. "Be a good boy."

But George, beset with growing pains, couldn't seem to change. Nahoum was called into the principal's office and persuaded to send him to a Maronite reform school in Buffalo run by Father Baker, a fanatic disciplinarian.

"Even today, years later, people still scare their kids by saying, 'If you don't behave we'll send you to Father Baker's,'" George remembered.

He went at the age of ten for about a year. There was a some classroom teaching in the mornings. In the afternoons, the children learned a trade—and the school made a profit selling the things they made. George's trade was printing. The school was dim and smelly, and so, it seemed to George, were the teachers.

"Kids couldn't really be kids in such a place," he said. "When you first came the older boys would set you up to fight the others, one by one. Who you could lick, who you couldn't, determined your status. That's where I learned to fight. It was one way I could work off some of my resentment. The teachers seemed to enjoy hitting us."

After a year he told his father, "If you don't take me out of here, I'll run away. They beat you all the time."

Nahoum brought him home.

"Why can't you behave?" he demanded. "It's so much better here than in the old country. Be grateful for what you've got, try to improve yourself."

"I just don't like being pushed around," George muttered.

His parents insisted that he attend the regular sevices in the Maronite Catholic church, hoping this would have an edifying effect. They led him in, washed spotless and wearing his best suit with its short pants, shod in new leather shoes over long black stockings. He was a nice-looking boy—curly black hair, large expressive eyes under heavy dark brows, regular features, his white teeth flashing in a quick smile.

George at first was enchanted by the lovely colors shining in through the rose window, and the harmonious singing of the choir. He even became an altar boy because he admired the attractive surplices the boys were allowed to wear. He also joined the choir and developed a love of singing. Thamam and Nahoum were very pleased. But George never became religious, and his enthusiasm for church attendance soon wore off. He had a vague belief in God, picturing Him as a benevolent old gentleman with a long white beard, who kept an eye from Heaven particularly on adults, and occasionally on children, down on earth below.

By 1923, George had finished grade school. The family couldn't afford to support four children, so they sent him to live with a Lebanesse merchant friend in Greenville, North Carolina. Greenville was very different from Lackawanna. There were trees and flowers everywhere. The weather was warmer, the pace slower. People were courteous, spoke with a gentle drawl.

There were other differences as well. Accustomed to the free and easy playing and brawling of kids of various ethnic origins in the North, George was taken aback to see white boys knocking down colored children returning home from school. He couldn't understand the contempt and hostility on the part of the whites, and he instinctively reacted against it. Though he was years from having any political concepts, "unfairness" angered him, then and always.

The Lebanese merchant undertook to put George through high school in exchange for work in his general store evenings and on Sundays. A stern Maronite, he had several children like George doing all the cleaning, cooking and housework. He was another tyrant, and George hated him from the start. As a teen-ager he never had time for baseball, basketball, football, or any other sport. George's days consisted of classes, store and homework. If the children played after school they were scolded or beaten.

"I was a good student in high school because I was never allowed to do anything but study," George said. "I finished at the top of my 1927 graduating class, and was chosen to deliver the valedictory address. The WASPs were quite upset because I was named valedictorian, instead of the girl 'of good family' they were rooting for."

His parents had moved to Greenville in 1924, where Nahoum opened a haberdashery store. It did fairly well, but the Hatems felt it would be an extravagance to buy a pair of light flannel trousers which George needed for the graduation ceremony but would have little occasion to wear otherwise. He had to borrow a pair. Inwardly humiliated, it gave him considerable satisfaction to think, as he looked down at the sprucely dressed boys in the audience, "You may be wearing your own pants, but I'm the one making the valedictory speech!" He vowed to himself that some day he would earn enough money to be able to hold his head up with the best of them.

"We were regarded as foreigners, Catholics, or Jews. Lebanese were generally lumped with the latter. Our black hair made suspect," George recalled. In the South while Blacks were openly discriminated against, immigrants and their children were treated with veiled prejudice.

"Sure, we went to school with the white Protestants, but we

never mixed socially. Even when I was asked to go to their homes to tutor kids who weren't doing well in school their parents made it plain I had to leave right after the lesson. I tutored because I needed the money, but I never liked those people. From what I saw of them I didn't think they had anything to be stuck up about."

In Greenville high school George also had his first impressions of China. One of the issues of a magazine used for teaching civics and current events was devoted to that exotic land. It told how the warlords were fighting each other, and printed two rows of their pictures. Most of the children liked Feng Yuxiang because he was known as the "Christian General", although it was rumored he frequently baptised his troops with a firehose. The pupils had to do an essay on the Chinese. George favored leaving them alone and letting them solve their own problems.

In his church, as in others, collections were made for "the starving Chinese". That was all he knew about China then. It seemed very far away. Never in a million years would he have dreamed that he would spend most of his life in China.

His education broadened, in more ways than one, when he went to college. He attended the University of North Carolina at Chapel Hill. It was quite liberal—for the south. He took a straight B.Sc. course because he wanted to go on to medicine. Apart from the little help his family could give, he worked his way—waiting on tables weekdays, which paid for his food, and selling shoes in a dry goods store Saturdays for extra income. He took no holidays at all and cut college time down a year by continuing in school every summer.

At Chapel Hill again he encountered discrimination, though more covert than it had been in high school. He was attracted to long-distance running, but the coaches recommended wrestling, which was considered a "foreigners'" sport. He could sense he was being sized up at the college entrance interview by seemingly innocent questions. "What color tie do you prefer?" "Who is your favorite baseball player?" The answers, he suspected, were taken as indications of the student's background and values.

Dormitories were allocated according to family names. Assumed to be Jewish, he was assigned a room with a boy called Harry Schwartz. The fraternities never approached him, except for one Jewish club. They said it didn't matter when he told them he was born a Maronite Catholic. But he had to decline. He couldn't afford to keep pace with their well-to-do membership.

Perhaps because they both suffered from discrimination, George was always closely associated with Jews and had many Jewish friends. When he decided to pursue his dream of becoming a doctor he discovered there was an unspoken quota at that time in American medical colleges against Jews, Blacks and children of immigrant parents. The only medical school which would accept him was the one in the American University in Beirut, Lebanon. Mom and Dad were happy that their Shafik would be returning to the old country as a "scholar". They gave him letters to relatives and friends, urging that he be received with suitable warmth and deference.

In Beirut in 1929 George met Robert Levinson and Lazar Katz, also from the States, two Jewish boys who were to become his close friends and professional associates. "Katzie", a volatile green-eyed redhead, was in interesting contrast to "Rob"—tall, slim and sophisticated. Tuition and living expenses were much cheaper in Lebanon than in the States, and the university, a Rockefeller institution, rated high.

It was also happily free of racial and religious prejudice. George did well in school, joined the basketball team, and had the beginnings of a social life. Though he was welcomed in Maronite Christian homes, Arab girls—Christian or Muslim —were not allowed to go out with American bachelors. But George had little trouble in finding dancing partners at the Saturday night parties thrown by one or another segment of the foreign colony. His olive-complected good looks and his jocular manner brought him frequent invitations.

He loved moving in rhythmic coordination with the music, and the feel of a healthy young girl in his arms—a fondness for which never left him. But he was too innocent to know as a rule when his charm was producing a response, and too shy to press his advantage when he did.

In 1931 he and Katzie and Rob Levinson transferred to the University of Geneva to complete their medical studies. For one thing, it had excellent hospital intern training conditions. For another, in Geneva a few wealthy Jewish friends of the Levinson and Katz families could be depended on for frequent good dinners. The Jewish boys would bring George with them.

"That's the least we can do," Rob said. "In Beirut you were

always taking us along to visit your Arab friends."

They introduced him as their "Sephardic" classmate. Since the Sephardis are Middle Eastern Jews, and George clearly bore signs of his Middle Eastern heritage, the deception worked for a while until the boys broke down and confessed, and everybody laughed.

Despite a heavy school program, the trio managed to cram in a variety of extra-curricula activities. They swam, climbed mountains, skied, went on bicycle tours and, on Saturday nights, danced—George's great obsession. The magnificent scenary both stimulated and soothed him. He had become fluent in French, and loved meeting and talking with people. George blossomed out. He felt more relaxed, more mature. There was a Belgian girl, also a medical student, he thought he was in love with, but the affair petered out and died of its own accord. They remained friends, and corresponded for a year or two afterwards.

It was not all fun and games, however. The young medics were becoming increasingly aware of the tensions building in America and Europe. Millions were unemployed. The whole world was in the grip of a severe depression. President Roosevelt ordered the closure of U.S. banks. America went off the gold standard. Hitler was named German chancellor and given dictatorial powers. Opposition parties were dissolved in Germany, strikes banned, and all aspects of economic, cultural and religious life brought under government and Nazi party control. Systematic persecution of Jews began. Only in the Soviet Union were some efforts being made to bring about social and economic reform. But the measures introduced were clumsy, impractical, with disasterous results.

Throughout Europe repressive regimes fought to retain their grip. In Switzerland, troops shot up a demonstration of the unemployed. George and his classmates worked all day on the wounded in their university surgery. In their boarding house they met so-called "perennial students"—revolutionary exiles from fascist Hungary and Bulgaria who sold newspapers like *Drapeau Rouge*, published by the Swiss Communist Party.

Lazar Katz had a brother in the USSR, which many young people then considered the hope of the world. At one time George thought about leaving medical school and going with Katzie to work in Moscow. Though he had neither the money nor a strong enough desire to carry this out, George was indignant at the outrages being committed in so many lands. He wanted to fight. The question was how?

In 1933, with graduation approaching, the future doctors had long discussions on what their next step should be. Where should they go? The U.S. was in the grip of a depression. Why not spend a little time first in another country, acquiring experience? Surely conditions would change in America in a year or two. The fact was they found the freedom of living abroad pleasant, and often exciting. They were in no hurry to go home.

Where, then? George proposed China. Besides being fascinated by what he had heard of the "mysterious" East, he believed that Shanghai, a great seaport harboring ships and sailors from all over the world, would present opportunities to treat with every ailment imaginable. His thesis had been entitled *Le Wasserman Irreductible*, and he was particularly interested in venereal disease. Rob and Katzie enthusiastically supported the idea.

They sailed from Europe directly to Shanghai and opened a clinic in the Continental Bank Building on Kiukiang Road, in what then was still the International Settlement. England, France and Japan enjoyed "extra-territoriality" in designated areas of Shanghai and other Chinese cities. They had their own laws, their own courts, and their own police.

George's first impressions of Shanghai was that everyone was in a great hurry, and there were tall buildings and buses and trolleys. That was similar to any big city in the West.

In many ways Shanghai was a foreign metropolis. Residences were in the shoddy European style of the century before, except for a few new elegant apartment houses in the French Concession. Street signs were in both English and Chinese. Bubbling Well Road, Avenue Joffre... were known to the local residents by the way their ear heard the foreign pronunciation. (Bus conductors announced Petain Road as "Bei Dong Lu".)

St. John's University, an American institution, bordered on Jessfield Park, established by the British. A sign at the entrance to the park read "No dogs or Chinese allowed". Turbanned Sikh policemen controlled traffic. European food and dress were popular. Movies were mainly Hollywood creations. There were even dance halls where charming partners were available for a set fee per dance. On the outskirts of the city riding stables and a large golf course offered healthful recreation to the tired executive.

But there the foreign resemblance ended. Many people rode in pedicabs or rickshaws. The first was a tricycle with the driver pedalling in front while a passenger, or two in the larger types, sat in the rear. Rickshaws were two-wheeled carts with long shafts gripped by the runner, usually thin to the point of emaciation, who pulled the vehicle. The rickshaw "boys" ran or plodded, depending on their age and physical condition, and were very dexterous at weaving in and out of traffic.

Later, George often rode in pedicabs, but after one ride in a rickshaw he could never bring himself to do it again. Being hauled along by a sweating panting fellow-man was too repugnant.

The buses and trolleys seemed to be in a perpetual rush-hour state. They were packed with people who, for the most part, managed to maintain their good humor in spite of their obvious discomfort.

Beggars were everywhere, people in patched and tattered clothes, old folks, women with babes in arms, wide-eyed older children clutching the edges of their mothers' tunics. Most of them came from the impoverished countryside, and swarmed after the more smartly dressed, who occasionally tossed them a few coppers or simply ignored them.

Affluence was very visible among the chosen few. Shiny limosenes, horns insolently blaring, nosed relentlessly through narrow streets choked with pedestrians, carts, rickshaws, pedicabs and vehicles of every description. The refugees, not used to big city traffic, scattered wildly when automobiles bore down. But blasé Shanghai natives stolidly proceeded at their own pace until the creeping monsters virtually pushed them out of the way.

Clothes were a mixture of East and West. Some of the men wore European style business suits, but most were dressed in tunic and trousers, over which was a long cotton or quilted gown in the cold weather.

For the country women it was mainly tunics and slacks. Their city sisters tended more to the *chi pao*, a kind of sheath dress slit up the sides. The gowns of the richer ladies were made of flowered silk or satin and tailored to hug the contours of the body.

The noise was incredible. Loudspeakers roared Chinese opera or whined saccharine love songs from innumerable store fronts in a futile effort to attract customers. Drivers used their horns instead of brakes. People had to shout to heard above the din. Others had to yell still louder to be heard above them. The endless hopeless competition went on and on.

And of course there were the smells, so chararacteristic of the exotic colonial Orient. Intermingled with the fumes of cars and buses was the odor of thousands of sweat-stained bodies, the fragrance of the tidbits cooking in the many street stalls for consumption on the spot, and over all, when the wind was right, the smell of the "honey boats" — barges laden with human excrement being hauled to outlying farms for use as fertilizer.

The sudden combination of these assaults on the senses was overwhelming. The three young doctors were always a bit dazed as they walked every morning to their clinic in the Continental Bank Building.

They divided the clinic into three sections—internal medicine plus eye, ear, nose and throat; surgery; and skin and venereal disease. Each section earned its own income, but expenses were shared jointly. George ran the third section. He was confident the seaport of Shanghai, with its hordes of foreign sailors, would provide him ample opportunity to treat the ailment he was beginning to specialize in—veneral disease.

One of the most cosmopolitan cities in the world, Shanghai was strikingly free of racial and religious prejudice—among the civilized Chinese. But the foreign barbarians had brought their age-old narrow phobias with them. Each felt supremely assured of the superiority of his own national culture, and all looked with contempt on their Chinese hosts.

Even the Jews, strongly united in their countries of origin by the persecution they suffered, found an opportunity to be high-handed with one another. The Ashkenazi, or northern European Jews, looked down their noses at the Sephardi —those from lands formerly under Moorish domination. This was absurd, particularly in Shanghai where many of the wealthiest and most learned families were Iraqi Sephardic Jews —the Hardoons, Sassoons, Kadoories.... The Sephardis had a similar antipathy for their European co-religionists.

They were also some of the best paying patients, and the enterprising young American doctors decided to use to their advantage the importance the Sephardis attached to their ethnic backgrounds. For Katz and Levinson, plainly of fair-skinned Ashkenazi stock, it was hopeless. But George, with his olive complexion, large eyes, and curly black hair, was the perfect "Sephardi specialist". He soon became a popular doctor in the Sephardic community, and his Ashkenazi colleagues basked in his reflected glory. Eventually, he admitted it was just a gag, but by that time his patients liked him, and it didn't matter.

Other opportunities to make money also became available to the fledgling medics. George was asked to take over the practice of a high-class dermatologist and venereologist who was going on vacation for three months. He hesitated, not sure he could earn enough to contribute his share to the Kiukiang Road clinic.

"My dear young man, you have nothing to worry about," the doctor assured him. "We have a roster of one hundred foreign prostitutes who have to come in regularly to be examined and have their passbooks endorsed that they are fit. We have another roster of two hundred Chinese prostitutes who must do the same. We have a contract with the Dutch steamship lines to treat the venereal diseases of their captains and first-mates. The Shanghai police force is also under contract to us. And if this is not enough, we charge three hundred U.S. dollars per abortion, and all the round-the-world cruises have our cards."

While George was learning about the rewards of organized vice, Katzie was approached in the clinic one morning by a well-dressed gentleman carrying an expensive briefcase.

"We have a proposition for you," the caller said. "You are a struggling young physician and we'd like to help you. I have here two kilograms of pure heroin which you as a doctor can cut and dispense. Since this is the International Settlement, you have extra-territorial rights. No one can touch you. Join us and you'll make a fortune in no time."

Dr. Katz politely declined.

What shook the young medics most was their experience in the American St. Luke's and the British Lester Chinese Hospital where they worked part-time in the charity wards. These were major medical institutions trying to do good work, but they were handicapped—not by lack of funds or staff, but by conditions in China. They could only take in the extremely ill —usually terminal when they came to a charity hospital.

Why, George asked himself, was the situation of these poor

people so awful? And why did only the terminal patients get to the hospital at all? What they needed was food, shelter, clothing, and some sort of security in their lives. But they had nothing. No matter how skilled the doctors were, or how wonderful their drugs, or how successful their operations, most of the patients were so weak they died anyway.

To the idealistic young doctors, it was an intolerable situation. But they were helpless to change it.

Katz and Levinson gave up in disgust and went back to America. Their families had brides waiting, and cars and medical practices ready. The pull was irresistable. George had no such lures in the offing. Moreover, he had almost no end of patients with skin and venereal ailments in Shanghai. He decided to stay "a while longer", as he wrote to his folks back home.

The family had been very proud when he graduated Magna Cum Laude before his twenty-third birthday. They had made many sacrifices to put him through medical school. The Great Depression that hit America in 1929 had broken the banks and wiped out the funds they had put away for his studies. Brother Joe quit college and dug ditches to help earn the money George needed. Aunts and uncles all pitched in as best they could. No sacrifice was too great. They were sure their Shafik was someone special who would reflect honor on the Hatem clan.

To say they were disappointed when he announced he would return home by way of China would be putting it mildly. Still, he said he would stay only a year. They could endure waiting another few months. But when, not long after, he wrote that he would remain in Shanghai and was considering going with a Rockefeller research group into Tibet, they were crushed. The Tibet trip never came off, but neither did he return to the States. In fact none of them was to see George again for nearly thirty years, when he met his father Nahoum in Syria in 1962.

Ironically, this wasn't what he originally planned at all. He went to Shanghai because he thought he could learn more about venereal disease, as well as malaria, hookworm and yellow fever—then rife in North Carolina. He fully intended to go home after a short stay. But China fascinated him, and he wanted more.

At the same time he began being troubled by a social conscience. He was appalled by the contrasts between the rich and the poor in China. The harsh realities of Shanghai recalled to him the poverty and hardships of his childhood and youth. Was there was a connection between the persecutions in Europe and the persecutions in China? Were they part of a universal pattern? George had a craving to understand the causes of the inequities of the world, to find a solution.

The attitude of the Western businessmen irritated and angered him. No American or Britisher, no matter how stupid or incompetant, was allowed to starve. He would be put on the payroll of one of the large foreign corporations and paid fifty U.S. dollars a week just to keep him off the streets. It was part of the "white man's burden" to ensure that none of their own kind disgrace the Western community. The great mass of the down-trodden Chinese they considered sub-human. The tiny minority who had achieved financial success, or had been to colleges abroad, they tolerated with thinly disguised contempt.

Shanghai was then called "The Paradise of Adventurers", with good cause. It was thronged with ruthless crooked hustlers from all over the world, working hand in glove with Chiang Kai-shek's venal officials, siphoning out everything that wasn't nailed down. George could find little pleasure in the company of most of his commercial compatriots.

Alone in Shanghai, with Rob and Katzie gone, he began frequenting a bookstore that sold liberal publications. The proprietor was a German woman named Irene Wedemeyer. There he met other browsers and buyers, people like left-wing American writer Agnes Smedley, fabulous New Zealander Rewi Alley, and U.S. newsman Randall Gould.

George and Rewi took to each other immediately. Rewi had reddish-blond hair, a very fair complexion. He reminded George of an oak tree, from his thick massive trunk to his sturdy solid legs. Most of the year he walked around in shorts, and seldom wore a hat. In addition to being a skilled technician, Rewi was a poet and scholar. George was just starting to develop intellectual interests, but he and Rewi shared an antipathy for hipocrisy and cant. Both had dry, sarcastic manners of speech, particularly when commenting on the Confucian or pseudo-Christian humbug with which the ruling Kuomintang (KMT) clique attempted to cloak their depredations of the public. Both were relentlessly honest in a milieu and at a time when back-slapping and boot-licking were the best way to "get along".

Agnes Smedley and Rewi Alley were actively helping the

Chinese Communist underground. They ran a small foreigners'
study group, which George joined, where they discussed Marxism and revolution. It didn't mean much to him at first.

But when Rewi took him out to Shanghai's Hungchiao
airport to watch the executions he began to understand that the
prejudice and discrimination he had encountered in the States
were trivial compared to the brutal suppression inflicted on the
Chinese people. Seeing youngsters put to death before his eyes
brought this starkly home to George, personalized it painfully.
He agonized, he felt he had to do something.

The airport was a tourist spot. People were escorted off their
round-the-world tours to see it. They stared with horrified
fascination.

George watched as the young people were taken out and
shot. Some had their eyes covered, others refused the blindfold.
They were mostly fresh-faced young men and women. A few
were only teen-agers. They stood bravely before firing squads
of KMT special police.

"Down with the Kuomintang! Down with imperialism!" they
yelled. "Long live communism! Long live the Red Army!"

And then they were slaughtered. One moment they were
vibrant youngsters with warm bodies and lively minds. The
next moment they were corpses crumpled on the ground,
nothing.

They were accused of being Communist Party members.
Actually, most of them were not. They were students or
workers who had said something against the local authorities
or their bosses. But even if they were Communists, did that
mean they should be obliterated just as they were beginning to
live? George was sickened and outraged.

"Those dirty bastards," he fumed. "What right have they to
kill those kids!"

He was boiling. He wanted to rush up and grab the guns and
mow those smartly dressed police goons down. Rewi put a hand
on his arm.

"Slowly, old boy. Don't lose your head. I wanted you to see
this so that you'd know better what the Chinese people are up
against. And what you too are going to be up against, if that's
how you want it. Think about it."

George's brain was reeling. He desperately needed to think.
There was no democracy in China, no legality. The haves
simply rolled over the have-nots like a juggernaught. They

"crushed the bones and drank the blood", as the Chinese say, of the workers and peasants in a merciless squeeze. They imprisoned, tortured and slaughtered with impunity anyone who dared say them nay.

The torments of the Chinese were endless. All the ordinary people were exploited, including the children. Rewi was a factory inspector in the International Settlement. He took George with him on his rounds and urged him to write a paper on the medical and health conditions in the chromium plating factories they visited.

The workers were children whose average age was fourteen. They were severely undernourished. Their ulcerated hands were being eaten away by the chemicals used in the chromium plating process. The kids worked long hours, and lived on the premises in miserable quarters. Their pay was a pittance. They were sickly, disease-ridden. The death rate was high.

"The owners of these plants ought to be drawn and quartered," George grated. "Why aren't they criminally prosecuted?"

Rewi snorted. "Who's going to do it? The government doesn't control business. Business controls the government."

George wrote a blistering article which was published by the British Lester Institute. Nothing came of it. The conditions of Chinese child laborers remained the same.

Daily, he witnessed the common sights of Shanghai in the thirties: foreign gunboats patrolling the Yangtse, well-fed Western businessmen and their sleek wives dancing in evening clothes at the French Club while turbanned Sikh concession police openly beat Chinese rickshaw pullers. In winter frozen bodies collected off the streets and piled like so much cordwood in garbage trucks and carted away. The all-pervasive pneumonia and tuberculosis, deaths by the thousands from over-work and starvation.... No wonder revolt seemed the only answer.

But how could it be fomented, who should lead it, how should it be organized, how had it been done in other countries?

George started reading books by left-wing American and British writers like Agnes Smedley and John Strachey. In his study group German theoretician Hans Shippe, later killed by the Japanese while working with the Communist-led Eighth Route Army, told about the battle of ideas in the German and other European political parties. Also active in the group was American Communist Max (Manny) Granich who, together with his wife Grace, was putting out the *Voice of China*. It called for an end to the civil war and a united front against Japanese aggression. Better known in the States was Manny's brother Mike Gold, author of *Jews Without Money*. The group discussed Marxism and the *Communist Manifesto*.

"The *Manifesto* hit me like a bolt of lightning," George recalled. "All my past experience swam up. I thought back on the States, Beirut, Europe. I considered what I was seeing now in China. It all checked with the analyses in the *Manifesto*. I felt the treatise was a terrific probe into the world's social and economic problems, a guidepost to how they should be tackled."

But although his comprehension of man's fight for freedom was growing, he wasn't sure what his role should be. In August, 1935, he sent a letter to Katzie, who was now practising medicine in New York:

I am still looking around, I do not want to go back, I am staying in China. The folks quit writing to me since I told them this, and now I am free to do what I please. I cannot agree with them that I should come home and start an office. I detest private practice....

There are more things in life than yourself and your family. With the whole world in misery your own problems are minor. I would like to go to Russia, but that would be running away. I'll wait till the rest of the countries become like Russia. In the meantime I will do what I can to help here....

To cure a couple of old fat people and sit on my can doesn't suit me any longer. I have energy and a different view on life. Any small salary job as a doctor will do, and I think I have one... In September I start in an insane asylum that has just been built for 600 patients. I will work only half days for room and board and 100 silver dollars a month....

No, I am not in love and have no girl friend, but I will soon remedy that. I may not be prosperous as you see it, Katzie, but I assure you I am very well off. Life means a lot to me now. A life not limited by racial or national ties is the one that offers the greatest freedom. I am sure you understand this, Katzie. We were brought up in the same school and learned the same lessons....

His optimism about finding a girl friend proved groundless. It was not that George wasn't interested—he had an eye for the ladies, and there were plenty of pretty young misses around. But each day brought another shock, another outrage at the cruelties he witnessed. What he saw with his own eyes was impelling him toward the revolutionaries. This was no time for dalliance and romance. He was a young American with a strong sense of justice, and he was infuriated by the heartless greed and corruption of the rulers, by the misery and sufferings of the millions of ordinary people.

George could bear no longer simply to watch from the sidelines. Rewi and Agnes and all his friends had told him the Chinese Communists were the main force working to bring about a change. He had heard that in Shanghai the Communist underground was protecting the downtrodden, organizing resistance to exploitation, mobilizing the people to unite against the Japanese. If the Communists are the champions of the persecuted, George thought, I'm for them!

As a doctor, as a foreigner, how could he help? The Communist Party in Shanghai was then a secret, underground organization. How could he make contact? Who would introduce him?

It turned out there were three people, two of whom were women, who could and did put him touch: Rewi Alley—a New Zealander; Agnes Smedley—an American; and Soong Ching Ling, widow of Dr. Sun Yat-sen—revered as the advocate of a modern, independant China.

Working with the Communist underground was very dangerous. Any Chinese caught by the KMT was killed, and foreigners were roughly treated. In addition to the police there were special political branches of Chinese and foreign intelligence organizations, operating hand in glove, whose main targets were foreign communists or those labelled as communist sympathizers. Arrested Chinese were seldom brought to trial. After interrogation and torture, victims were simply executed. Or, simpler still, a contract for the "wasting" of a particular target would be given to one of the many gangs and secret societies. In Shanghai the murder of a man of minor importance could be carried out for a few cents; for a more important individual the price might be as little as two silver dollars.

Agnes bitterly resented the poverty and cruelty which had

been her lot since childhood. In China she automatically sided with the oppressed with a courage often bordering on abandon. Her father, half Irish and half American-Indian, had driven a team of horses in Missouri for a living. His neglect of his wife and family, in contrast to his care for his animals, started the barefoot little girl on a lifetime of ardent feminism.

They moved to Colorado where, as Agnes succinctly stated, the Rockefeller "Colorado Fuel and Iron Company owned everything except the air." She and her four brothers could get only a few years of primary school. Their drunken father kept the family in constant debt. Their sadly overworked mother died when Agnes was sixteen, and she was thrown out into the world to fight her own way. She began as a waitress, became a tobacco worker, then taught herself enough stenography and typing to get a job as a stenographer. Avid for knowledge, she read every book she could lay her hands on. Agnes was in her early twenties before she knew who Shakespeare was, and forty before she read one of his plays.

While at NYU night school during World War I, she became friendly with Indian students and helped them establish an organization seeking India's freedom from British rule. Charged with a violation of America's Neutrality Law, she was arrested and imprisoned in the notorious Tombs prison in New York City, and not released until the war ended. She came out with the manuscript of her first book *Cell Mates*.

Agnes obtained employment as a stewardess on an ocean liner, jumped ship in Danzig, and travelled to Berlin where she joined a group of Indian exiles involved in the freedom movement. She hoped to be able to proceed from there to India. But she fell in love with Virendranath Chattopadhyaya, generally known as "Viren", and lived with him for eight years.

Viren was brilliant, a master of several languages, and his home in Berlin was the Mecca of many of the rebels of the world. It was he who explained to her the great influence the Chinese revolution would have on the nations of Asia and stimulated her interest in China. They parted good friends in 1928. After an exciting trip overland across the USSR and down through China's Northwest, Agnes arrived in Shanghai.

The year before the KMT had treacherously broken its alliance with the Communist Party and butchered thousands of people in Shanghai, Canton and Hankow. Hundreds of thousands more died of sickness and starvation. Agnes saw outside the city limits corpses stacked in large piles, doused in gasoline and burnt en masse. Intrigue and corruption in town and country were rampant, and Chinese officials and foreign financial groups joined hands to bleed the nation dry. She vividly describes this period in her second book *Chinese Destinies*.

Agnes always lived intensely, often against great odds. Her health broke down under constant attack by the foreign press in China and systematic pursuit by special agents, and she had to leave. She spent some time in the Philippines and in the USSR, where she stayed in a sanitarium and worked on her third book *China's Red Army Marches*.

She was back in Shanghai in 1933 when George first set foot on Chinese soil. Agnes was a close friend of Lu Xun, China's greatest satirical essayist, and Mao Dun, famous novelist and leader of the left-wing literati. They were too important to be harrassed by the KMT, but Agnes and all her acquaintances were automatically suspect. Police surveillance of her never ceased. Even to get to the flat where she lived in the French Concession it was wiser to climb to the roof of the building next door, cross over to her roof, and then walk down the stairs to her apartment. After any meeting or party at her place visitors always left quietly through different hallways.

George liked Agnes a lot. For some time she had been hiding in her home Red Army people on the run. In the teeth of Kuomintang fascist terror Agnes showed great courage. She was almost completly unfeminine, brusque, rugged, and absolutely fearless. She flung herself openly, wildly, into battle. Agnes had a lot to do with his wanting to go to the Red Areas. George admired her reckless daring. He was more cautious, but just as incensed by inequity.

Rewi Alley became his life-long friend. Born in Christchurch, New Zealand, in a school teacher's family, Rewi was raised in a proper environment markedly contrasting to the chaotic one Agnes had endured. He fought in France during World War I in the New Zealand Expeditionary Force, was wounded, returned home, tried his hand at sheep farming for six years and, looking for adventure, went to Shanghai in 1927. He worked in the Fire Department, then became Chief Factory Inspector. What he saw—ravaged bodies of callously exploited child laborers, mass executions of young people who dared to protest against injustice, the penniless starving populace

—quickly radicalized him.

He found like-minded Westerners who were willing to aid in the efforts of the revolutionary underground, and worked closely with Agnes and Madame Sun Yet-sen—known to her friends by her maiden name Soong Ching Ling. Because of his respectable status Rewi was able to undertake missions which the notorious Agnes could not. Many was the time he rode through the streets in a brightly polished rickshaw, looking every inch the pukka sahib, with a bundle of weapons on the floor boards beneath his feet. Who could suspect so affluent a gentleman?

Nevertheless, he had a few narrow squeaks. In his handsomely furnished apartment in the French Concession, Rewi harbored a concealed radio receiver and transmitter on which underground agents were maintaining communications with the Communist interior. One day a couple of inspectors from the Power and Light Company came by. Rewi told George about it as a big joke.

"You're using an unsual amount of electricity in this flat," they said. "There's a power leak somewhere. We'll check."

Rewi was all in a sweat. He and his Chinese friends had been tapping electricity from a public power line that passed over the building's roof. He was sure his lead-in cable would be discovered. The technicians examined his refrigerator first.

"Aha, here it is," they exclaimed. "Your wiring has gone faulty."

They made some adjustments, said goodbye, and left. Rewi breathed a sigh of relief.

"It takes nerve to play those kinds of games," he said to George with a laugh. "And a bit of luck doesn't hurt at all!"

On one occasion Agnes brought to his flat a short-sighted Chinese professor and his wife who had to get out of Shanghai quickly to escape arrest. (Professor Chen Hansheng today is a leading historian and economist.) George had a car, and Rewi enlisted his help.

"Our job is to take them to a ship that is sailing tomorrow. We will be carrying flowers as though we were seeing them off," Rewi said. "We'll escort them to their cabin. Then, when the hooter sounds and 'All visitors ashore' is called, you and I will stroll down the gangway, leaving them on board."

The next day Agnes gave the professor a huge bunch of gladioli to obscure his face. To better disguise him, they dressed him in white shorts, silk stockings, a palm beach coat, and white pith helmet. He was not to wear his spectacles, for those would certainly be included in his police description.

George and Rewi drove the professor and his wife to the warf and escorted them down the long walk to the ship. The gallant professor was a memorable sight, trying to look nonchalant under his unaccustomed headgear, peering myopically through the great red flowers, and hoping against hope he would not trip.

They walked coolly past the plainclothes men grouped around the bottom of the gangway. Since they appeared so much the usual wealthy Shanghai types, the detectives barely gave them a glance. They marched sedately up the gangway, and the plan went off without a hitch.

When Rewi reported the successful departure of Professor Chen and his wife to Agnes, she was overjoyed and promptly threw a party to celebrate.

Rewi and Agnes found George to be an enthusiastic helper. He began delivering the underground's letters, including some to or from Madame Soong, keeping an eye on doorways at places where they met to ensure that nobody was trailing them. Soon they were holding private meetings in his clinic after office hours. On several occasions, using George's car, they drove Chinese Communists the Kuomintang was after down to the docks, and slipped them aboard Russian vessels bound for the Soviet Union. George also secretly mimeographed and distributed a news sheet Agnes was publishing.

His whole life had changed. No longer just an angered observer of China's miseries, he was playing an active, though small, part in trying to alleviate them. Working for the underground, taking risks, gave him solid satisfaction. To serve as foreign doctor in China now had a new meaning. He believed it was his function not only to cure people, but to help as much as possible to cure the underlying social causes of their physical aliments.

Rewi and Agnes's tales of what the Communists were doing in the "liberated areas" made him eager to see for himself. Was it true that there were no very rich and no very poor? No child laborers? Equal access to medical treatment? Could this revolutionary experiment really create a new way of life? Madame Soong, to whom Agnes introduced him, made it possible for him to find out.

Soong Ching Ling was one of three sisters. The eldest, Ai Ling, was the wife of H. H. Kong, Kuomintang Minister of Finance. Mei Ling was married to Chiang Kai-shek. And she herself had been the wife and helpmate of the idolized Sun Yat-sen. For this reason, Ching Ling, or "Suzy", as she was known to her intimates, could not be touched by the KMT police, although she made no secret of her liberal views. A graduate of Wesleyan College, in Macon, Georgia, she spoke English better than she did Chinese. Of medium height, with perfect skin and expressive eyes under fine brows, she gave the impression of stately calm. Her home in Shanghai was a natural meeting place for a few foreign friends who gathered every week or two after dinner to chat, dance, and discuss current affairs.

When Agnes took George to Madame Soong's home for the first time, she said only they were going to visit a hospitable Chinese friend. Entering a walled compound, they crossed a well-tended garden, and went into a large house, tastefully furnished in traditional style. People were dancing. Without a moment's hesitation George walked up to the most beautiful woman in the room and asked her to dance. Madame Soong smilingly protested she didn't know how. She was wearing a simple *chi pao*, and no make-up. No one had bothered to introduce them. Emboldened by the slight American intonation of her flawless English, George persisted.

"Nothing to it," he said, pulling her to the floor. "I'll show you."

The fact was she danced very well. When it was over, George thanked her and escorted her back to her seat. He danced with her another few times.

"Isn't she lovely," he whispered to Agnes. "And her English is perfect. Who is she?"

"Madame Sun Yat-sen," Agnes replied, smiling.

George's face reddened with embarrassment. "Holy smoke! How could I have been so flip!"

Soong Ching Ling was not a member of the Chinese Communist Party, but she was its main liason in Shanghai. Messages, Party statements, articles by Mao Zedong, nameless individuals... were relayed through her to their destinations. She maintained contacts with the anti-Japanese United Front, set up secret meetings.

Agnes later told Madame Soong what an ardent and dependable supporter of the Chinese revolution George was. The gracious lady took a warm liking to him, which was more than reciprocated. The friendship formed between them lasted till the day she died.

In March of 1936, on Rewi's recommendation, Madame Soong arranged for George to go to what was then known as the Red Base in Shaanxi Province. He went first to Xian, where he was to be met by a member of the underground. He took a room in the Xijing (Western Capital) Hotel, run by the Kuomintang, where most foreigners were required to stay. Three weeks passed. The contact never showed up. For camouflage George hung around the missionaries and British-American Tobacco Company people as though he was an idle traveller. Finally, he went back to Shanghai.

His friends gave him a cool reception—even Rewi. These were dangerous times. Anything could have happened to a man exposed to the comfortable Xian foreign colony and the flesh-pot blandishments of the Kuomintang. George didn't understand his friends' reserve, but he didn't mind much. While he had the beginnings of a serious revolutionary in his inner core, in his daily existence, in his speech and manner, he was still the happy-go-lucky young American, wise-cracking, a little brash, never doubting for a moment that he would somehow get through.

The Communist underground very likely checked and found him clean. His friends were soon cordial again and brought him back into their activities. He never learned what happened to the contact.

At last, in June 1936, Madame Soong summoned him to her home. She said the KMT was enforcing an effective block-ade of the Communist Revolutionary Base Area in northern Shaanxi province, preventing any news about it from getting out. Mao Zedong, then in Bao An, wanted "an honest Western journalist" to visit the Area and tell the world what he had seen, and "a well-trained Western doctor" to help with the fledgling medical work.

"It's lucky Mao doesn't insist that the doctor also be 'honest', or I might not be able to go!" George quipped.

Madame Soong laughed. She said Edgar Snow and Dr. George Hatem, both Americans, had been chosen. They would be met in Xian by an underground operative and escorted in.

She handed George half of a British five pound note. The

person meeting them would have the other half. In that way, and only in that way, would recognition be established. She also gave him a 16-exposure Kodak camera and a few roles of film. He was to pose as a reporter for a magazine, sent to take pictures of children.

His luggage consisted of a leather Red Cross kit and two wooden cases of medicine. Under the tightly soldered false bottom of one of the cases were a number of documents, including Dimitrov's anti-fascist united front speech at the Seventh Congress of the Communist International in 1935. The full text had not yet been seen in the Red Base Area.

George was thrilled, and filled with curiosity. At that time he had no idea of permanently joining the revolutionary forces in the Red Base Area. He was going there to see, to help if he could. What would happen after that, he left open.

A few days later George Hatem set out for the new China that would shake the world and shape his destiny.

A LEAP INTO THE UNKNOWN

It was a mildly warm June day in 1936 when George Hatem boarded the train at the Shanghai station. His destination was Xian. Edgar Snow would join him en route at Zhengzhou, arriving on another train from Beijing. They would proceed together to Xian where contact would be made and further instructions given on how to reach Bao An.

As the train rolled to a halt at the Zhengzhou station, through the open window George spotted a startling apparition. There, waiting on the platform was a man with his hat brim pulled low, almost meeting the gauze mask covering his face to the bridge of his nose, leaving only his eyes visible. Edgar Snow.

George went out and greeted him, and they identified each other. They boarded the train and sat down in the compartment which, until then, George had been occupying alone. Of average height, Snow had wavy brown hair, dark eyebrows and smiling grey eyes. He was dressed in a tweed suit which had seen a lot of wear, and a khaki shirt open at the neck. He looked younger than his thirty-one years.

Curious about each other, they talked quietly. In the typically uninhibited American manner, Snow related his complete personal history.

Like Agnes Smedley, Ed also was born in Missouri, but there the similarity ended. The son of a printer and publisher, he was raised in a comfortable middle-class family and attended the schools of journalism at the University of Missouri and Columbia. As a free-lance journalist he travelled to Hawaii where he wrote his first published article for *Harper's Bazaar*. He went on next to Japan and then, in 1928, to Shanghai. He found a job on *China Weekly Review*, run by staunchly independent American J.B. Powell.

Assigned to advertise the pleasures of tours by railroad in China, Ed covered some 8,000 miles—then the total extent of Chinese lines. Everywhere he saw terrible famine and desperate poverty. His plan to stay for only six weeks was forgotten under the impact of the universal misery he witnessed. Edgar Snow was to remain in China for thirteen years.

By 1931 he was Assistant Editor of *China Weekly Review*. At the same time he contributed articles to the *New York Herald Tribune*, the *New York Sun*, and the *Chicago Daily News*. On trips to Japan, Indo-China and India he interviewed prominent figures, including Mahatma Ghandi and Jawaharlal Nehru. He married crack woman journalist Helen "Peg" Foster, who wrote under the pen name of Nym Wales. They established a home in Beijing in 1935, where Ed was invited to teach journalism at Harvard-affiliated Yenching University. Liberal students found in the young couple sympathetic listeners and supporters of their patriotic demands. Through the more radical elements among them Ed established contact with the Communist underground and expressed a wish to report on the Red Bases in the "liberated areas". The request was granted. He was instructed to meet fellow-American George Hatem at the Zhengzhou railway station and go on with him to Xian, and from there to the Red Base in Bao An.

The journey required considerable courage. Ed spoke a little standard Chinese, George knew only a few phrases of Shanghai dialect—neither of which was of much use among the thickly-accented people of the northwest. Travel was laboriously slow and exhausting. The rail line ended at Xian. They would have to go the rest of the way by whatever transport was available. Severe hazards awaited them in the open countryside. The risk of being killed by bandits was real. Recently a foreign famine relief worker had been murdered. And there were other threats to health and life. Typhus from body lice, for instance, chalked up a high mortality rate. Sanitation was elementary to non-existant.

But both men were determined to reach the fabled land. George because he was looking for a social utopia, Ed because he sensed there was a block-busting news story waiting for him.

Just as they were starting to relax, a large swarthy Chinese, obviously not a first-class passenger, plumped himself down on the folding seat in the aisle opposite the door of their compartment. He never left it, even at station stops, only opening the window occasionally to buy a watermelon or other provisions. He remained stolidly in his seat, eating.

"Do you think he's watching us?" George whispered. He didn't suppose the man knew English, but you never could tell. He kept his voice low.

"Maybe he's a KMT agent," Ed said softly. "Better close the door."

Their brows were damp with perspiration. They were very tense.

"No, don't do that," George said nervously. "If he's an agent it will only make him more suspicious."

"Let me see if I can sound him out," said Ed.

He boldly took the bull by the horns. In his limited Chinese Ed struck up a conversation with the man. They chatted about generalities, neither revealing anything of significance.

At the stop just before Xian, the big fellow vanished. Much relieved, the young Americans decided he must have been an underground escort. A KMT spy would have stayed with them to their destination.

George evidently made a good impression on Ed. In his book *Red China Today* Snow described him as a "... healthy, uncomplicated bachelor of twenty-six." It was Ed Snow's opinion that:

> George possessed a shrewd intelligence that had already penetrated the glossy surface of society to its ugliest sores. Beneath a superficial cynicism he was serious about one thing. He wanted to find some purpose to his work as a doctor.... Hitler had also sent him up to Xian—as, in a way, he had sent me. The world was no longer a pretty place for young people who understood where Hitlerism was leading it, and in the East the Japanese, going in the same direction, threatened to take Chiang Kai-shek (who at the time had German and Italian fascist advisers) with them.... Communism seemed about the only force interested in fighting fascism. Since Hitler and Japan hated communism so much, George thought there must be some good in it. He had also developed a strong distaste for existing society in Shanghai.

Ever the sensitive journalist, Snow had cut to the core of the sentiment which bound them together—a hatred of fascism and a feeling that the communists were the most active ele-

ments in the fight against it—in China and in the West. They
were going to the Red Base area to see specifically how the
Chinese communists were waging their part of the battle.

Ed wanted to know whether, in addition, George had any
personal reasons for this trip into the hinterlands.

"Well, yes," said George, a trifle heatedly. "My father didn't
starve himself to educate me for what I've been doing—fighting VD with a pea shooter." He frowned. "You know, venereal
disease is one thing that can easily be prevented and cured.
Shanghai exists to breed and spread it. It's a big business there
run by organized gangs with the full protection of the police
in both the foreign settlements and the KMT-run Chinese city.
There's a lot of money in the doctor's end of the business, too."

George shrugged. "I could make a fortune there treating
nothing but chancres and blueballs for the rest of my life. In
fact I've been doing very well. But I didn't spend my old man's
money learning to become a VD quack for a gangster society.
Maybe these people up north are interested in putting an end
to the whole business. I want to see what they're like."

Ed nodded. "Nothing like a couple of years in Shanghai for
turning young Americans into emotional radicals."

"I guess I would agree with that," George laughed. "But I
hope this radical is becoming less emotional and more objective
as time goes on."

The future would prove that while George Hatem did indeed gradually become more objective, he remained always a
deeply emotional person.

From the Xian station they took pedicabs to the Xijing
Hotel. It was run by the KMT. They registered under their own
names, in English. They were given a suite consisting of a
sitting room and two bedrooms.

Three days passed. No one came. At first they didn't dare
go out for fear of missing their caller. They stayed in their
rooms, reading. Finally, bored and restless, they wandered
around the city. Xian was very seedy and run-down. As one
jingle described it: "dim lights, faulty phones, bumpy roads".
It rhymed in Chinese—*dian deng bu ming, dian hua bu ling,
ma lu bu ping.*

In ancient times Xian, then named Chang An, was the
capital of China, and reached its pinnacle of splendor in the
Tang daynasty, which extended from the seventh to the tenth
century. With a population of two million, including some

40,000 foreign residents, it was the largest city in the world, and a great center of science, culture and trade, the terminus of the old Silk Road, carrying goods between China, Europe, the Middle East, and other parts of Asia.

Although sadly deteriorated, Xian still retained some signs of its former glory. One or two of the old temples remained, and the Big Goose and Small Goose Pagodas were standing firm, though now out in the suburbs, the city having shrunk to a third of its former size.

During their wanderings George and Ed ran into Dr. Wunsch, a dentist refugee from Nazi Germany. He must have sensed that they were sympathetic to the revolution, for he told them all about himself and what he was doing.

At the request of the Chinese Communist Party he had set up a dental clinic in Xian to serve as a center for underground operations. A Party member had been detailed to be his nurse and liaison man. But when Ed and George met him, he was alone. Very timid, Wunsch was frightened by the frequent killings in the city and the pervasive presence of KMT agents. He was also worried about the books and documents which had been entrusted to him for delivery. They were still where he had left them in the luggage deposit section of the railway station.

"It's dangerous," he said. "What shall I do?"

The young Americans had little knowledge of how the Xian Communist Party branch functioned, and could offer him no advice.

Dr. Wunsch was killed by a stray bullet while watching a clash from the doorway of his office during the Xian Incident —about which more later. He was one of several Westerners who lost their lives in the cause of the Chinese revolution.

Ed had a cool pragmatic attitude toward the situation they were in. He was brave and helpful in the travels with George.

"If you look like an arrogant, well-to-do foreigner, you might as well act like one in a good cause," he said. "Just carry a visiting card in your pocket and if anyone tries to stop you flip it out and go right past them. Don't stop or look back. They'll let you through because that's what they expect of someone important."

Recalling this, George smiled. "That's the way we got all the stuff—medicines, documents and all—past the KMT officials and guards. My admiration for Ed grew rapidly."

Continuing to mark time while waiting to be approached by their underground contact, they visited the Big Goose Pagoda —a beautiful structure housing the scriptures brought back from India in the seventh century by Buddhist monk Xuan Zhuang. On the wall was a WANTED poster offering 200 silver dollars for information leading to the capture of "notorious Communist bandit" Deng Fa. Ed took a picture of it.

He laughed. "Two hundred isn't much for such an important revolutionary!"

The next day a man knocked on the door of their suite. He was neatly and expensively dressed in a long silk gown, and carried a large cloth-wrapped bundle.

"My name is Wang," he said. He spoke good English. "I have some antiques for sale. Would you care to look at them?"

There were many Chinese who made a living selling antiques, not all authentic, to foreign tourists. George said he wasn't interested, but Ed agreed to see what the man had to offer. Wang opened his bundle and laid out a few quite good bronze mirrors and some ancient coins.

He was being very careful. Having checked their names in the hotel register, he knew they were the persons he was seeking. But he couldn't speak openly. The hotel was a KMT organization, and the whole staff, including the floor attendants, was permeated with spies. It wouldn't do to be overheard.

They hadn't yet caught on. Ed liked one of the mirrors and asked the price.

"Will you pay in Chinese or foreign currency?" Wang queried.

"I can give foreign money, either English or American, whichever you prefer," said Ed.

"English pounds will be fine."

Ah, English pounds. Ed understood. He asked George to get the five pound note which was in the bedroom. The light finally dawned on George, as well. He went inside and returned with the half of the five pound note given to him by Madame Soong. Wang smilingly produced the other half. They matched perfectly. He took the note and the remainder of the antiques and left without a word.

Ed and George were baffled. Why hadn't Wang said anything, or at least scribbled a few words on a slip of paper? They were up half the night speculating over this mystery.

The following morning at about nine o'clock, Wang returned. This time he was clad in silk tunic and trousers. He wore a snap-brim fedora and carried a folding fan.

"Please come with me," he said.

A car was waiting downstairs at the door, with a chauffeur and a man in KMT Army officer's uniform in the front seat. The Americans got into the back. Mr. Wang did not join them. The car drove off and travelled for about an hour. No one spoke. In the foothills of Lintong, famous ancient spa where a Tang emperor's favorite concubine once bathed, they stopped. The officer got out and started climbing a slope. Ed and George followed. Halfway up, the man halted. Removing his officer's hat he turned around and laughed.

"I'm Deng Fa," he announced in Cantonese-accented English. "I'm in charge of underground activities, and responsible for getting you to Bao An. Tonight, at 2 a.m., leave the hotel by the back window and climb over the compound wall. On the opposite side of the street you will see someone waiting with a stick of burning incense. Go over to him. Do everything exactly as he tells you."

They returned to the city in the car. "Aren't you afraid of losing your head?" Ed asked Deng Fa.

The Cantonese grinned. "Not as afraid as Zhang Xueliang is afraid of losing his!" Zhang was the Manchurian warlord general who, while ostensibly allied with Chiang Kai-shek and leading the "bandit suppression"—a euphemistic term for fighting the Communist forces—in Northwest China, was secretly giving the Red Army a great deal of help.

A short distance from the hotel, Ed and George got out and walked back. Neither of them could sleep that night.

At two in the morning they were wide awake. Their rooms were on the ground floor. They crept out of the back window in the hallway with their belongings and tip-toed across the courtyard to the compound wall. George scaled it first. It was only about six feet high. Ed handed over the luggage, and followed.

On the other side of the street they saw a tiny glow. They walked toward it. There was Mr. Wang waiting with two pedicabs, one for each of them. They mounted the vehicles with their belongings and moved off, accompanied by Mr. Wang on a bicycle. Ten or fifteen minutes later they came to a military barracks near the city wall. They were ushered into what appeared to be an officer's quarters and were told to rest.

For two hours they smoked and drank tea.

Just before dawn an open army truck carrying piles of uniforms pulled up. Mr. Wang told them to get in. The uniforms were stacked around and over them. The truck ground into motion. At daylight they reached the city gate, which had just opened, and the truck rolled through without a hitch. The uniforms were being supplied by the KMT to the troops of Zhang Xueliang, known as the "Young Marshal".

Zhang's headquarters were in Xian. While he had the typical feudal veneration for a senior statesman and military leader, he also harbored a bitter resentment against Chiang Kai-shek. For it was as a result of the "Generalissimo's" advice and policies that all of the Young Marshal's Manchurian territory and possessions were relinquished to the Japanese without a fight. Because the Communists saw Zhang as a potential participant in a united front against the invaders, they maintained a neutral, and at times even friendly, relationship with him. The Communist underground and the Young Marshal had stage-managed the secret movement of George Hatem and Edgar Snow to Yanan, and beyond.

Once outside Xian George and Ed were able to emerge from beneath the uniforms and breathe the crisp fresh air. The truck climbed steadily. Northwest China consists largely of "loess" soil—a friable, loamy deposit covering the entire Yellow River basin. In places it is hundreds of yards thick, forming high plateaux. With irrigation it can be quite fertile, but the difficulty of raising water to the highlands allows for only marginal farming. Deep gullies and huge canyons divide the plateaux. Down within them are roads which human and vehicular traffic grind ever lower into the earth, rendering them invisible to the traveller above until he is right upon them.

They spent the night in a small town and continued north the next day. They reached Yanan that evening, occupied by a large contingent of the Northeast Army of the Young Marshal's Manchurian forces. Worn out by the tension of their escape from Xian and the hours of jouncing in the back of the truck, they slept like logs.

An officer of the Northeast Army greeted them early the following morning. He gave them a donkey for their baggage and set them on the road to Bao An, apologizing for not being able to provide them with a guide. The Manchurians could not very well deliver two foreigners into the arms of the Reds they were supposed to be guarding against, he explained.

"Red Army soldiers will be waiting for you not far ahead," he said. "Just keep walking."

They were travelling light. Aside from his camera and his pipe, Ed carried only coffee and chocolate—without which no true American would ever venture into the unknown.

After several hours march there was still no sign of the welcoming party. The dirt road wound through a deep gorge, broken occasionally by side roads branching off into other gorges. Except at the openings, it was impossible to see from one to another. Sound carried far in the thin silent air, but they could only guess, from the bottom of the canyon, the direction from which it came.

And so, when Ed and George heard shots, they were not unduly alarmed. In fact they were not even sure it was firing they heard. Had they known what was happening they would have been much less serene. The platoon sent to meet them had passed by in one of the side roads. When the soldiers realized this, they turned back and began searching for them.

The platoon soon located them but discovered they were being trailed by a gang of bandits. The Red Army men softly followed behind, hesitating to make their presence known. If hostilities broke out, the foreign friends might be accidentally hit.

But the bandits kept drawing closer to their quarry. The platoon opened fire. The bandits shot back. For several minutes there was a wild skirmish. Then the bandits fled along one of the side gullies, with the soldiers in hot pursuit. The Americans learned of this only later.

Meanwhile, blissfully ignorant, they pushed on until dark. After dining on Ed's chocolate bars, they spent the night in the open. Although they didn't know it, they were quite near Bao An.

The next morning they resumed walking. Soon they reached the sparkling Yan River. Hot and tired, they peeled off their clothes and jumped in. They didn't notice, as they splashed happily in the cool water, the children holding red-tassled spears who had appeared along the bank.

"*Chu lai, chu lai*," the kids shouted. "Come out, come out."

Ed and George curiously emerged. The children had confiscated their clothes. Ed's Beijing Chinese bore no resemblance to the throaty local dialect. There was a complete failure of communications. Only after much gesticulation were they able to persuade the kids to let them have their pants back. This was their first encounter with the peasant children who had organized themselves into valiant guards and sentries all over liberated rural China. No stranger could escape their vigilant eyes.

They were escorted under guard to a cave dwelling in a nearby hamlet. Its interior was white-washed and spotlessly clean. Loess soil when hollowed out of hillsides creates comfortable homes, cool in summer and warm in winter. Young fellows wearing white towel turbans returned the rest of their clothes. No attempt was made at conversation. At noon they were given steamed bread and a few vegetable dishes. George was ravenously hungry. He remembers that meal as one of the best he ever ate.

An hour later a troop of cavalry trotted up. The handsome bearded man at its head dismounted, entered the cave and shook hands.

"I'm Zhou Enlai," he said in passable English. "Headquarters Command. We were expecting you. The men we sent out to meet you took a wrong turn, then got into a brush with bandits they found following you. By the time they chased them off, they had lost you again. I'm terribly sorry. We haven't done our job very well. You've had a rough experience." He smiled engagingly. "This is the outskirts of Bao An. The town is just ahead. Please come with me."

Horses had been brought for the Americans. They rode into Bao An with their first Red Army men and one of the key figures in China's revolution. Polished, urbane, even in his unpressed grey uniform, Zhou already possessed the quiet authority and appealing charm for which he later became famed in world diplomatic circles. Ed and George were too keyed up by the new world in which they found themselves to sleep well that night.

A few days later, Zhou introduced them to Mao Zedong, and Edgar Snow began the series of intensive interviews which would appear the following year in his famous *Red Star Over China*.

They started that evening after dinner and talked well into the wee hours. Mao was a tall, well-built man who seemed to exude an almost luminous charisma. He wore a shapeless grey tunic and trousers, and cloth shoes with stitched soles, like

everyone else in the area. In winter these clothes were changed
for cotton-padded garments, equally shapeless.

Mao was then married to He Zizhen, his second wife. His
first, Yang Kaihui, had been executed by the KMT in 1930.
Zizhen served them with stewed apricots as the night deepened.
Mao traced the development of the Red Army and the "struggle between the two lines". In his book, Ed brought the first
inkling to the outside world of the excessively hard and excessively soft approaches alternately plaguing Chinese Communist methodology. Mao, speaking slowly in the heavy accents
of his native Hunan, told, through an interpreter, of China's
history, society and philosophy as seen by its Communist
Party, of the Long March and Chinese revolutionary strategy.
He outlined the policy for the anti-Japanese war and the united
front, both still to come.

It was an eery sensation to sit in that dimly lit cave amid
absolutely silent dark hills and listen to Mao quietly analysing
China's past and present. His large important formulations did
not seem out of place in these humble surroundings. For all of
Mao's philosophy was grounded in the grass roots and aimed
at their nurture. He illustrated his ideas with folksy anecdotes
from Chinese history and fable, often humorous, always pithy.

George was present at these and all the other interviews Ed
had with Chinese leaders over a period of several weeks. For
George, it was the best kind of university. He was able to attain
an understanding of the Chinese revolution fairly quickly.
Before that he had only a rough mental outline.

Ed and George lived together in a cave dwelling gouged out
of the soft yellow soil, and ate very simple food—cabbage,
potatoes, soup, garlic, peppers, and millet gruel. Because they
were "special guests", once in a while they had steamed bread
made with wheat flour rather than corn meal.

Accompanied by young interpreter Huang Hua, they travelled through the provinces of Shaanxi, Gansu and Ningxia.
Huang Hua had been one of Ed's students at Yenching University. In the years to come he would be the Chinese Ambassador to the United Nations and then the Foreign Minister of
China. While Ed interviewed, George, on Mao's orders, inspected medical and health conditions in the Red Army and
among the civilian population. As the first foreign visitors they
were warmly received.

In a village in northwest Shaanxi they were invited to attend a mass meeting of the Red Army. Large banners read: WE ARE NOT ISOLATED. WE HAVE THE SUPPORT OF INTERNATIONAL FRIENDS.

A podium and a big stage with some logs and trees and a few branches to camouflage them were set up. "We're going to bring all of the armies together and we want you to talk to them," the young Americans were told. "It will be very encouraging."

As George recalled, "The meeting was on an area about the size of an American football field. The soldiers seated in the front row had machine guns, the ones in the second row had a couple of mortars and rifles, and those in the next three or four more rows had rifles with bayonets. When I looked at all the remaining rows I could see every agricultural tool China had ever invented over the past 2,000 years. But no arms."

The chief speaker made a very fiery oration. He said: "We're going to liberate China. All the oppressed people of the world will support us. We're going to get rid of imperialism. We're going to get rid of the Kuomintang. Down with all of them! Victory lies ahead!"

Edgar Snow, seated beside George on the stage, turned to him and said: "They're mighty brave people if they think they're going to do it with that army."

Exactly thirteen years later "that army", considerably enlarged, entered Beijing.

In Ningxia, in China's far northwest, George acquired the name Ma Haide. Zhou Enlai was there with a Communist delegation seeking to obtain more support from the Moslems, who had good reason to hate the Han Chinese. China's fifty-five ethnic minority races, constituting only six percent of the population, occupy half of the country's territory. But much of this is desert, steppe and mountain. Over the centuries, the Han majority drove the ethnic peoples from the fertile lowlands into the harsher border regions.

George was on a medical mission. The terrain was a lot like America's southwest, rough, open. Everyone rode horses or donkeys. George loved it. He felt as if he were in a Wild West movie. Some of the "cowboys" were racially a mixture of Asians and Europeans, but they had the same devil-may-care air about them as their American counterparts.

The Grand Mullah gave a banquet in Zhou's honor and requested that George also be present. The Mullah had heard that he was an "Arabic scholar". George had grown a beard and he really looked the part. The people of Northwest China are mainly of local Turkic stock, plus descendants of ancient migrants from Arabia and Persia. They are predominantly Moslem. Their most holy book—the Koran—is written in Arabic, and their religious services are also conducted in that language.

George was asked at the banquet whether he could speak Arabic. He said, "No, but I can eat Arabic!" He demonstrated with skill and gusto, and remembered how to write his name. He was a great hit. The hosts insisted that he be given a Moslem name. Zhou Enlai suggested "Ma"—a common Moslem family appelation. "Haide" was adopted as an approximation of "Hatem" to serve as his given name.

"Ma Haide" comes easily off the Chinese tongue. From then on George was known to his Chinese patients as "Ma *Daifu*" (Dr. Ma), and to his Chinese friends as "*Lao* Ma" (Good Old Ma), or in later years as "Ma *Lao*" (the Venerable Ma). Foreign intimates jokingly hailed him as "Horse" (which is what "ma" in the third tone means), or even "The Veterinarian".

Back in Bao An he submitted a detailed report on medical and health conditions in the Red Army and among the civilian population in the areas he visited. Mao was very pleased. He appointed him "Medical Advisor to the Army Department of Health". At that time George was the only doctor in the Base Area who had graduated from a medical school.

He and Ed were issued Red Army uniforms, complete with hats and leggings. Ed wanted to take a picture of Mao. The Chairman was bareheaded, and George thought he wouldn't look dignified enough. At his suggestion, Mao put on Ed's "eight-pointed" Red Army hat. The picture that resulted became world-famous, and is still popular in China today.

Ed left in October to write *Red Star Over China*. It was agreed he would not mention George for fear of implicating those persons, Chinese and foreign, who were known to have been friendly with him in Shanghai. The Kuomintang would have been nasty to anyone who helped provide the Reds with their only foreign doctor. Ed kept his promise. Not until 1970, in the revised and updated edition of *The Other Side of the River* did Ed reveal that his companion on his journey into the Red Bases was Dr. George Hatem. The only "leak" was an imaginative tale in a Shanghai English language newspaper about a "Turkish Moslem doctor" working for the Red Army among the Mohammedans in the Northwest.

After Ed Snow departed for Beijing, George joined the medics of the First Front Army, and went with them to Gansu province to meet the Second and Fourth Front Armies, straggling up as the last troops to complete the Long March. The men were ill, exhausted, their clothing in tatters. But they hadn't the slightest doubt they would eventually liberate all China.

Sitting around a charcoal fire with these ragged survivors in a peasant's hut, George heard stories of the epic trek. A heavily outnumbered Red Army had withdrawn a twisting eight thousand miles through the worst mountains and swamps in China, relentlessly pursued by a mechanized, well-equipped KMT Army. They suffered ninety percent casualties. Only about 30,000 of their original force of three hundred thousand arrived. But the skinny scarecrows spoke always simply, humorously, as if they had just finished a romp in the park.

On the way back to Bao An George saw Generals Chu Teh (Zhu De) and Ho Lung (He Long) give up their horses to the wounded and walk on foot, carrying their own gear. There was a simple democratic equality among officers and men. No one wore any distinctive insignia. They ate the same food, shared similar rough quarters. They argued out tactics before battle, and critically reviewed them after—together, with no holds barred. Only when the fighting started did the officers become superiors. Then the men obeyed orders without question.

The Xian Incident broke in December 1936. Although public sentiment was overwhelmingly in favor of putting an end to the civil war and turning the guns on the Japanese invaders, Chiang Kai-shek was still fulminating against the revolutionaries and harassing them with his huge military machine. He flew to Xian early in December to harrangue Yang Hucheng —warlord of the Northwest Army, and the Young Marshal —warlord of the Northeast Army, into greater efforts against the Reds. Both of these commanders felt they were fighting the wrong enemy. Their officers and men, and the people of their home territories, were heatedly demanding a change.

When the generals' attempt to convince Chiang failed, they staged a coup. The Generalissimo was asleep in the hot springs spa in Lintong when he was awakened by shots. He leaped out of the back window in his night shirt, leaving his false teeth behind in a glass, scampered up a percipitous slope, and concealed himself in a crevice. There he was discovered by soldiers of the Young Marshal and courteously escorted to a guest house in Xian.

Prolonged and delicate negotiations brought Madame Chiang Kai-shek, her brother Foreign Affairs Minister T.V. Soong, and Chiang's Australian advisor W.H. Donald hastening up from Nanking to join the two warlords and Zhou Enlai, who had flown in representing the Communists. Under their combined urgings Chiang capitulated. He reluctantly promised to halt the civil war and form a united army to fight the Japanese. It took several more months to hammer out the details. But in August of 1937 the Red Army was renamed the Eighth Route Army, and in October the Communist guerilla fighters in south China were officially designated the New Fourth Army. Ten years of internal civil strife were, temporarily, at an end.

Under the terms of the agreement Yanan was ceded to the Communists. They moved over from Bao An in January 1937. With them went the Medical Advisor to the Army Department of Health, Dr. Ma Haide. There was no hospital in Yanan, no clinics or health facilities of any kind. George spent his days in the saddle, a kit bag containing medicines on his back, riding to villages, schools and barracks. Treating patients everywhere, in their cave homes, under a tree, in open fields, he had to ignore the dirty surroundings, the hardships, and the danger that he might himself become infected.

He seemed to have endless energy. He rode a horse, rode a bike, played basketball. After doctoring all day, he worked half the night in the Xinhua News Agency, where Liao Chengzhi and he set up an English Department which issued regular dispatches and gave radio broadcasts. Around midnight they dined on snacks of boiled potato.

Liao was the son of Liao Zhongkai—Dr. Sun Yat-sen's closest colleague, and He Xiangning—liberal woman leader in the original Kuomintang Party. When the Japanese attacked Shanghai in 1932 and Chiang Kai-shek refused to reinforce the 19th Route KMT Army heroically defending the city, she sent him a woman's gown with a letter berating him for "not acting like a man". Liao Chengzhi joined the Communist Party early in his career. Humorous and informative, he told exciting stories in fluent English about his adventures and explained how the Party functioned.

George had come to the Red Base Area as a sympathetic observer. His experience in Shanghai had taught him that the KMT was hopelessly venal and corrupt, that the old society was finished. After hearing Mao talk, and engaging in long discussions with Liao and other English-speaking Chinese, George became convinced that China's future lay with the Communists. Although only a small fraction of the population were members of the Communist Party, most people supported its principles and goals.

He felt irresistibly drawn to the courageous Chinese he encountered all around. Under constant attack by an implacable reactionary government, driven into arid mountains and desert in a remote corner of China, menaced by a cruel foreign invader, impoverished, short of everything, they remained buoyantly optimistic. The society they established was dedicated to helping the common man, leading and teaching him to help himself with down-to-earth, practical measures. Their morality scorned private wealth and position, and extolled a "love thy neighbor" sense of responsibility.

George spent a good deal of time at the front. The Japanese were launching a big drive. In August, he and a team of medics marched with the 129th Division of the Ba Lu (Eighth Route) Army. They were moving up to reinforce positions in the Wutai Mountains region held by troops of Hu Zongnan, the Shaanxi province warlord allied to Chiang Kai-shek.

Now that there was a "United Front", the Kuomintang had promised to give the Ba Lu medical supplies and equipment. But when the doctors sent carts to collect them, all they got was three small boxes of iodine and bandages. The Ba Lu met hordes of Hu Zongnan's KMT troops withdrawing to the rear, abandoning their positions while the Japanese were still miles away. Some of the soldiers were angry. They wanted to fight, but their generals had ordered them to retreat.

"None of this gave us a very good impression of the KMT," George said sarcastically.

But he was tremendously impressed by the Ba Lu, and the rigors he shared welded him closer to the revolution. They fought, marched and countermarched. He was very moved by the way the Eighth Route Army men reacted to being wounded. One boy had been hit in the head, and his brain was oozing out. But he wouldn't let the medics take his rifle or his bandolier of bullets. Only when the unit political instructor came would he give up his gun—and only to him. He wouldn't listen to any of the medical staff.

George ate millet, which he had never seen before, and it gave him painful stomach trouble. At the front they ate twice a day. It was hardly anything, just millet gruel with water from the river's edge. The water was brackish, full of sodium and magnesium salts. The peasants avoided it. They drank only rainwater, but the soldiers had no choice. It was a bitter time.

He was getting thinner and thinner. He couldn't eat the food, his stomach wouldn't accept it. The millet was cooked in linseed oil, which tasted rank. Long March veterans carried in their pockets bits of rock sugar wrapped in six thicknesses of paper. From time to time, they would give him a little piece, and it certainly helped.

"It was such a sacrifice for them—the final source of energy, of life," said George. "That was when our fighters' internationalism really came through to me. They didn't look at me as a foreigner. We were all working for the same cause, helping each other. It came so naturally to them, so easily."

Those long-legged wiry Eighth Route Army men took a lot of keeping up with. They had been on the move under hardship conditions for nearly two years, right up from Jiangxi, meeting all kinds of difficulties, navigating over unbelievably tough country. George had gone soft in Shanghai, little using his muscles and developing a taste for good coffee and apple pie a la mode, Too many visits to Jimmy's, the American café on Nanking Road. Physically hardened he was not.

"Battles are very frightening things, and were especially so to me who had never been in one," he said. "But whatever it was—bombings, shellings—these people took it in stride. I'd look for a hole and get in. But they'd go around as usual, carefully of course, but with great courage, protecting and helping one another. The bond between them was stronger than between brothers and sisters."

George remembered the toughness, the heart, the comradeship, the bravery. He related to them, understood them. They were what made him stick to the revolution, decided him never to waver through crisis after crisis. They made him believe that any blunders could be overcome.

He was called back to Yanan toward the end of 1937 to establish the Shaanxi-Gansu-Ningxia Border Region Hospital and organize some of the medical aid starting to come in from the outside. In spite of its grand name the "hospital" began life as a row of cave dwellings with very limited equipment. It was built on three levels. Offices were on the ground floor, in-patients occupied the two higher levels.

Being able to work out of a hospital was a change, but the greatest change was in his personal life. Although he had lived in Shanghai for three years, he hadn't really had any Chinese friends. In fact, except for Madame Soong, whom he respected and admired at a distance, he knew very few Chinese. Here in Yanan everything was different. He was close to Liao Chengzhi and a few other English speaking Chinese colleagues. He was on familiar terms with Mao Zedong and Zhou Enlai—leaders of a revolution affecting the lives of hundreds of millions of people. And he was able to meet and talk with dozens of ordinary Chinese every day.

It took the local folk a little time to become accustomed to this ebulent American. At first, they looked on him as a strange foreign doctor, not at all solemn and reserved like traditional Chinese practitioners. He sang loud peasant ditties as he cantered on horseback from place to place. He boldly flirted with the farm girls, who were shy in public and not used to such free and easy ways.

But since he was good-hearted and honest, and a conscientious, effective doctor, he soon was well-liked by almost everyone. He had a good ear for languages, and rapidly picked up the local patois. Illiterate peasants, well-educated intellectuals, soldiers, veteran Communists, women, children... came to him for medical treatment. But also they all wanted to talk, to know more about him, to tell him about themselves. George and his patients managed to communicate quite well. To their mutual gratification they discovered not so much their few differences but their many similarities. It was a pleasure knowing these people. While completely serious in their devotion to the public good, they laughed and sang a lot. The girls were beautiful, the men hearty.

George was not merely accepted, he was embraced simply and fully as an equal, as another human being with the same feelings and aspirations as their own. Wasn't this precisely the kind of life he had been seeking? In this land of "wide open spaces" a man could see far and think large. Here he was welcome, useful, encouraged to give full rein to his creativity, provide medical treatment to hundreds.

Never had he been so happy. He felt completely at home, bathed in a warm sea of mutual concern and care. He decided to stay, to make the Chinese cause his life, his career.

Joyously, George told this to everyone he knew. He applied to join the Communist Party in February 1937. He had made an excellent impression in his less than one year in the Base Area. He was immediately accepted as a probationary Party member. Final approval required a wait of another year.

He was awakened in Yanan shortly before dawn in February 1938 by two men and led to a cave on a hillside. The air was chill, and mist filled the gullies. There on the floor of the cave was a decapitated body, with the head lying beside it. This had been the mayor of a liberated village. The landlord tyrant and his private "militia" had stormed back in the day before, and cut his head off. They left his corpse on display in the public square as a warning to supporters of the popular forces.

A Red Army unit recaptured the village the same day. The remains had been brought to Yanan to show the savagery of the landlord class to the new arrivals, who were mostly from the cities.

One of the men turned to George and said, "You have applied to become a member of the Chinese Communist Party. This is what will happen to you if the enemy catches you. Are you sure you want to join?"

Pale and unable to speak, he could only nod. He was very shaken.

"They wanted to impress on me how cruel and bitter the struggle was," George later recalled. "I must say this did the trick. Any Communist caught by the enemy was a dead man. When you joined the Party you were laying your life on the line. Your dedication had to be complete. I never forgot that."

They let George return to his quarters. Two weeks later, he was formally admitted to membership in the Communist Party of China.

LOVE REQUITED

The tumultuous Agnes Smedley suddenly appeared in Yan-an, and the story she told George with passionate vehemence was typically Agnes. She came with the Communist delegation returning to Yanan after successfully concluding an agreement in Xian with Chiang Kai-shek for a United Front. She happened to be there when the famous "Incident" occurred on December 12,1936 and naturally, for Agnes, immediately became deeply involved. The event was of major importance to China.

Agnes had been resting at the spa in Lintong in the outskirts of Xian and beginning another book when the director excitedly told her she had to get out. The whole place—hotel, gardens and hot springs, was being placed at the disposal of no less a personage than Chiang Kai-shek, who was due to arrive shortly. Over her objections, she was put in a car and delivered to the Xijing Guest House, then the only modern hotel in Xian. Here she was informed they had no vacancies. The guest house had been reserved for Chiang's large entourage.

"Fine," she said. "Then I shall go back to Lintong."

In consternation, the manager hastily discovered a room for her next to his own. The local Blue Shirts—part of the "Generalissimo's" fascist bully boys organization, spent the next several days trying to have her evicted. But then Chiang was arrested by the Young Marshal, and the KMT network thought it wiser to keep a low profile.

The struggle among feudal power blocs in China was endless. Looters from the warlord armies which had staged the coup promptly supplanted the Blue Shirts. The KMT-owned guest house was a perfect target. They pounded on Agnes' door

48

demanding entry. She refused to open up. They put three bullets through the door, shattering windows at the other end of the room, and burst in. Agnes took refuge in a corner and watched them remove practically everything she had of value.

All this changed when the Young Marshal's garrison found out who she was. They invited her to go on the air at the radio station and tell the world what was happening in Xian. It was a journalist's dream—a ringside seat at one of the most dramatic events in modern Chinese history. Agnes was thrilled. She was able to observe the peace negotiations closely, to meet and talk with the Communist representatives, and report the inside story as one of the few foreign journalists on the scene.

The "liberated areas", which she had long idealized, turned out to be even better than she expected. The air of great changes being shaped, the pervasive simplicity and genuineness, inspired her as never before.

"Incredible," she cried to George. "Absolutely marvellous!"

Agnes at last could wear the dark homespun uniform sewn with white thread. She was especially proud of her cap with its five pointed red star. "He who takes this takes my head with it," she shouted in all seriousness when George playfully tried to snatch it.

But mainly she interviewed and wrote and collected material which was later to be published in two books: *Battle Hymn of China* and *The Great Road*—her biography of Zhu (then romanized as "Chu") De, Commander-in-Chief of the Red Army.

Other writers were now also coming to the northwest. The indefatigable and brilliant Helen Foster Snow, called "Peg" by her friends, who wrote under the name of Nym Wales and was then the wife of Edgar Snow, managed to reach Yanan after many adventures. What she observed in China's northwest was incorporated in *Inside Red China* and *The Chinese Communists*. In *Red China* she recalls how she met George:

> I first heard of him when Edgar Snow returned to our house from his 1936 trip to the Red Areas. They had travelled together on this trip, but Ma Hai Teh (his Chinese name) wanted to keep secret, so nothing was published about him. Ed had liked him. He told me that of all people Hai Teh loved to eat and he was starving for European food. When I went on my own trip a year later Ed told me to be sure to take food to Hai Teh or he wouldn't welcome me. If

you want to get on the good side of foreigners in China, take some good food with you. Rewi likes marmalade and Hai Teh likes good cheese....

Peg was plainly charmed by George, for she concludes:

Hai Teh is no ordinary person. He is quick, bright and easy to talk to (though all the foreigners in China are, and have to be, discrete to extinction). He is likeable, witty and still has a sense of humor. He also has a sense of responsibility and seems self-assured and positive, not like a person on approval. I asked if he intended to do a book about his life experience, and he said he had definitely decided against it.

George was adamantly against writing a book about himself, or having anyone else write it. To the end of his days he refused to sit down long enough for the interviews an author would need to do the job professionally.

"Too much is going on right now," he would say whenever approached on the subject of his biography. "Who's got time to reminisce!"

Peg liked his high spirits and sense of humor. At Ba Lu song fests it didn't take much coaxing to persuade him to launch into a loud rendition of "The Daring Young Man on the Flying Trapeze". And when Peg was bedded down for a time with dysentery and restricted to a diet of rice gruel, George would stand outside her window every morning and awaken her with "Arise, ye prisoner of starvation..."—his specially revised first line of the *Internationale*.

The whole Communist establishment—all the Party military and civilian units, the schools, the institutes, the residences... were located not inside the city of Yanan but in its outskirts, in caves carved out of the yellow earth hillsides and faced with doors and windows. Yanan was an old town with a wall around it, which made it a city by Chinese definition. In ancient times it had been the center of a northern frontier garrison district. Criminals and enemy soldiers captured in battle used to be sent further up to towns nearer the Great Wall boundary in permanent exile. Some of the soldiers—European mercenaries in the Mongol armies, intermarried with the local women. The girls who were their mixed-blood descendants in places like Suide and Mizhi, were famed as among the most beautiful in China.

As if to make up for the monotonous colorlessness of their surroundings, people in the northwest area were possessed of a dashing air and a great fondness for music. The men turbanned their heads in small towels, knotted in front. The towels were a protection against the dust and handy for wiping sweat. Tunics, padded or lined with sheepskin, were held in place by a sash, often with a brass-bowled long-stemmed pipe tucked beneath it like a dagger. Baggy trousers were lined or unlined according to season. The women were dressed in printed tunics of blue and white over long dark trousers. The little children covered the necessary minimum with jaunty aprons.

Everyone's feet were shod—the kids went barefoot most of the year—in the ubiquitous cloth shoes, by far the most comfortable of footwear. The soles were layers of cloth pasted and stitched together. Sturdy black cloth made the uppers. The shoes were light, they could "breathe". Atheletes foot among these folks was virtually unknown.

Everybody sang—men and women, young and old. The northern part of Shaanxi, where Yanan was located, was famous for it. There were plaintive shepherd songs, sometimes to the acompaniment of a lute. And there were the duets—between boy and girl, between husband wife—tender, funny, broad, as the case might be. Singing seemed to come naturally to the hill dwellers.

George was sharing a cave dwelling with Otto Braun, a thin wiry German communist with glasses, whose Chinese name was Li De. Braun had received military training in Moscow, and had been sent by the Comintern to serve as adviser to the Chinese Communists when they maintained their central revolutionary base in the southern province of Jiangxi in the early thirties. Surrounded by half a million KMT troops, the small Red Army, on Braun's advice, waged positional warfare against a much stronger and better equipped foe, over the strong protests of Mao Zedong and Zhu De. As a result the Red Army suffered such heavy losses that it was compelled to abandon the southern bases and undertake, now under Mao's leadership, the Long March to the northwest. Braun marched with them.

Although completely discredited militarily, Braun still enjoyed the prestige of a representative of the mighty Comintern and a Long March veteran. As part of his v.i.p. treatment he lived in a two-room cave with George outside the South Gate of the city.

They argued a lot, but became friends, based originally on a mutual longing for good food. Braun could make delicious German stew with pork or mutton, plus onions and potatoes. They had an orderly who couldn't cook, but brought them meat and vegetables from the general kitchen.

George was amiable, relaxed. Braun was proud, explosive. He slept with his gun under his pillow. In spite of the difference in their personalities they got along well enough. As the only two foreign men then in Yanan it was inevitable they should share the same quarters. They used to play cards for cigarettes and hunt mountain gazelle together. Both of them had rifles.

Braun fell in love with the pretty Li Lilian. She had been a famous singer in Canton before coming to Yanan, and had made several phonograph records. Lilian was married to a young man named Ouyang Shanzhen. George romantically sympathized with the lovers and delivered secret letters between them. They both knew enough English to be able to communicate. Finally, Lilian moved in with Braun, and lived with him in the inner room of the cave. George occupied the outer.

What attraction could have brought this oddly matched pair together was a mystery to everyone. Braun was a positive, domineering person who had simply impelled himself on Lilian. A sweet, gentle girl, she had been unable to resist his assaults.

When Ouyang, the outraged husband, stormed beligerantly into the cave, Braun threatened him with his pistol. George quickly intervened. Braun undoubtedly would have shot him if he hadn't. The angry shouting brought in others, who persuaded Ouyang to leave. He and Lilian were divorced, and she then "married" Braun. Such formalities at that time consisted only of reporting the *fait accompli* to the Communist Party organization.

There was as yet no national government. The Party ran military and civil affairs. It was the legislature, the executive and the judiciary all rolled into one. Party directives had the force of law. Statements by higher leaders on important issues were embraced as policy formulations. This concept proliferated as more and more of the country came under Communist domination.

After the establishment of the People's Republic in 1949 and the formation of legislative, executive and judicial bodies it proved difficult to convince the officials, and the rank and file, of the value of separating Party and government functions. The average citizen still went to his local Party chief with his legal problems. On a national level the Congress served mainly as a rubber stamp for the Communist Party Central Committee. Members of the Party, especially those in positions of authority, became "more equal than others" in the alleged equality all Chinese were supposed to enjoy before the law. While this was a violation of Communist Party principles it was also entirely in keeping with the feudal tradition of special privileges for a ruling elite.

In 1937, at the time of the autumn harvest the Japanese suddenly bombed Yanan and its environs. The attack was unexpected, and no defensive measures had been taken. There was tremendous damage.

George helped with the rescue. Never had he seen such carnage. Limbs and shreds of clothing were hanging from the trees. One man had a piece of bomb fragment sticking out of his skull. The medics in the field didn't dare remove it. A dazed soldier sat hugging his rifle. They had to put him and his gun on a stretcher together. Many caves, including George's front room, collapsed under the bombing. He moved over to the Army Health Department, leaving Braun behind, in the inner room, with Lilian.

She remained with him until he was recalled by the Third International in 1938. He never returned. Lilian was heartbroken. George did his best to comfort her. Rumors rose that they were lovers. Such suspicion was not unreasonable since Lilian was still in George's old cave dwelling. He was tempted at times, but she was much too distraught to take up with another man, and he couldn't bring himself to take advantage of her distress. Shortly thereafter, she moved back to the Lu Xun Arts Academy, where most of Yanan's writers, artists and theatre people lived. She and Ouyang remarried in 1939.

As surprised as George had been by the affair between Lilian and Braun, he was even more surprised when Ouyang took her back. Though a generous person, he himself would have been deeply humiliated if the woman he loved went off with someone else. Such a blow to his pride and self-respect would not have permitted him to take such a course. While rationally he approved Ouyang's broadness of spirit, emotionally it was beyond his comprehension.

A very different kind of foreign military expert arrived in 1938—U.S. Marine officer Evans Carlson. He was on a special mission to observe and report directly to President Roosevelt on the organization and fighting qualities of the Chinese Communist forces and the Kuomintang. He was so impressed with the tactics of the Eighth Route Army that, when given command of the Second Marine Raider Battalion in 1941 after America entered the war, he patterned his unit after it. "Carlson's Raiders", whose battle cry was *gung ho!* (Chinese for "do it together!"), landed from submarines on Makin Atoll and at Guadalcanal won the first U.S. victory in the Pacific war. Carlson was awarded the Navy Cross and promoted to Commander. He was a Brigadier General when he retired in 1946.

Blue-eyed, tall and rangy, with rugged features, Carlson was a man of strict principle and integrity. He went directly to Eighth Route Army Headquarters on his arrival in Yanan in 1938 and said: "I am an American Marine working for U.S. Naval Intelligence. I do not want to pry. Anything you want me to see, please show me and I will be satisfied."

A deeply religious person, the son of a New England Congregationalist minister, Carlson appreciated the ethical calibre of the new society he discovered in the Border Area.

The honesty, selflessness and incorruptibility of the leaders appeal to the patriotism and noble instincts of men and women who are not in accord with the political ideology of the Communist group (he noted later in his treatise *The Chinese Soldier*). Experiments which are being conducted in education, government and economic organization are destined to affect the whole of Chinese society when the present conflict is over. Politically they are developing representative government, economically they are developing a cooperative society, and socially they are developing an equitable social order which might be termed communal.

Carlson naturally was interested in the obviously American resident known as Dr. Ma Haide, who "advised on medical affairs", and whose "past... was unrevealed." In his *Twin Stars of China* Carlson gives an entertaining glimpse of how George managed to convey something of the warm brio of Yanan to Western visitors:

Ma was short, of dark complexion, and sort of an eternal optimist. His cheerful, hearty way, and the fact that he had learned to speak Chinese with amazing facility, made him extremely popular with the army. Over in Shansi men had asked me eagerly: "Do you know Ma Hai-teh? He speaks Chinese almost as well as we do."

Carlson met Ma Haide late one afternoon down in the village and invited him to have dinner. George agreed and they started for a restaurant famous for its "Ba Bao Fan" (Eight Precious Ingredients Rice)—a sweetened concoction. As they walked along George was hailed at almost every step by students and shop keepers, men and women alike. To each he replied: "Come along and have dinner with us."

Carlson was amused by the generosity with which George dispensed his hospitality. George obviously assumed that he was not pressed for money. As Carlson recalled it:

By the time we reached the restaurant I felt like the Pied Piper of Hamlin. In our wake were a dozen or more of young men and women, laughing, joking and thoroughly in the spirit of the occasion. It was great fun, and wholly informal. Individuals ordered what they wanted and then got up and left, or sat around and told stories of past experiences, without any sense of obligation.

George wanted to let Carlson savor the atmosphere and the people who gave him such pleasure. The marine officer was just the kind of person who could appreciate them. He was honest and sympathetic, and much impressed by what he had seen at the front and in civilian life. Both men were open, direct types, and instinctively liked each other. Carlson gave George a good briar pipe. It got smashed in one of the first Japanese air raids.

"It was in my pocket, and I hit the ground too hard," George said ruefully.

Dr. Norman Bethune, Canadian surgeon, appeared early in 1938, fresh from the battles of the Spanish Civil War. George was among the group of medical and army people who met him at the airport. Not only did Bethune display a cool expertise at the front under primitive conditions but, equally important, he was able to pass it on to Chinese medical personnel.

Bethune brought with him the latest scientific knowledge and broad experience in war surgery and care for the wounded.

He had an extensive knowledge of blood transfusion service in the field. He understood the need and urgency of immediate operation for the wounded, the value of the control of shock and bleeding, the need for intravenous fluids, the importance of the control of pain and the role of fixation and plaster casts for open fractures, osteomyelitis and similar injuries. This was the pre-antibiotic era. His experiences in military surgery in the Spanish Civil War enabled Bethune to convey all of this knowledge to his colleagues and to the training classes and mobile surgical teams he organized.

Later he wrote illustrated textbooks and lectures for teaching. He worked with carpenters and blacksmiths to improve equipment for travelling surgical units which could transport medicines, supplies and instruments, and serve as operating tables when removed from the pack animals carrying them.

Bethune was a man of many ideas and talents. He worked and taught and led mobile surgical teams, frequently participating in close support to battle lines, operating on the wounded practically at the front. Bethune set a fast pace, coinciding entirely with the tradition of hard work and self-sacrifice of the Eighth Route Army. In the period of over a year that Bethune worked in the Shanxi-Chahar-Hebei liberated area, he did a tremendous amount of teaching, travelling and operating. His head-on, tireless approach raised the level of the medical work and the morale of the Ba Lu fighting forces.

He died of blood poisoning on November 12, 1939. He had nicked his finger while operating on an infected limb.

"Norman Bethune died because there were not enough rubber gloves to use in operations," George said bitterly. "He cut his finger and died of septicemia. Fifty cents worth of penicillin or sulphanilamide would have saved his life."

The conditions the Chinese medical personnel were working under were woefully inadequate. They had virtually nothing in the way of equipment. The number of doctors with standard medical training could be counted on the fingers of two hands.

As Norman Bethune himself had commented, "Think of it! Two hundred thousand soldiers behind the Japanese lines, 2,500 wounded in the hospitals always, over 1,000 battles fought during the past year, and only five qualified Chinese doctors, 50 untrained doctors, and one foreigner to do all the work."

George Hatem had been that "one foreigner" before the

coming of Bethune. It was a severe shock to everyone when
Norman Bethune died. Memorial mass meetings stressed the
importance of international brotherhood. Mao Zedong wrote
an article extolling Bethune as its selfless epitome.

While the problem of qualified medical personnel was never
fully solved, it was considerably ameliorated by intensive
methods. The Red Army Medical School was training doctors
in nine months. They had come up from the ranks as orderlies,
nurses, nurses' aides, the first-aid corps and pharmacy workers.
Millions of people in the areas behind the enemy lines were
treated by nine-month trained doctors. Until 1949 the revolutionaries had few fully trained doctors. But these had formulated the policies, principles and methods of working with very
little and taking care not only of the army but of the civilians
wherever the army went.

Especially appalling was the dearth of medicines. But even
this was dealt with. The measures were bold and ingenious.
Many battles and engagements were fought just to capture
medicine. Ba Lu intelligence services were so good they often
knew exactly what medical supplies a Japanese or puppet army
was carrying on the march. Ba Lu forces would engage them
to get the supplies if there was enough to make it worthwhile.

Foreign friends and missionaries would go into cities like
Beijing and Shanghai to buy medicine for their mission stations. They would bring it through the Japanese lines, and then
give part or all of it to the Base Area. The Communists would
also send their own people in secretly, but that was much more
dangerous. Many revolutionaries lost their lives trying to get a
little bit of anaesthesia through the enemy blockade.

The Western-trained medical people in Yanan, including
George, then "discovered" a method of treatment which had
been in use a mere two or three thousand years—traditional
Chinese medicine. It was only reasonable to make use of its
practitioners since, for one thing, they outnumbered their
modern colleagues ten to one. For another, their treatments
were equally effective, and sometimes more effective. Moreover, given a choice between Western and traditional doctors, the
average Chinese patient chose the latter every time. It was
found the best results were obtained by combining the skills of
both.

Fortunately, traditional medicines could easily be manufac-
tured locally. Yanan's medical authorities were already prom-

oting the concept that modern and traditional doctors should work together. During this period a number of perscriptions which the traditional practitioners recommended as useful were selected. In simple factories the herbal and plant ingredients—ordinarily brewed in an earthenware pot by the patient at home—were concocted into infusions or syrups or pills and powders which could be conveniently carried around and quickly applied under battle conditions.

Western-trained doctors tended to scoff at the traditional methods, holding them "backward" and "unscientific". Although originally also a sceptic, George became convinced of their value through practical evidence and personal experience.

The first time he ran across traditional medicine was during the Anti-Japanese War. In 1936, when the Red Armies came up from the south into northern China, many of the old fighters had malaria. They would get chills and fever and be out of action, and the Western-trained doctors had no medicine for them, not even quinine.

I saw a traditional doctor take a soldier sitting by the side of the road with malaria chills and give him three acupuncture needles along the last cervical and first thoracic vertebrae, (George remembered.) Within half an hour the man could get up and continue marching with the rest of the troops. Though it was not a cure, the relief would last about two weeks. I've seen this with my own eyes. I wouldn't have believed it if anybody had told me of such a result.... I myself have written hundreds of prescriptions using Chinese ingredients—and they work. I've become a firm devotee of traditional medicine.

Another source of medicine was Madame Soong Ching Ling in Hong Kong. George maintained a steady correspondence with her and kept her informed on the medical situation in the Base Area. This helped her to tell the world, through the China Defense League which she organized in Hong Kong in 1938, of the heroic fight of the revolutionaries against the Japanese invaders, and their desperate need for medicines and medical equipment.

In September 1939, just two months before Bethune died, George sent an urgent plea for medical supplies to Manny Granich who was editing *China Today* in New York. Edgar Snow, then on a second visit to Yanan, took the letter out.

Medicines for the 8th Route Army, front and rear, have been distributed for July, August, and September. By the end of the month we will have no more Western medicines. We are sending out from our medical factory medicines made with Chinese drugs which provide approximate application in the foreign sense, but which are completely inadequate to carry on a medical service for civilians, refugees, and the wounded.

Bethune has just sent me note from the front, saying: "I have one pound of ether, two scalpels, and a few pounds of cotton and gauze. When this is finished I don't know what I'll do. For Marx's sake, do something!"

And here we are in Yanan dishing out medicine of Chinese herbs. For anybody's sake, do something!

Funds and medical supplies donated by sympathizers abroad came slowly through the heavy KMT blockade to Yanan. George oversaw their receipt, checked their content, and expedited their distribution.

When the Indian doctors arrived in the winter of 1939, he was there to welcome them, help them settle in, and begin their valuable work. He had become, in fact, the greeter *ex officio* of all the foreign doctors who came to Yanan to volunteer their services—Norman Bethune of Canada, A. Orlov of the Soviet Union, Hans Muller of Germany, five doctors from India.... Showing them around, answering questions, telling his own experiences, George did his best to smoothe their adjustment to a strange new environment.

The Indians were part of the first large international medical delegation to visit Yanan. A crowd of youngsters, wearing the worn cut-down padded clothes of grown-ups, very patched and faded, came tumbling down the hillside, bare feet in hemp sandals, eager to see the new arrivals. These were the "imps" —the boys who served as orderlies, messengers, and did a million and one other useful things in the Ba Lu. They did not look much like any army personnel the delegation had seen previously. But they were full of life, and the sight of the tall handsome doctors in fur hats and coats alighting from the ambulances intrigued and delighted them.

On hand to welcome the delegation, George was solemnly on his dignity. This was abruptly deflated when someone gave him "a friendly kick in the pants". Startled, he turned around to see his old friend Rewi Alley. George hadn't known Rewi was coming or, for that matter, where Rewi was in China. The two of them soon slipped away from the reception and sought privacy in a noisy cooperative restaurant where they tucked into a modest dinner.

Afterwards they went to George's new quarters and talked far into the night. A peasant came to the door with a paper lantern on a stick, and George quickly packed his medical bag and went trudging off through the snow. Rewi had coffee boiling by the time he returned. But before George had finished his first cup they heard another voice at the door. "Ma *Daifu*! Ma *Daifu*!" Again George took up his bag and departed.

Rewi was asleep when he came back. When Rewi awoke in the morning George was kneeling on the floor blowing embers in the brazier, getting ready to make more coffee. In those days coffee was in very short supply, brought in by stray visitors. Next, George went off and returned with a big hunk of hot flatbread and a few long oil fritters. They tasted particularly delicious in the bracing cold mountain air.

"That's what my days and nights were like," George recalled. "I was liable to be sent for at any time. I didn't get much rest, but I enjoyed meeting and talking with the local folk, learning about their lives, basking in their homey warmth, feeling that I was being useful."

Yanan was relatively prosperous that year. Roads through to the cities in the south were still open, and some good food was coming in. The co-op market shop even had jam made with local fruit and Sichuan sugar.

But the Japanese were bombing more frequently. A day or two before Rewi's arrival, a big bomb had burst right in front of George's cave dwelling, blowing everything inward, and killing people in an adjacent compound. He showed Rewi the case of a dud bomb which had been rigged up as a gong.

"Reminds me of home," George said. Around the rim was stamped "Toledo, Ohio".

Athough on the surface he remained an unbuttoned wise-cracking American with an easy natural manner, he took problems seriously. He was not the same person he had been only a year or two before. George had found his feet, become part of the Yanan community. He had developed a poise and self-confidence he had not possessed in Shanghai.

It surprised him that U.S. arms manufacturers should be selling bombs to Japan at a time when everyone knew that

country posed a dangerous potential threat to America. They
certainly were making them available to international weapons
merchants who put them in Japanese hands for the slaughter
of innocent Chinese civilians. Neither humanitarian consider-
ations nor intelligent self-interest seemed to play any role in
shaping Washington's foreign policy. Greed for immediate
profits was given first priority, as usual.

Encouraged by the lack of opposition from Chiang Kai-
shek's Kuomintang Nationalist government to its occupation
of "Manchuria" (Northeast China), Japan decided to seize
North China as a next step to converting the whole country
into a Japanese colony. In July 1937, Japanese troops attacked
the Marco Polo Bridge southwest of Beijing. Nationwide rage
was aroused. Thousands flocked to join the Chinese fighting
forces. Many formed effective hit-and-run guerilla bands. Persons in other countries who saw the spread of Japan's "Greater
East Asia Co-Prosperity Sphere", in conjunction with the blessings bestowed by the Nazi *herrenvolk*, as a menace to the entire
globe, helped in whatever ways they were able.

But these contributions from the outside, though often at
great personal sacrifice, were small in comparison with the
monumental assistance the Western democracies gave to the
Axis powers. Britain, France and the United States attempted
to protect their interests in the Pacific by appeasing Japan,
which they hoped would turn north and attack the Soviet
Union. Already threatened by the German-Japanese Comintern Pact, signed in 1936, the Soviet Union nevertheless gave
active support to the Chinese.

For years relations between Chiang Kai-shek's government
and Nazi Germany had been close. A German military mission
under General von Falkenhausen was stationed in China. It
helped train Kuomintang troops and gave advice on how to
fight the Communist Red Army in Chiang's "encirclement and
suppression" campaigns. When Japan started its large-scale
invasion, Hitler's government tried to mediate between its two
"friends" through its ambassador in Nanjing. But no compromise could be reached. In the spring of 1938 the German mission
was withdrawn at Japanese insistence.

Britain—Japan's long-time ally in the Far East, had no
objection to sacrificing China's interests if it would keep the
Japanese from harming Britain's. When Japanese troops occupied China's coastal cities, British officials presented Japan

with the revenues of the Chinese Maritime Customs Administration, which it previously controlled. In north China the British-dominated Kailuan Mines readily supplied the Japanese with coal.

Great Britain agreed in 1939 that Japanese forces in the British Concession in Tianjin had the right to "suppress or remove any acts or causes as will obstruct them or benefit their enemy". The effect of this was to hand over a number of Chinese patriots to the Japanese for execution. Fresh from his sell-out of Czechoslavakia at Munich in September 1938, Prime Minister Chamberlain in November predicted that after the Japanese won they probably would not have enough funds to develop Chinese resources. He magnanimously proposed to let British capital lend a helping hand.

In 1940, under Japanese pressure, Britain closed the Burma Road through which China had been receiving some supplies from the West. France likewise discontinued the Haiphong-Yunnan Railway, a link to the outside through Vietnam. Both offered their services in arranging a Sino-Japanese "settlement" at China's expense.

The United States, reacting in much the same manner as it had when Japan invaded China's Northeast in 1931, again proclaimed high-sounding principles, but took no effective steps to stop Japanese aggression. On October 5, 1937, President Roosevelt made a speech recommending a "quarantine" to halt the spreading "epidemic of world lawlessness". The following day the State Department announced that it considered Japan's action in China to be contrary to the Nine Power Treaty of 1922 and the Kellogg-Briand Pact of 1928. But America did nothing to implement a "quarantine", nor did it impose any sanctions.

Although wide sections of the American public were sympathetic to China, the spirit of "business as usual" prevailed. U.S. corporations continued to buy large quantities of raw silk from Japan and sell shiploads of scrap steel which fed Japan's war industry. After 1941 when the U.S. entered the war, some of this steel came back as bullets into the bodies of American boys. Congress passed Neutrality Acts in 1935 and 1937 creating a policy of "non-intervention" which in essence prevented America from aiding victims. On the eve of Pearl Harbor the State Department was still attempting to negotiate a Far Eastern version of the Munich Pact with Japan.

In a letter to Manny Granich, George angrily related his personal encounter with American scrap iron delivered by courtesy of Japanese bombers:

This last week I was blown out of my cave. Everything in it was destroyed. I was in the connecting cave and the paper I was reading was taken all the way outside by the bombing. Forty-five planes dropped three hundred bombs on an area of two-thirds of a square mile. There were thirty to forty killed and wounded from the collapse of the caves. This was the 19th bombing of the city.

We hope that an embargo on Japan goes thru. Those damned steel pieces sticking in the wounds must come from American scrap iron. I feel like a cur every time I and the surgical assistant take out one of them and he looks at me and doesn't say a word. Somehow I can't get away from a sense of guilt. If every American could go thru a bombing and the work after it I am sure Japan would get no bombs or oil for killing the Chinese.

The only power which gave China any real help in her hour of need was "Godless Russia". In August 1937, one month after the Japanese attack on the Marco Polo Bridge near Beijing, Moscow signed a Non-Aggression Treaty with Nanjing. The Soviets extended credits of $100 million in 1938 and $150 million in 1939 for the purchase of war materials.

This enabled China to buy tens of thousands of tons of munitions from the USSR, delivered via Xinjiang in the Northwest. In addition, Moscow dispatched 1,000 planes and 2,000 fliers. They played an important role in protecting major cities such as Hankow, Chongqing, Chengdu and Lanzhou against Japanese air raids. Moscow also sent a military mission of some 500 men to replace the military advisors the German's had withdrawn from Nanjing.

The contrast between the Soviet and the American positions was so marked that even ardently anti-Communist Madame Chiang Kai-shek was impelled to public comment. In the January 1939 issue of the U.S. mass-circulation magazine *Liberty*, she wrote:

Eighty percent of Japan's war supplies come from America.... Ninety-five percent of the aviation gasoline which was used by Japan in her ruthless bombing was American.

Throughout the first three years of resistance, Soviet

Russia extended to China for the actual purchase of war supplies and other necessities, credits several times larger than the credits given either by Great Britain or America.

I may point out that Russian help has been unconditional throughout.

Then in August 1939, the Soviet Union signed a Non-Aggression Pact with Nazi Germany, causing consternation among many who looked to Moscow for support in their struggle against Axis invasion. In a letter to Granich in September, George reported that Edgar Snow, again in Yanan, had long talks with Mao on the old and new world situations —especially the upheaval in Europe and the resulting changes. Snow said Mao, while noting the universal befuddlement, considered the Soviet move a ploy to gain time to prepare for an attack on the USSR by the combined forces of Germany and the other Western countries.

"According to Mao," George wrote, "Chamberlain, the rogue, is trying to form a coalition of all the capitalist powers to fight the Soviets, as part of a plan hatched long ago."

While there may have been confusion in the West as to where the Soviet Union stood against the Nazis, there was no question as to her attitude regarding Nazi Germany's strongest partner in the Rome-Berlin-Tokyo Axis—Japan, China's main enemy. In retaliation for Soviet military aid to China, the Japanese attacked Outer Mongolia, a Moscow ally, in 1939. They were utterly plastered by the Soviet Red Army, losing 25,000 troops, 660 planes, and a large number of tanks. In spite of the short-lived Non-Aggression Pact, which ended abruptly with the German invasion of the Soviet Union in June 1941, Moscow continued to give China support all through the anti-Japanese war.

But the Russians had their hands full in Europe, and could only offer limited assistance. Nothing could be expected from America which, until Pearl Harbor, was helping Japan. For this reason China particularly cherished the "international friends" who stood by her side. In Yanan, Ma Haide, George Hatem, was one of a highly valued few. Not only for his medical contributions, but because he was a symbol, vividly present among the Chinese, of people in other lands who supported the justice of their cause.

After the Japanese bombing in 1937 levelled most of the old city of Yanan, the Lu Xun Arts Academy moved to Chao Er

Gully in the outskirts. George was appointed school doctor. There was comparatively little illness at the Academy, since it was populated mainly by young people, and he dropped by only once a week. He enjoyed visiting the writers, artists, and actors and actresses of stage and screen who lived there because they tended to be vivacious and natural, much resembling their counterparts in the West. They, in turn, welcomed the jocular American medic as someone compatible.

George also went in for sports and was on a basketball team which included Liao Chengzhi, who was known by the sobriquet "Fatty". Their team played against young students and army men.

"They beat the pants off us regularly," George said.

Life was rich and full, with one exception—he had no wife. He was constantly on the lookout for someone to marry. George found a girl he thought was a desireable prospect, not among the charming actresses at the Lu Xun Academy, but on the basketball court. Her name was Wang Ping, and she had been trained as a coach at the famous Shanghai Physical Education Institute. Though not pretty, she had a magnificent body, and wore her short hair parted on the side like a boy. George was enchanted by the lush fluidity of her movements during a game. They went out together a few times. He proposed, she refused, and they broke up.

Sufei, his future wife, accidentally met her in 1939 in the Ba Lu Hostel in Xian. She told George about it, laughing, after they were married.

Wang Ping had been heading for another part of the country on an underground assignment. Sufei and a group of girls were on their way to Yanan. They all slept in the same room. A second Yanan girl, teasing Wang Ping, asked her why she hadn't married Ma Haide, since the two of them had been so close.

"I didn't want to give birth to a little half-breed," Wang Ping said simply. They all chuckled.

"Who is this Ma Haide?" Sufei asked the other Yanan girl.

"A high-nose."

Chinese are struck not by the size of foreigners' noses—some of them have quite substantial probosces of their own—but by the fact that the bridges of Western noses are usually higher than theirs.

That was the first Sufei heard of the man whose life she was to share for forty-eight years.

She came from a family of fishing boat builders on the Zhoushan Islands. In her early teens she ran away to Shanghai to avoid an arranged marriage, and stayed with sympathetic relatives. A few years later she began acting in a theatre company run by the Left Wing Writers Guild, playing mainly kid sister roles. A film director saw one of her performances and thought she showed promise. He gave her a small part in *Ba Yi San* ("August Thirteenth"—the day in 1937 the Japanese had bombed Shanghai).

During a brief unsuccessful marriage ending in divorce she gave birth to a little daughter, Liang Bi. In 1939, when the baby was less than a year old, Sufei left her with relatives in Shanghai and went off with the theatrical troupe to Kunming in Yunnan province, which is just north of Burma, Laos and Vietnam. Because their plays commended the United Front and urged resistance against the Japanese invaders, the troupe and everyone in it were put on a KMT black list. Chiang Kai-shek didn't want to divert any of his bullets from his planned destruction of the revolutionaries.

It was dangerous for the theatrical company people to remain in Kunming. A member of the underground told them about Yanan, where one could openly oppose Japanese aggression. Sufei and another girl immediately proposed to go. The underground contact bought them bus tickets to Guiyang in Guizhou province to the east. The fragile armistice with the Kuomintang was still holding, and the Ba Lu was able to maintain an office in the city. Clad in the green uniforms of KMT nurses surreptitiously given them by the Ba Lu, the girls then went by truck to Chengdu, Sichuan, where a large group of girl students joined them. Everyone, including the drivers, was decked out in KMT green. Chungking (now Chongqing), also in Sichuan, was the next stop. The convoy expanded here to seven trucks containing about forty people.

Young German doctor Hans Muller was added to Sufei's truck. At twenty-four, tall and thin, he had been living in Switzerland, where he had obtained his medical degree. He was determined to fight fascism. If he couldn't do it in Germany, he would do it in China. He had heard about the remarkable resistance center in Yanan. Travelling via Switzerland, Hong Kong, and Vietnam, he had succeeded in reaching Chongqing without knowing a word of Chinese.

Hard-headed, intelligent and humorous, Hans, linguistically mute, was at a disadvantage as the only man among this gaggle of rollicking teen-age girls. He looked very proper in his Western suit and tie, and behaved with formal correctness. He had even brought his diploma in an aluminum tube container which he never let out of his hands. Since the truck was jammed with luggage and bedding, and the girls occupied the only available seats, Hans had to sit on the floor next to the tailboard, where he was suffused with dust. The girls teased him constantly, and relented only after he showed them a picture of his sweetheart, a pretty Swiss dancer.

When the convoy reached Xian, the last "United Front" city before Yanan, the girls stayed in the hostel of the Ba Lu Office. Hans, as a foreigner, had to live in the Xijing Hotel run by the Kuomintang. Their agents searched his luggage in his absence. He was incensed.

About half the original passengers went on. The others remained for a few weeks' "training". Actually it was to give the Ba Lu authorities a chance to check their backgrounds more thoroughly. There had been a few instances, and would be more later, of Kuomintang infiltration.

All had changed into Ba Lu gray. The trucks slowly climbed the loess highlands. They reached Yanan two days later. Sufei joined the theatre people in the Lu Xun Arts Academy. Hans was assigned to the Army Hospital, where the Indian doctors were already at work. Shortly thereafter, the Indians, and Hans with them, left for the front.

George was riding his horse for one of his weekly medical visits to the Arts Academy when a young fellow he knew hailed him excitedly.

"Hey! Ma Haide! A new batch of girls has just arrived at the Academy. They say one of them, Jiang Qing's kid sister, is very pretty. Introduce me to her, will you?"

Sufei had played the maid in Ostrovsky's *The Storm* in Shanghai. Jiang Qing, then called Lan Ping, had been the leading lady. Inaccurate theatrical gossip held that they were sisters. Jiang Qing was later to become Mao's third wife.

"Fat chance," George said under his breath. "You don't catch me passing up any pretty girls."

He saw Sufei at the Academy, and was bowled over by her grace and beauty. She had bright expressive eyes and wore her shining back hair in a short bob. He had no chance to talk with her at any length until the following year at the Spring Festival, which in 1940 fell in January. All of the schools threw parties, but the Academy's was by far the best. Its young people in the theatre and the arts were naturally talented performers, and its girls were famous for their good looks. Even the clothes they wore, although the same as those of everyone else, somehow, with a little decoration here and a slightly different cut there, had a touch of swagger, an air of smartness.

George played in an extract from a Peking opera *San Da Zhu Jia Zhuang*—"Three Attacks on the Zhu Family Village". He was dressed in ornate classical costume, a fantastic traditional colored design adorned his face. George strode on in high platform shoes and bowed in every direction. Since he couldn't sing Peking opera arias, he launched into one of the few Chinese songs he knew—a local ditty called "Our village is full of lovely maids...." The incongruity of this foreign friend in full opera make-up and regalia beating out a pop tune had the audience in stitches. Mao Zedong, Zhou Enlai, and other top leaders who had come to see the show, nearly collapsed with laughter.

The party went on for hours. There was dancing to a small pick-up band of mixed Chinese and Western musical instruments. General Ye Jianying, played a *yang qin*—a kind of Cantonese zither. Now back in ordinary clothes, his face washed clean, George spotted Sufei peeking out from behind one of the pillars supporting the roof of the large hall in which the festivities were being held. George asked her to dance, his heart beating fast. She said she didn't know how.

"Never mind," he retorted boldly, though he was quaking inwardly. "I'll teach you." Her loveliness was breath-taking.

George led her to the floor. He was a very good dancer, and she caught on quickly. Her body seemed to mould itself to his. They were holding each other much closer than Yanan decorum usually allowed, but neither of them cared.

This is what Heaven must be like, if there is one, George thought. They danced all the rest of the dances together.

After midnight they walked along the banks of the Yan River, a favorite spot for post-dinner strollers and romantic couples. George proclaimed his love. He told her about himself, his family. Sufei did the same. This was standard procedure for young people who were courting. He kissed her, long and deliciously. She broke away and ran back to her hostel in confused agitation.

One of the women in Sufei's room was very pregnant. At two in the morning the birth pains started. The party had ended late. George had told Sufei that rather than ride back to his own quarters in the dark he would stay over with Emi Xiao, a teacher in the Academy. None of the girls knew where exactly Emi lived, but they had to find a doctor. They were wandering around in front of the long row of teachers' cave dwellings when luckily Emi heard their voices. He got up and went out to see what was the trouble.

They hauled George out of a deep sleep and rushed him to the patient. He put everyone to work, boiling water, preparing clean cloths.... "Is the father here?" he demanded. Of course, he wasn't. Most of the married couples were separated, the husbands and wives working and living in different units. George shooed everyone out, except Sufei and another girl who remained to assist him. He safely delivered the baby.

Although it was his first venture into a maternity procedure, George had done a clean and competent job. By now it was nearly dawn. Sufei helped him wash up. She told him later that seeing him perform that night had roused her admiration for him as a doctor, and as a man.

From then on, there was an "understanding" between them. Before two months had elapsed, they decided to get married. Every one of Sufei's girl friends was opposed. He may not want to spend his whole life in China, they said. They pointed to the example of Braun, who had deserted Lilian. What's more, they contended, there is no way of checking whether Ma Haide doesn't already have a wife in America.

But the young couple were determined. At the end of February 1940, George went to the Organization Department of the Chinese Communist Party. The man in charge and he were friends.

"I want to get married," George said.

"Who to?"

"Guess."

"Li Lilian."

"Wrong. It's Sufei."

"I can't place her. Who is she?"

George told him all about her. Party approval was granted. He took Sufei to the Border Area government office to formally register and obtain a marriage certificate. This was a procedure followed only by local residents. It was not necessary for people attached to the Revolutionary units. But George wanted everything proper and legal, American style.

To Rewi he dashed off a telegram: GETTING MARRIED. PLEASE SEND 200 DOLLARS. His old friend and mentor promptly complied. The money was used to order a banquet in a local restaurant for ten tables of ten guests each. Zhou Enlai and Mao Zedong attended the wedding party. It was a lively noisy affair.

But none of Sufei's girl friends came, and she was miserable. She wept when she and George were lying in bed together in his cave dwelling that night. What would life be like without friends? George was very understanding. He said she could still call the marriage off if she wished. He told her again about himself and his family in America, and swore he would never deceive or abandon her.

"If you love me, you ought to trust me. But you're free," he said. "It's up to you."

Sufei threw her arms around him. They fiercely embraced.

COMPLEX YANAN

The honeymoon lasted all of three days. Then Sufei moved over to the Women's College to begin a course in political science. George called for her every Saturday afternoon on his horse and took her home to their cave dwelling in the Health Department compound. She rode pillion behind him—a rare sight in conservative Yanan. On Monday mornings he returned her to school.

Competition for Sufei's hand had been keen. "I won out only because of my persistence and high-powered American salesmanship," George said modestly.

Some of the young fellows in the Arts Academy were displeased with Sufei's marriage. With so many eligible Chinese around, why marry a foreigner? A certain amount of Han-chauvinism, always latent, seeped to the surface. Among the girls it took the form of snide back-biting. She married Ma Haide for the relative comforts the match could bring, for a chance to go with him to America....

The young educated people did manage, for the most part, to find mates among their own kind. It was much more difficult for the army men, for the veterans of the Long March. Not only were they older and more numerous than the city-bred girls who came flocking to the Revolutionary Bases, but they were mainly of peasant background and tended to be simpler in their tastes and cruder in their manners. Few had any formal education. It was almost impossible for them to find a common language with the girls.

A pretty girl stolling on a hilltop with a veteran one evening remarked dreamily on the beauty of the moon. "What's beautiful about it?" the man said brusquely. "Looks like a big round

71

flatcake." While by no means were all of the army men so insensitive, the story got around.

Another incident illustrative of the aesthetic hiatus between town and country occurred while George was chalking up a fresh triumph in his thespian career. He was performing in an amusing little vehicle called *Yanan Waltz*, introducing the kind of people then living in the Revolutionary Base. The actors played themselves. Several of the most alluring actresses took part. An appreciative capacity audience filled the large hall.

When it was over Sufei asked one of the veterans what he thought of a certain actress's performance. He said he hadn't noticed because he had been unable to tear his eyes from her beautiful breasts—they bounced so delightfully when she sobbed.

That these men, after long months of fighting and on the march, should have been starved for female companionship and love, was natural enough. The Chinese are tireless match-makers, and everyone tried to find them brides. This proved virtually impossible, particularly among the girls from the big cities. One or two did marry older men, mainly out of a sense of duty, or perhaps to improve their social positions. There were also some marriages with girls who were themselves of rural background. But the question of the no-longer-young bachelors remained.

More serious problems threatened the inhabitants of the Border Region, as the Revolutionary Base now commonly was called. The Japanese, attempting to consolidate their rear, were concentrating their attacks on the liberated areas and conducting a "kill all, burn all, loot all" campaign. An estimated thirty million civilians lost their lives. Vast tracts of land were left covered only with rubble and cinders.

At the same time the KMT rulers, in spite of the "United Front", tightened their economic blockade of the Border Region. They were worried by the steady flow of the cream of China's intellectuals and the best of her youth to Yanan. And Chiang Kai-shek never for an instant relinquished the idea that the revolutionaries, not the Japanese, were the main enemy.

Food was short. Everyone, from Mao Zedong right on down, cultivated his own little vegetable garden in his spare time. George was proud of the irrigation ditch Sufei and he had dug from a mountain stream to the patch they tended every evening. They raised beans and radishes. An old farmer taught him how to castrate pigs.

"I don't know whether you could call it a medical skill," said George, "but I got plenty of calls to demonstrate it."

Salt, sugar and cooking oil were in short supply. The Indian doctors, whose traditional diet is sweet, missed sugar the most. When the first snow fell, they said, "It looks just like sugar. If only it were!"

The students constantly thought and talked of food. One young man was dying for fried eggs. He was able to buy a couple of eggs, but had no oil for frying. Although each hostel room had an "oil lamp", it was just a dish with a little oil and a single wick, dim and difficult to read by. Certainly none of this precious oil could be spared.

Our young student had a brilliant idea. He went to the infirmary, complaining of constipation. As expected, he was given a small bottle of castor oil. He hurried back and, ignoring the warnings of his room-mates, fried two eggs. Oil heated till it smoked was no longer laxative, he firmly announced. The eggs smelled and tasted delicious. He went to the infirmary again the next day—this time to be treated for diarrhea.

Mao and his colleagues in the Communist Party leadership instituted a drive for self-sufficiency. It was comprehensive and eminently practical, embracing every aspect of the Border Region economy.

To ease the peasants' burdens, gain their allegience, and encourage them to produce more, a 25 percent rent reduction was enforced, with a rent ceiling of 37.5 percent of the crop instead of the usual 50 to 80 percent. Interest on loans was limited to 1.5 percent monthly, or 18 percent per year—a substantial reduction from the customary usurious charge. In addition to benefitting the poor peasants, who constituted the bulk of population, it put a severe dent in the strength of the rural landlords.

Early experiments in land reform were started with the formation, on a strictly voluntary basis, of mutual aid teams and farming cooperatives. Remuneration was based on the value of land, draft animals and tools invested, as well as the amount of labor performed, so that both the more prosperous and the poor peasants benefitted. By 1943 eighty percent of the farmers in the Region had joined one or the other of these organizations. They opened up 250,000 acres of new land, producing an abundance of grain and some cotton.

Reliance was not placed entirely on the local population. Every government organization, school, and military unit was urged to grow as much of its own food as possible. The famous 359th Brigade set the pace, undertaking the reclamation of Nanniwan, a barren hilly area southeast of Yanan. With no shelter, few tools and little food, the soldiers pitched in with such vigor and ingenuity that by 1943 they had reclaimed 25,000 acres, yielding more grain than the brigade could eat. They had also learned how to make clothes, blankets, shoes, tables, chairs, charcoal and paper. The "spirit of Nanniwan" is remembered and cherished in China to this day.

The local government set up iron-smelting and oil-refining works, machine shops, arsenals, pottery and porcelain kilns, and small factories making cloth, blankets, shoes, paper and soap. By the end of 1942 there were 84 of these factories, employing 4,000 workers.

Women, weaving at home, were producing more cloth than the small textile mills by the end of 1943. Their contribution in this and other ways was so marked that, along with the rise in their economic status, their social position in what was still a predominantly male chauvinist feudal society, also improved.

The Communist Party instituted free elections and other democratic procedures, cut government personnel and military expenditures, and saw to it that all civil servants worked side by side with everyone else in all types of endeavor. An astonishing development in a country where traditionally bureaucrats grew long fingernails to prove they never had to stoop to physical labor. A foundation was laid for the cooperative approach which would characterize China's drive toward modernization.

Material conditions improved dramatically, and with them morale. The Border Region was far from prosperous, but there were no serious shortages and spirits were high. The people were confident they could fight the Japanese invaders as long as need be. Strength and power had come to the formerly weak and powerless.

All of the foreign doctors received extra monthly rations. These consisted of four packs of eight candles each, half a *jin* of tea (about half a pound), two *jin* of white sugar, and a carton of British *Capstan* cigarettes—a rare treasure. There were never enough cigarettes for heavy smokers like George. Sufei made him a week's supply when she came home over Saturday and Sunday, rolling them from dried willow leaves and scrap paper.

Eating was the main weekend activity. George would go to great pains to get nourishing food for Sufei, who was very thin. But whenever he managed to buy a chicken or a cut of meat and cook it, she refused to eat. Her stomach would accept only the simple fare to which they were all accustomed. Worried, George would try to force her, and she would cry, and it would end in a quarrel.

Gradually Sufei's appetite improved. On Sundays she and George would entertain Basu and the other Indian doctors. They would pool their extra rations of pork and make one big lunch, for themselves and any friends who dropped by. They had acquired a small phonograph, and the Indians brought records. Everyone danced, and there were some hot card games —for cigarette butts.

On Saturday nights, George and Sufei wandered from one party to another, bringing their records, which made them particularly welcome guests. Wang, their orderly and jack-of-all-trades, escorted them, carrying a lantern. They seldom got home before ten or eleven. It was a time of relative peace and well-being. George felt very much at home—Saturday night dances, a pregnant wife, kidding around among friends, walking home under the stars.

"I couldn't have done any better in North Carolina," he thought.

Disruption of this tranquility began in 1941. During the anti-Japanese war young people from all over China flocked to join the Communist Party. By 1941 its ranks had swollen from 100,000 to 800,000. While patriotic and ardent revolutionaries, many were not too conversant with political theory. The majority of those who migrated to the liberated areas were of peasant origin, the rest were mainly students and city intellectuals. A war was being fought against a powerful foreign invader while maintaining a precarious united front with the Kuomintang. It was a delicate situation requiring intelligent sensitive handling. Everyone had to be perfectly clear on goals and reasons and methods.

The Party Central Committee decided to conduct a "rectification movement"—an educational campaign in the various liberated areas all over China, starting with the Northwest Border Region. Both Communists and non-Communists took part. At first the movement concentrated on such matters as linking theory to practice, mutual cooperation, and learning whatever was valuable—ancient and modern, Chinese and foreign.

But under the leadership of the fanatic Kang Sheng it soon deteriorated into a virulent witch hunt. He was, he said, going to "expose the darker side" of life in Yanan. No charge was considered too fanciful, no person was exempt from attack. Targets at "accusation meetings" often "confessed" to being "spies"—one of the most heinous crimes, and implicated others. A man would say, "I was recruited by X to spy for the Kuomintang, and I then recruited Y and Z...." All three would be excoriated by members of the audience, eager to demonstrate their own purity.

These high-jinks bore a remarkable resemblance to subsequent hearings at the House Un-American Affairs Committee, or old fashioned revival meetings in the southern United States. In Yanan a kind of Save the Sinners conclave was held every Sunday. Those who had "confessed well" were praised and permitted to rejoin the ranks of the righteous. In Sufei's drama group of thirty only she and one other person—a man, escaped being "saved" in 1943—in her case because she fortunately was too pregnant to be able to attend.

Sufei's group showered on her a full share of vituperation. Again she was attacked for having married George. It was only because she wanted to share the benefits he received as a foreigner.... Even George himself was sniped at. Why should a foreigner give up a comfortable life in America to endure hardships in Yanan? He may be a spy....

George learned that these slanders were started by none other than Kang Sheng. He was shocked. He could see how people in the arts, who had lived in the cities and were accustomed to a softer environment, might wonder about a person from abroad who surrendered the "comforts" they simplistically imagined all Americans enjoyed. But why should Kang Sheng, a Marxist and a man of the world, entertain such dirty thoughts? Surely he knew that Communist parties, in the East as well as in the West, were full of persons who came from affluent backgrounds. In fact most of the leaders were the sons of families financially able to pay for their educations.

Or did Kang Sheng think that foreigners were a lesser breed, necessarily inferior to snobbish Chinese types like himself? George felt deeply insulted. For the first time it was forcefully brought home to him that not all Chinese Communist leaders were of equal calibre. He continued attending the clinic and hospital as usual.

"I'll be damned if I let that bigotted son of bitch make me drop out!" he told Sufei.

Casualties were high among those victims stubborn enough to refuse to confess to crimes they hadn't committed. People suffered mental break-downs under the pressure and humiliation. There were several suicides—four or five in the Arts Academy alone. One girl in late autumn jumped into a well —a time-honored means of female self-destruction in feudal China. When they pulled her out, her clothes were frozen to her body. They had to be cut away. Luckily, she survived.

The result was utter confusion. Schools and academies were closed. Government units were paralysed, unable to function. Finally, in 1945 a "re-screening" was instituted. It was essential to determine who was who and what was what. Fresh checks were made on all accusations. They turned out to be almost completely without foundation.

Mao convened a huge meeting at which he announced the innocence of the slandered. He apologized and bowed deeply to the assembled thousands. The "rectification movement" would not, he hoped, sour their attitude toward the Chinese Communist Party. "If your mother wrongfully struck you, surely you would not hold it against her...."

A residue of bitterness remained nevertheless. While those expelled from the Party were restored to membership, the dead could not be brought back to life. People who had falsely accused others said they had been forced to do so by Kang Sheng and his cronies. No action was taken against these harpies, but from then on they were treated with scorn and contempt.

After a pro forma "self-criticism" Kang Sheng continued to climb ever higher in the Party hierarchy. He was one of the chief hatchet-men in the campaign against the "Rightist" intellectuals in 1957, and helped head the massive character assassination pogrom during the Cultural Revolution in the sixties and seventies. To this day the Communist Party has said very little about the man and his career. Yet even after the Yanan "rectification", on a number of occasions the Party repeated the same mistake, abandoning "democratic centralism"—one of its fundamental principles, and permitting control to reside in the hands of a single individual or a small group, with disasterous results.

The concept of democratic centralism has been very difficult to put across. Centralism is entirely in keeping with China's feudal heritage. Democracy is viewed suspiciously as a foreign import.

George was fully committed. Neither Kang Sheng or the excesses of the Rectification Movement could shake his faith. Mao himself in open meeting had admitted that the Party had made a serious mistake, and apologized for it. That, to George, was proof not only of a big man, but of an honest political party. He now recognized that individual Communists could do wrong things, or even terrible things. But he was convinced that the Party as an organization was sound. The principles on which it was based—Mao's concepts and perceptions of the world—George thought made good sense.

They certainly seemed reasonable to the majority of the Chinese, for they were a continuation and extension of the ancient traditional conception of yin and yang, of male and female, of light and darkness. In the modern sciences—both social and physical—they represented positive and negative. Mao maintained the unending "contradictions" between them brought not only conflict but progress. He illustrated this time and again in his writings and speeches with folksy anecdotes and analogies as easily understood by the illiterate masses as by the educated intellectuals. Mao dealt with rank and file practical problems as well as questions of abstract philosophy. There was no matter he didn't discuss, nothing he hadn't an answer for. Mao seemed omnipotent. Within the framework of society in the "liberated areas", his ideas worked.

Mao was everybody's Mao among the Chinese people, and he certainly was Ma Haide's Mao. George respected and admired him without reservation. And because he was the leader and fountain head of wisdom of the Chinese Communist Party, George trusted the Party completely. Then and later he unhesitatingly carried out Communist orders. If ever political decisions seemed strange to him, he took it for granted that his own ignorance, not leadership error or incompetance, was at fault.

"Looking back, I can see what a tremendous change this

marked in me," George said. "From a young American, scept-
ical of authorities and dogma, more than a little cynical, I
became a 'believer', mainly in an intellectual sense, but with
more than a touch of religious fervor."

While it was comforting to have faith and be able always to
do things by the book, it made George a bit rigid and dam-
pened his nose for suspicious odors. He was to pay a price in
future years for the shallowness of his understanding.

Sufei's middle was visibly swollen in mid-1943. She developed a longing for *zha cai*, a popular salted vegetable. There
wasn't any in Yanan, but the Supply Department had the
courier bring some back from one of his periodic trips to Xian.
The vegetable didn't travel well in the hot summer months. It
arrived spoiled and inedible. George scolded Sufei for having
put so many people to so much trouble. The wife of the Supply
Department chief soothed him.

"All pregnant women have odd cravings," she said.

The couple were also having other problems. Coming from
very different backgrounds and accustomed to very different
lifestyles, like all newlyweds they had to learn to exist harmon-
iously. In addition, they had to adjust to an environment which
was strange to them both. Sufei was born and raised in a
well-to-do family in the Zhoushan Islands, George had spent
his youth amid the magnolias and gentle breezes of North
Carolina. They both found the Spartan life of Yanan pretty
hard to take, at first.

You Ma weighed only five pounds when he was born in
November 1943. "You" means "young". When used in conjunction with "ma" or "horse", it is the term for "colt". To the
pun-loving Chinese, "You Ma", which can be taken as either
"colt" or "Young Ma", was the ideal name for the son of Ma
Haide.

Sufei was still thin and undernourished. Her breast milk ran
out after three months. They fed the baby on millet gruel
—only the liquid without the grains. Finally, they managed to
obtain a pint of milk per day, which they bolstered with millet
water.

Late each afternoon when George returned from the hospital he washed the diapers and sterilized the empty medicine
bottles they used for the baby's milk. To the devoted diligence
of the first-time-father he added the stern requirements of the
trained physician. This no doubt improved the infant's health,

but it worked considerable hardship on him and Sufei and their friends. Although a heavy smoker, as a doctor in the hospital George couldn't put a cigarette to his lips all day. By the time he got home he was dying for a good deep drag. But he had to observe the SMOKING FORBIDDEN signs he had put up on the door and all the windows. And so George would stand outside the doorway, puffing blissfully while Sufei, on the other side of the threshold, answered his medical questions and held up the baby for his inspection, at a sanitary distance. Only after he finished his cigarette would he go inside.

"I felt very righteous," George recalled, "but I was a pain in the butt to everyone else."

To Sufei's mind, George was an ideal husband—most of the time. Some nights he worked very late at the hospital, operating, and would return home frozen. They slept together under a single set of quilts. Sufei would forbid him to come close until his icy feet warmed up. As time went on, she encountered other irritations.

High on the list was Sunday bridge. George and three of his cronies used to play all day and frequently far into the night. One of them was a woman who spoke excellent English. It enraged Sufei that George should neglect her and little You Ma on the only day in the week they could spend some time together. At a card session in their house she thrust the baby into his arms. He had to quit playing, and the visiting bridge enthusiasts went home. Sufei and he had a flaming row.

The next morning they heard that the other families had also quarrelled. The lady bridge fan found herself locked out. Her husband wouldn't let her in no matter how she banged on the door. The other two couples had harsh words, as well. They all laughed when they learned what had happened. Card-playing was one of the few amusements Yanan had to offer, and George was mad about bridge. But he knew he had been behaving selfishly. That put an end to his Sunday bridge in Yanan.

For eight years since his arrival in Bao An in 1936 he met very few Americans, and most of these were pre-disposed in favor of the Chinese revolutionaries. Now in July and August of 1944 two sections of the U.S. Army Observer Group, popularly known as the "Dixie Mission", suddenly descended on Yanan. The Group was comprised of eighteen men who previously wouldn't have recognized a Chinese Communist if they fell over one. But they shared a lively curiosity and, to George's delight, were typically American.

What brought the Dixie Mission to the Border Region was the decision in Washington to establish liaison with the Chinese Communists in order to learn the capabilities and potentials of their fighting forces. The Japanese were driving against Chiang Kai-shek's armies on many fronts, especially in the provinces of Henan and Hubei. There was some danger that the whole jerry-built KMT military machine would collapse. General Joseph W. ("Vinegar Joe") Stilwell, then commanding the China-Burma-India Theatre of War, was beginning to recognize that should this happen he would be left with only the Communist Ba Lu areas in the north and the Communist New Fourth Army territory in the south in which to operate. Moreover, some thought was being given to landing a parachute division on the coast of the Shandong peninsula, in a sector under Communist control, to create a staging area for the final attack on the Japanese islands. This was before the decision to drop the atom bomb was made. The U.S. needed to know what logistic support the Communists could offer.

American fliers shot down over regions occupied by the Japanese were frequently rescued by Ba Lu guerilla detachments and returned to their units. They had been reporting on the excellent fighting capacity and high morale of their Chinese hosts. But more thorough professional information was necessary to appraise their military value accurately.

Of equal concern to Washington was a frightening political scenario. Some years previous, Captain Evans Carlson of the U.S. Marine Corps had visited Yanan and reported that "the Communists constituted the most cohesive, disciplined, and aggressive anti-Japanese group in the country." He stated further that "the Communists were in an area which Russia would probably enter when she attacked Japan, and were in a position to become the foundation of a new rapprochment beween the Chinese Communists and the USSR." Fear of Moscow was very real in Washington, and already talk was current of preparing for "World War Three". Meetings with the Border Region Chinese might probe the prospects of a Sino-Soviet alliance, and provide some ideas on how to forestall it.

Stilwell therefore applied to Chiang Kai-shek for permission to dispatch a team of military experts to the Border Region for

direct investigation of the Communist forces, with which the
KMT was supposedly maintaining a united front. Chiang
refused. Only after President Roosevelt sent Vice Pesident
Wallace to voice his insistence did the "Generalissimo" reluctantly consent.

Mao and Zhu De were at the airport to greet the first section
of the U.S. Army Observer Group, later popularly known as
the "Dixie Mission", when it flew in from Chongqing on July
22, 1944. There were nine members in all. Another nine
arrived on August 7. Colonel David D. Barrett headed the
entire Group of eighteen. Nearly all were specialists in various
military branches, including two political officers—John S.
Service and Raymond P. Ludden, both Second Secretaries in
the U.S. Embassy in Chongqing, and both attached to the Staff
of the Commanding General, CBI. Ye Jianying, Chief of Staff
of the Ba Lu gave a speech of welcome, with George acting as
interpreter. But only for the first few minutes, then he had to
give it up. He couldn't cope with the flowery ceremonial
language.

George visited the newcomers as soon as they were settled
into their cave-dwelling quarters. They were surprised and
pleased to find a fellow American who knew the language and
the people, who could show them around and answer their
many questions.

They spent a great deal of time together over the next few
months. They did a lot of singing and beer drinking. George
and several of the boys became quite good friends. John
(Johnny) Colling and George formed a warm attachment
which lasted more than forty years.

Colling told him how he became involved in the Dixie
Mission. In 1944 he had been an infantry captain in Burma,
serving as a specialist in guerilla warfare and demolition with
OSS. On completion of a rugged eighteen-month stint, he was
recalled to OSS headquarters in northern India and granted a
leave for rest and recreation. He went up into the mountains.

A few days later he received a telegram: RETURN TO
BASE IMMEDIATELY. Johnny wondered: "What the hell
did I do now?" At headquarters he was told about the mission.
He was to proceed to Kunming, pick up the demolition materials he would need for demonstrations, go on to Chongqing,
and join a flight to Yanan.

On July 4 in Chongqing naval officer Herbert Hitch, also

attached to the Observer Group, introduced him to Madame
Soong Ching Ling. She was watching a baseball game with the
American specialists. They chatted about the forthcoming mis-
sion.

"Keep your eyes open and see for yourself," she advised.
"You'll be surprised."

"In Yanan I sort of adopted Johnny," George said. "He was
only 22, the youngest man in the Group. I was 34. We immediately were very *sympatico*, like brothers. He had many meals
with me and Sufei in our home."

He tagged along one day when George went to examine a
pregnant mother. As a "foreign doctor" Ma Haide was believed
to be blessed with the ability to foretell the sex of the future
child. George took the young woman's pulse, then solemnly
made his prediction.

In an aside to Johnny, he murmured, "I am never wrong
more than fifty percent of the time, at most."

Johnny chuckled. George's laid-back style of humor really
tickled him.

Colling and the other Mission men called at the Hatem's
cave dwelling very often. George bombarded them with questions about the war, about how things were going at home. The
Dixie Mission had brought in radios, and they would listen to
American news broadcasts and ball games. George hadn't
realized how hungry he was for such fare.

For their part the Americans were curious about the kind of
people who migrated to Yanan, how they fought their wars,
what their social relationships were, whether he thought Mao's
ideas would succeed.... And everything about George—who he
was, why he came, why he stayed, what his plans were. Most
of them couldn't understand what he was doing out in this
"wilderness", as they called it, when he could be home in North
Carolina drinking mint juleps and sparking the girls.

"I've got nothing against mint juleps, but I like this stuff
better," George said with a grin, sloshing the beer around in
the big mug from which he was drinking. "As for girls, you
must admit the ones we have here can stack up against any
southern belle." He lowered his voice. "Go easy on that girl
talk, fellas," he pleaded. "I'm a married man. I'm not sure how
much English Sufei has picked up!"

The GI's hooted. "Yeah, man!"

"I came because I'm intrigued by this experiment they're

trying. I want to learn what it's all about. Some call them 'Commies' and 'Reds'. Well, maybe so. I don't know about that. What I do know is that people here have a helluva a lot better life than the ones in Chiang Kai-shek's part of China."

A staff sergeant from Kentucky nodded. "They do seem like right God-fearing folks."

"Well, I wouldn't exactly put it that way myself," George said, smiling. "But they really are very nice people. And living out in this 'wilderness' isn't bad. At least you're in no danger of being mowed down by a speeding Packard."

The GI's laughed.

George didn't talk much about communism. The hate-China crowd was strong in America, and he had to protect his family. He did tell the Dixie Mission members all about his background. He inquired whether they knew any ways to bring in more medical supplies. The base areas needed them badly.

Colling, who had grown very close to him, asked how he had been able to adapt to an environment so different from his social origins. George took a drag on his cigarette, exhaled slowly and gazed through the window at the rolling hills of yellow soil.

"When I first came to China I guess I was a pretty typical American of my day and age," he replied thoughtfully. "I didn't know much what things were all about. Because of my upbringing I was shy in public, and sometimes tried to hide it by acting the clown. It wasn't easy for me to cope with a new situation. In Shanghai I met mainly foreigners and better-off Chinese. In Yanan I was mixing with very different people. I had to live and work with them, and win their cooperation and understanding. For a while I had the feeling I was on the outside looking in, and that was hard. But gradually that broke down. I began to get straight the basic ideas that activated everyone. I gained confidence. Everything became easier. It was as simple as that."

Johnny told George privately he was an important man to the Group. They appreciated the fact that he never tried to impose his opinions on any of them. George was very careful about that. He encouraged them to think for themselves. A number of them were very intelligent, and every bit as idealistic as he was, though based on different philosophies.

George encouraged them to go anywhere and inspect anything they wanted to see of Ba Lu operations. "All you have to do is ask," he said. "Maybe you think we're just putting on an act here. Well, we can't put on an act all over the country."

Johnny took his advice. He requested and obtained permission to test methods of demolition in enemy occupied territory. He set out with a team of eight Ba Lu soldiers and an interpreter and crossed the Yellow River into neighboring Shanxi province. Moving stealthily from place to place, they were gone for nearly three months. Johnny had a chance to demonstrate demolition technique on a Japanese blockhouse.

Creeping up on it from its blind side, he set his charges with pencil time fuses. When the explosives blew, the blockhouse interior burst into flames, forcing the Japanese occupants into the open where they were easily captured. Col. Barrett had instructed the members of the Group to avoid combat, but everyone smilingly neglected to criticise Johnny's lapse.

At the end of Colling's tour of duty, as he was preparing to return to the States, George asked him to deliver a letter and some pictures to his brother Joe. It had not been possible for him to communicate with his family since leaving Shanghai in 1936.

Johnny was glad to comply. A few weeks later, he was submitting his reports in Washington. Joe came to see him in the Pentagon, and Colling turned over the precious letter and pictures. Johnny and George had embraced like brothers on parting in Yanan. The two had grown very close. They didn't meet again until 1973.

George spent considerable time with the members of the Dixie Mission and helped them with their medical work. There were some fine young Americans among them. They saw eye to eye with George on quite a few things. The Americans were sick of the run-around they had been getting from the Kuomintang generals, and they liked the straight-forward way the Ba Lu operated.

Col. Dave Barrett, leader of the U.S. Army Observer Group in Yanan, took a liking to George, which George reciprocated. Barrett was a no-nonsense professional army man. In his monograph on the Dixie Mission, published by the University of California at Berkeley in 1970, the colonel made favorable comment about George.

On our own, members of our group sought amusement and exercise in playing softball. We were joined in this by "Doctor Ma", an American who had been in Yanan for some years. He performed brilliantly in the outfield.... "Doctor Ma"... had been born George Hatem, I believe in North Carolina. To judge from his American family name and his appearance, his forebears might have come from some Middle East country.... I do not know the story of how Dr. Ma came originally to cast his lot with the Chinese Communists, and even if I did, it would be outside the scope of this monograph. He was a well-spoken, pleasant, friendly man, who as far as I ever heard did not talk politics. He had an attractive Chinese wife with whom he lived on the premises of the Norman Bethune International Peace Hospital.

George chatted with Barrett several times. He didn't get to know him as well as many of the others in the Dixie Mission, but he could see that the colonel was a very good officer, well-liked by his men.

On the seventh of November, 1944, another American arrived in Yanan with whom Barrett was not so favorably impressed. He was Major General Patrick J. Hurley, Special Emissary of the President of the United States. Chiang Kai-shek had compelled President Roosevelt to recall General Stilwell, who advocated utilizing the Communist forces in the fight against the Japanese, and whose private epithet for the Generalissimo was "that peanut!" But Washington recognized the advantages of combining the Communist and KMT armies against the common enemy, and Hurley was sent to try to bring the two sides together. Barrett's description of Hurley's descent on Yanan is a minor literary masterpiece.

The arrival of the plane from Chungking was always a big event in Yanan, (the colonel wrote,) and on the afternoon of the 7th of November, Chou En-lai and I were among a large crowd of Chinese and Americans on hand to greet it. After it landed and the doors opened, there appeared at the top of the steps a tall, gray haired, soldierly, extremely handsome man, wearing one of the most beautifully tailored uniforms I have ever seen, and with enough ribbons on his chest to represent every war, so it seemed to me, in which the United States had ever engaged except possibly Shay's Rebellion.

...No one had thought to inform us (of his) intention to visit Yanan.... Visibly startled by this picture of soldierly bearing and sartorial splendor was Chou En-lai, who at once asked who the distinguished visitor was. I told him it was

General Hurley. "Please hold him here until I can bring Chairman Mao," said Chou, as he disappeared in a cloud of dust.

In a shorter time than I would have thought possible, Mao and Chou appeared in the Communists' only piece of motor transport in Yanan, at least as far as I ever saw, a beat-up truck with an enclosed cabin. Close behind them came a company of soldiers, evidently hastily mustered at a barracks near the airfield. While Mao greeted the General with due ceremony, the company lined up in guard of honor formation and the General reviewed them. After the General had returned the salute of the officer commanding the company, he drew himself up to his full impressive height, swelled up like a poisoned pup, and let out an Indian warwhoop. I shall never forget the expression on the faces of Mao and Chou at this totally unexpected behavior on the part of the distinguished visitor.

The Chinese were amazed. It was inconceivable to them that a high plenipotentiary of a foreign power should behave in such an unseemly manner.

George's appraisal was less polite. "They thought he was a screwball," he said.

Hurley flew back to Chongqing on November 7 carrying counter-proposals from the Communists to the Kuomintang. While at first supportive of the Communist position, Hurley quickly swung over in favor of the Chiang Kai-shek crowd, ever increasingly so after his appointment as Ambassador to China on November 17. The negotiations fizzled out, were renewed again in 1945 and 1946, with General Marshall acting as mediator. These also ended in failure.

The Dixie Mission marked the beginning of a rising tide of sympathy from friendly Americans. George did what he could to foster this rapport among the men of the Dixie Mission and any other Americans who visited Yanan. He was upset when the U.S. government became more overt in its backing of the KMT against the Communists. Would it create hostility in the Chinese against all Americans? George was a Chinese Communist, but in many ways he was still an American. He wanted the Chinese to like the American people just as much as he wanted the Americans to like the Chinese.

Mao himself set him straight. He called George and Huang Hua and Chen Jiakang in for a special talk. He impressed on them that there was a difference between U.S. government actions and the American people, between top U.S. civil and military leaders and ordinary officials and soldiers. "We mustn't blur those distinctions," Mao said.

George always remembered that talk. He knew that the Chinese Communists did not hold the actions of a government against its people. But he was relieved and reassured to hear it from Mao himself.

He met and spoke with more than a hundred Americans rescued by the guerrillas after their planes had been shot down behind enemy lines. They were very grateful. The guerrillas often risked their own lives to save them. These fliers had to be escorted through hundreds of miles of countryside to bring them to Yanan, from where they were returned to their units. They saw how the liberated areas were run, and were very impressed—despite originally strong anti-communist prejud-ices.

One pilot, an Italian-American Catholic youngster from Boston, was full of admiration for the resistance bases behind the Japanese lines, and the Chinese friends he made there. In his naivete and honesty, he told General Zhu De that he used to spend his weekends beating up communists on Boston com-mon! The boy was typical of many American servicemen in China. While hating "communism" in the abstract in their own country, they couldn't help liking the "communists" they met in the Border Region.

Members of the Observer Group travelled throughout the liberated areas and behind the Japanese lines, gathering infor-mation. They also heard talks almost daily by high ranking Chinese military leaders on such topics as American policy toward the Chinese Communist Party, Communist-Kuomin-tang negotiations, postwar treatment of Japan, future economic and democratic reforms in China, foreign relations, Mao's views on Sino-U.S. relations, ethnic minorities, plans for relief and rehabilitation in Communist areas, and labor and women's organizations.

With this wealth of material many wrote favorable factual reports to the American military and government leadership. Some of the observers—like Foreign Service Officer John S. Service, would be persecuted for this by the McCarthyite witch hunters. The reports nevertheless created a sounder under-standing on the part of the U.S. authorities.

Service, a tall, spare professional diplomat, had been raised in China, and knew the country well. When the Dixie Mission got to Yanan in July 1944, he was fascinated and a bit surprised to meet this "hitherto nameless man of mystery" Ma Haide. Service was astonished that, despite his years of isolation in Yanan, George was still so "American", and immediately on the most friendly terms with all of them, especially the juniors and the enlisted men. The diplomat soon became "Jack" to George, who proved very helpful in enabling him to form a relatively well-rounded picture of the Border Region.

A number of American journalists had pressured Chiang Kai-shek into permitting them to go to Yanan some weeks before the Observer Group. These included such crack reporters as Gunther Stein of the *Christian Science Monitor* and the *London News-Chronicle*, Israel Epstein representing the *New York Times, Time-Life* and *Allied Labor News*, Harrison Foreman for the *New York Herald Tribune* and the *Times* of London, and Maurice Votaw representing the *Baltimore Sun*.

George was a useful guide to several of them. Their articles and, later, books broke through the Generalissimo's efforts to prevent information about the Revolutionary Bases and the Ba Lu Army from reaching the outside world.

When a few of the Mission boys went back to the States they got in touch with George's family, at his request. His people were entirely non-political. But FBI agents came around, asking questions. McCarthyism was rampant.

Jack Service, out of the goodness of his heart when he was suddenly ordered back to the US, asked George if he wished to send a message to his folks. George gave him a letter with some photographs—pictures of Sufei and You Ma whom his family had never seen.

Even John S. Service, a career diplomat, was unable to escape the hate-China hysteria. As soon as he reached the States he became suspect for carrying a private uncensored letter from a "communist area". George's brother Joe, who was in the US Army and had been handed the letter by Service in Washington, was questioned repeatedly by his officers and by the FBI. Anything that smacked of friendliness to the Chinese Communists incited attacks by the Super Patriots.

Still, the letters had reached their destination. It was a great relief to George's family to have positive confirmation that he was still alive. What's more, he was happily married, and the father of a bouncing boy! Through the members of the Group still in Yanan George learned that the letters had gone through. He was very grateful.

The Dixie Mission helped him in other ways, as well. Mixing daily with fellow Americans, most of whom were about his age, recalled his cultural roots, stirred his nostalgia, brought him up to date on life and events in the U.S. Some of the young Americans told him of their feelings, their hopes, their families, and he told them of his. A warm empathy grew up betweem them.

One very important, though perhaps unanticipated, benefit George gained from this, and from his meetings with visiting journalists, was the realization that it was not only possible but desireable for him to be both an American and a Chinese. There was no conflict between the two. It was not his mission in life to turn the whole world Red. Rather, he should use his unique position to promote mutual understanding and friendship between America and China, to serve as a catlytic agent between the land of his birth and the country of his adoption.

He recalled, with some shame, how childishly ignorant he had been in such matters the last time he had written home.

In 1936 he had sent a letter to his brother Joe, from Shanghai. Full of his own superiority, he told Joe he was going to take out subscriptions for him to *New Masses* and the *Daily Worker*. He was going to proselytise him and turn him into a Marxist, just like himself.

Frantically, Joe wrote back saying, "Please don't. That would be terrible. I'd never be able to make a living here in the South."

George was upset. He thought, "Here am I trying to be a revolutionary, and all you think of is money." He wrote Joe a nasty letter, demanding, "Are you going to be a slave all your life?"

It embarrassed George to think of it. He knew now what his relationship with America and Americans ought to be, and he felt entirely at home in China with the Chinese.

VICTORY

Although George was naturally attracted to Americans and they to him, he also met and mixed in Yanan with people from other lands. His medical acquaintances alone included doctors such as Basu and colleagues from India, Norman Bethune of Canada, Hans Muller of Germany, Arlov of the USSR, Bick Tiao-wen of Indonesia, and Melvin Casberg of the U.S. Army Observer Group. A few of his foreign friends lived in Yanan for several years.

Eva Xiao, a charming young German woman, was one of them. She had married Emi Xiao, Chinese poet, in Moscow in the thirties. They came to Yanan with their two-year-old son Leon in October 1940. Eva painted an intimate picture of Sufei and George in the April 1941 issue of the Hong Kong magazine *Eastern Horizon.*

Shortly after our arrival, (she recalled,) I pulled out a wooden tub in the afternoon and placed it in front of our cave where there was a big empty space. While I was giving Leon his bath under the warm October sun, I noticed that two people were coming up the hill path in our direction. The man with slightly greying hair and oriental features looked to be around thirty; the slender woman beside him was much younger and very beautiful.

They were our first guests in Yanan—the American doctor George Hatem (in Chinese he took the name Ma Haide) and his Chinese wife Zhou Sufei. The two were shocked that I bathed my child in the open air at that time, in late autumn. I laughed at them and they laughed with me. That laughter put the seal on our friendship which has lasted to this very day, through all storms and upheavals.

Eva remembered the good times they had together. "We lived then at the Club for Cultural Workers which was headed by Emi," she said.

Aside from many cultural activities—lectures, exhibitions and the like, Emi organized "dances" on Saturday nights, which was quite a novel experience for Spartan Yanan. But these dances were greeted joyfully by many —they brought change and recreation to those whose life consisted solely of work and struggle. Not only young people frequented these dances, the elite of Yanan also came. Lao Ma, as I called Haide, although other friends called him George, and Sufei were among our regular guests. And it was lovely to see them dancing together in the silvery moonlight.

Then she and Emi moved house and became their neighbors. "We lived in the lower three caves," she recalled.

In the caves above us lived Ma Haide with Sufei and the Indian doctor Basu.... Sufei was a student in the Lu Xun Academy of Literature and Art, and came home on weekends only. Apart from her common sense, her amiable character and her exquisite looks, Sufei is the best housekeeper I have met in my whole life. Under the primitive, crude conditions of life in Yanan she produced, as if by magic, the most wonderful delicacies like meat and fruit preserves, all sorts of vegetables, each with a different and delicious taste. And she could sew and knit besides!

Lao Ma... spoke Chinese fluently, loved his work, and was simple and out-going and ever ready to help. Everybody knew that, and I also came to find it out for myself very soon. *Lao* Ma, himself a foreigner, helped me to get acquainted with life in Yanan. In the daily contacts with him and Dr. Basu I was able to brush up my English, which I had learned in school. In summer we swam together in the small river which runs through Yanan. During the long winter evenings we sat by the fire, enjoying a rare cup of coffee and discussing God and the world—including the past, the present, life in Yanan, the events at the front and faraway places abroad. The future, which at that time was rather dubious, also came into our discussions....

Their conversations covered a lot of ground. It was interesting because each of them looked at questions from somewhat different angles. Though Sufei and Emi were both Chinese, she was younger and less experienced. Emi was a scholar, a poet, a world traveller. Eva was German, romantic, passionately committed against injustice. George, the American, was getting to the point where he felt more at home in the East than he had in the West.

Those were the years when the big mass movement which Mao Zedong initiated got under way. Truly everyone took part, breaking the Kuomintang's economic blockade. Men and women spun yarn and wool, knitted and sewed garments for summer and winter wear, produced the famous straw sandals, padded shoes and shoes of cloth, for the Army as well as for civilians. Everyone, including Eva and Emi and Sufei and George, planted vegetables and potatoes in front of the cave dwellings and on every slope and empty spot. They ate potatoes, pumpkins, tomatoes, cucumbers, peppers and other things which they had grown themselves. Eva also learned from Sufei how to make preserves of all these fresh wonders for the winter.

In 1942 Dr. Basu returned to his native India. George and Sufei moved house to a place rather far from Eva and Emi, and they saw each other only rarely. At the end of 1943, without much deliberation, Eva left Yanan with her two small children, and returned to "Nationalist" China, then supposedly allied with the Liberated Areas against the Japanese. She completely overlooked the insuperable enmity prevailing between the Kuomintang and the Communist Party despite the official united front.

As she later said, "I just packed up and left, believing it would be 'for a short time', but it turned out to be five long years!... In those difficult years I often thought, if only *Lao* Ma had been near me, he would surely have known how to keep me from undertaking this senseless trek. It was only many years later that I learned how *Lao* Ma's and Sufei's one and only son You Ma was born the day before my departure, on 22 November, 1943."

George certainly would have advised against going into Kuomintang China. Whether she would have listened was another matter. He and Sufei were very involved with bringing You Ma into the world. They didn't know Eva had left until after she was gone. They missed her very much. Eva and Emi brought pleasure and intellectual stimulus into their simple lives.

As enjoyable as George's foreign contacts were in Yanan, he found his deepest satisfaction in the Chinese friends and colleagues and ordinary folk whose trials and joys he shared.

Because of his special position as a foreign doctor who was also a member of the Communist Party of China, George had occasion to give medical treatment to some of the highest leaders. In the summer of 1939 he attended Zhou Enlai. Zhou had suffered a compound fracture of the right arm sustained in a fall from his horse while fording a turbulent stream. Yanan had no x-ray equipment to check the alignment of the setting, and Zhou was left with a permanently bent right arm. George gave him corrective exercises to improve mobility.

He treated Mao, as well. The Chairman was rarely ill, suffering only from occasional bouts of indigestion, brought on, no doubt, by an inordinate love of hot peppers. Sufei and George often played mah jong with him and his new wife Jiang Qing in 1944. The young actress would evolve into a waspish virago by the late sixties, a kind of Lady Macbeth of the "Cultural Revolution". Then, she was soft-spoken and pleasant. Together with her and Mao, the Hatems made a frequent mah jong foursome.

The games went on all night. By four in the morning, George and Sufei were groggy. Mao usually preferred to complete eight games in a row. A brilliant player, he was helpless against George—because he broke all the rules.

Mao was fond of the young couple. He himself did not comment on important national or world affairs. His style was more to ask questions, provocative questions they found difficult to answer. He sometimes invited them to dinner. The food was good, by Yanan standards.

The day the Japanese surrendered—V-J Day, August 15, 1945, Mao gave a speech, typically rich in classical literary allusion, on the current situation in China.

"In the past eight years we have changed places with Chiang Kai-shek," he said. "Formerly we were in the mountains and he was by the river. During the War of Resistance we were behind the enemy lines and he went up into the mountains. Now he is coming down from the mountains, coming down to seize the fruits of victory."

What Mao meant was that in the thirties Chiang Kai-shek and his Kuomintang controlled China's waterways and fertile plains, and had driven the revolutionary forces back into the hills. But during the Japanese invasion, while the Red Army and guerillas were fighting perilous engagements behind the lines of a much stronger enemy, Chiang Kai-shek retreated to the province of Szechwan, deep in southwest China and far from the battlefronts, saving his troops and equipment for an annihilation campaign against the revolutionaries.

Now that the Japanese had capitulated—due, in large part, to the costly efforts of the people and their armies and guerillas —the Chiang Kai-shek gang was scrambling to return quickly to China's heavily populated areas to accept the military hardware and territory which the Japanese were surrendering, and prevent them from falling into Communist hands. In this the Generalissimo received the unstinting assistance of President Harry S. Truman and the U.S. government, who were appalled by the possiblity that an independant left-wing administration would take over.

To attain the time needed to move Chiang's armies back to where the action was, Washington employed a two-faced strategy. In August 1945, Ambassador Hurley flew to Yanan and brought Mao to Chongqing for negotiations with Chiang regarding a proposed coalition govenment. The talks dragged on for forty-five days and ended inconclusively.

At the same time, on August 10, General Wedemeyer, Stillwell's successor as commander of the U.S. forces in China, was instructed to aid the Kuomintang in accepting the Japanese surrender and occupying all the areas held by Japanese troops. Four days later, General Douglas MacArthur, Supreme Commander of the Allied Powers in the Pacific, issued an order designating Chiang Kai-shek's government the sole agency qualified to accept the Japanese surrender in China's mainland (excluding Manchuria), in Taiwan, and in Indochina north of the 16th parallel.

Meanwhile, U.S. air and naval forces were busily ferrying half a million KMT troops to assume control of major cities and communications lines still under Japanese control in north and east China. 53,000 U.S. marines landed at Tanggu and Qingdao on the north China coast and proceeded to occupy Beijing, Tianjin, the Kailuan coal mines and the Beijing-Shanhaiguan Railway. They then turned these over to the Kuomintang.

Much encouraged, Chiang deployed six armies along the Great Wall and prepared to attack the Communist positions.

Hurley demanded still more aid for the KMT, and resigned his post as ambassador when it was not forthcoming. His proposal, he alleged, was "nullified by a few individuals in the State Department." President Truman appointed General George C. Marshall to serve as his special representative in China. U.S. policy, however, remained the same.

Marshall arrived in China near the end of 1945 and opened an "Executive Headquarters" in the PUMC Hospital in Beijing. It consisted of military members of the U.S., the Kuomintang, and the Communists. A wobbly "cease-fire" was in effect between the contending Chinese factions. Whenever a clash occurred a team representing the three parties was to hasten to the scene and restore calm.

The idea didn't work very well. U.S. Marines took part in a Kuomintang attack on a liberated Chinese village near Beijing. At first the American representatives vehemently denied it. But they they were embarrassed into shame-faced silence when U.S. Marine maps, documents and a radio transmitter captured in the encounter were produced at a press conference, considerably damaging the image of impartiality they sought to maintain.

George and Sufei had moved into the Wangjiaping section of Yanan, and were living in the same compound with Mao Zedong and Yang Shangkun. George was appointed medical advisor to the Chinese Communist Observers Group in the Executive Headquarters, and shuttled between Yanan and Beijing on the regular Dixie Mission plane. Sometimes he brought home ice cream, which Sufei loved almost as much as he did.

In March of 1946, the KMT flatly rejected the offers of a compromise by the Communists and other democratic parties. Marshall admitted his "mediation" had failed. America sharply increased its aid to the Chiang Kai-shek regime, tooling up for full scale civil war. A U.S. Military Advisory Group was created to help the KMT strengthen its armed forces. The Export-Import Bank of the United States had already extended a loan of $82,800,000 to the KMT after V-J Day. In April 1946, it granted half a billion more. The U.S. also gave a $51,700,000 long-term credit for the purchase of "civilian" machinery, motor vehicles, and communications equipment. In August a huge supply of war surplus was made available to the Generalissimo at bargain prices. Zhou Enlai complained to

General Marshall that from the day Chiang broke the cease-
fire, the U.S. had transported 1,740,000 soldiers to positions
surrounding the liberated areas.

Yet Mao made no categorical condemnation of America. He
said—and this has consistently been the Chinese Communist
stand: "We oppose the U.S. government's policy of supporting
Chiang Kai-shek against the Communists. But we must draw a
distinction, firstly, between the people of the United States and
their government and, secondly, within the U.S. government
between the policy-makers and their subordinates."

George saw many indications of the friendliness of ordinary
Americans and those in the lower echelons of U.S. government
agencies and military units. He spent a few months in 1946 in
the Beijing office of CLARA (Chinese Liberated Areas Relief
Administration) to which he had been appointed medical
advisor. This brought him into daily contact with UNRRA
(United Nations Relief and Rehabilitation Administration)
which was supposed to make fair distribution of medical
supplies in both the Communist-held areas, through CLARA,
and areas controlled by the Kuomintang, through CNRRA
(Chinese National Relief and Rehabilitation Administration).
He dealt as well with officials of the American Red Cross, met
American doctors, relief workers, journalists, writers, Quaker
Friends, Army personnel.... George was invited to speak at a
number of gatherings, including one hosted by a U.S. Marine
unit.

He found most of these people honest and appreciative of
what was being done in the liberated areas. On the other hand,
Kuomintang plunder and sale on the black market of medical
supplies intended for the sick and destitute outraged their
American sense of fair play. Six hundred UNRRA personnel
signed a strongly worded protest that made world headlines.

Many of the Americans handling the relief supplies gave
substantial help to the liberated areas. Bob Drummond, for
instance, head of the American Red Cross in Beijing, was
responsible for allocating their supplies in North China. He
would tell George when meetings on supplies were about to be
held, and what was available for distribution. He would say,
"You go back and write a request for such and such, with
examples of what you are doing with them, and where." At the
meetings, there would be people from different parts of China.
Bob would announce the medicines which had arrived in the

latest shipment, and ask everyone, "Do you have any statements showing a need for them in your area? I'd like it in writing, please." George's, of course, would be the first formal detailed request, and the supplies would go up on the next U.S. plane to Zhangjiakou (Kalgan), which was in a liberated area.

UNRRA was not so helpful. Their top men would hand everything over to CNRRA, run by the Kuomintang. Many of these supplies would turn up on the black market, sold by Chiang's corrupt officials.

When one of the liberated areas had a plague epidemic CLARA applied for sulpha drugs that were specific for plague. UNRRA had a lot. George wrote reports telling them where the plague was, how many people were involved, how many people were at risk, and asked for the medication.

UNRRA gave only about 3,000 pills and demanded a receipt specifying that CLARA would return them later when it had other sources of supply. The political discrimination at the top was obvious.

But at the same time there were plenty of other Americans who were fair. Lower-level UNRRA personnel were quite friendly, once they saw what was going on in China. And leaders of various health and welfare missions, such as Dr. Michael Sachs, later with the World Health Organization; Dr. Leo Eloesser, who headed UNICEF (United Nations Children's Emergency Fund) in China and was one of the four world pioneers in chest surgery; Bob Burden and Jim Grant, then head of UNICEF; and Dr. Herbert Abrams. They were good men, and very helpful to the people's forces right up to liberation. Herb Abrams told George about his experience in this regard.

A Surgeon (equivalent in rank to major) in the U.S. Public Health Service attatched to UNRRA, Abrams had been stationed in Qingdao, Shandong province. Qingdao harbor was full of U.S. warships and the U.S. Marines were on shore. They were actively transporting Kuomintang troops from the south to bolster the Nationalist defenses. Several miles north of Qingdao was a surrendered Japanese garrison of 20,000 men. They had been allowed to retain their arms in order "to hold back the Communists".

To the Marines who had landed in China after the bloody campaigns in the Pacific, in was inexplicable that the Japanese had suddenly become their allies.

On December 7, 1945, the anniversary of the Japanese attack on Pearl Harbor, several U.S. Marine planes in a "show of force" demonstrated over Shandong. One of them crashed in the mountains in a snowstorm. The pilot parachuted out and was picked up by peasants in the Liberated Area. Two Ba Lu messengers came into Qingdao and informed Marine headquarters. Marine Commandant General Howard asked Dr. Abrams and another UNRRA worker to go into the Liberated Area and bring back the pilot.

Abrams did as requested, in the course of which he got a good look at how people lived and functioned there. He discovered they were badly in need of medical supplies. On returning to Qingdao he put in a request with UNRRA. A ship was sent up from Shanghai in February 1946, with thirty tons of wheat flour, but not a single pill or roll of bandage. Angrily, Dr. Abrams went to every commanding medical officer at the Marine hospital on shore and on the many Navy ships in the harbor. He said: "We are organizing a first shipment to the Liberated Areas, but UNRRA has sent us no medical supplies. Can you help?"

The outpouring was generous: plasma, sulfa drugs, quinine tablets, saline solutions, surgical dressings and instruments, syringes and needles.... Most U.S. medical officers and the rank and file knew that the "Reds" had fought the Japanese and that the Chiang Kai-shek administration was a gang of conniving grafters.

"We're supporting the wrong crowd," they told Abrams. They gave him enough medical supplies to fill three big trucks.

Dr. Abrams led the convoy and delivered the precious supplies and the wheat personally. They travelled through many villages. In one of them at a party in their honor, a Ba Lu chorus sang "Old Black Joe" and "Pretty Redwing", as well as the popular revolutionary anthem *Qi Lai* (Rise Up) and other Chinese songs. Their hosts asked the UNRRA visitors to perform. Australian leader Arthur Lowndes made a big hit with his "Waltzing Matilda" solo. The Americans gave a rather lame rendition of the "Star Spangled Banner", but it was enthusiastically received. The Chinese asked them to write down the words and music so that they could learn it. The clasp of Hands Across the Sea was never stronger.

Early in 1947 the Executive Headquarters closed down for good. George was back in Yanan in March when KMT warlord

Hu Zongnan attacked from two sides with 230,000 troops. The Communists had only about 20,000 fighting men in the entire Northwest. Outnumbered ten to one, they decided to evacuate the city.

Many people wept. With their own hands they had built a self-sufficient and, until now, secure community. The soldiers wanted to stand and fight. Mao promised that if they left an empty city and led the enemy in a fruitless chase through the mountainous terrain, Yanan would be retaken in the not too distant future.

That is precisely what happened. The city was evacuated in March 1947. Chiang Kai-shek crowed that final victory was at hand. Then, one Kuomintang defeat followed another in north China. The Communists' armed forces, now called the PLA (People's Liberation Army), recaptured Yanan in April 1948, a little over one year later.

But few shared Mao's optimism as they prepared to pull out. Everything that couldn't be taken along had to be hidden or destroyed. Kids buried their toys. George's little son You Ma buried their knives and forks, as well. They had to dig them up again. The entire revolutionary community departed on March 22, and the local people went with them. Mao was the last to leave.

George was given a horse, but wouldn't ride it because he wanted to stay close to Sufei and four-year-old You Ma. They had a donkey to carry their meagre belongings. Wicker baskets hanging on opposite sides of the animal contained You Ma in one and Yang Shangkun's little boy in the other.

During the day KMT planes constantly bombed and strafed. The exodus could proceed only after dark. In daylight hours the convoy took shelter and slept in peasant homes. The two children, who had dreamed peacefully all night in their baskets, were wide awake when the sun rose and wanted to play. They prevented Sufei from getting much sleep. She was very tired.

George's beard grew out. It was prematurely grey. In a village where they rested a few days, a peasant woman took Sufei aside.

"Who is that man?"

"My husband."

"So old! Must have been an arranged marriage."

"No. I wanted him."

"What did you want an old man like that for?"

His prestige received a considerable boost when he went wild pigeon hunting. He was a good shot, and brought down four or five of the birds with one charge of buckshot. The peasants nodded approvingly.

"That old man has marvellous eyes," they said. He was thirty-seven.

The column wound out of the village at dusk, assuming it was too dark for planes. But a KMT fighter squadron, flying low, swept over and strafed. The marchers had no anti-aircraft weapons or even machine guns. George left Sufei and the kids and rode up and down the line, helping the wounded. There were not many casualties. People knew if there was an attack they had to hug the sides of the canyons and gullies through which the roads ran and to hang on to their animals so that they wouldn't bolt.

After circling around in the mountains for a few weeks, the column crossed the Yellow River into the province of Shanxi on the eastern side. Sufei and George and little You Ma were travelling with the Army field hospitals. To avoid enemy air attack the crossing had to be made at night, stealthily, in boats. These were pulled back and forth by ropes from the opposite shores, with several dozen people and their animals in each craft.

The column settled temporarily in Two Towers Village, about one day's donkey ride from the riverbank. There, Communist Party headquarters was established. George and Sufei again met the young married couple Zhang Wenjin and Jiang Ying. George went to work with them in the large Foreign Affairs Section, mainly on English language documents. He also helped at the Xin Hua News Agency with the conversion into comprehensible English of news for press and radio release, and with the translation into Chinese of news broadcasts in English picked up by their receivers.

Jiang Ying gave birth to her first child, a little boy. Sufei presented her with a small alarm clock she had received as a gift from a foreign visitor so that the new mother could tell when it was time to feed the baby. Clocks and watches were a precious rarity.

Sufei took part in the Land Reform program the Communists instituted in the neighboring countryside. George heard a lot about it from her, and sat in on some of the "speak bitterness" meetings. These rallies were tremendously emotional affairs where peasants came forward, one after another, and poured out tales of landlord brutality—of tenant debtors beaten to death for being short a peck of rent grain, of daughters sold into bondage, of ravished wives.... The rallies moved George deeply. But they did more than provide a forum for anguished cries. They were concrete evidence that all peasants were persecuted by the same common enemy—the landlord class, and that feudalism—its bulwark and rationale, had to be destroyed.

Further, the meetings were proof that ordinary people could speak out freely, that the "Ba Lu" had come to stay, that everyone would get a fair share of land and could keep it. The peasants' response was terrific. This had been their dream for generations—to actually have their own land, free and clear. As a consequence, they lined up solidly behind the Communist government.

On Sundays the bridge games which the spouses thought they had stifled resumed, if anything, more avidly than before. The bridge buffs would start early in the morning in the courtyard of the Foreign Affairs Section where the four of them worked, moving their table and themselves at times to remain in the sunlight, and continue until dark. They played only for points, not for money. The bidding was in English, and so was some of the conversation.

Sufei resented being neglected on the only day in the week the family could be together. She smouldered one Sunday, unable to sleep, when George still hadn't returned even after nightfall. When at last he came blithely in, very late, pack of cards in hand, she exploded. Leaping from the bed, she snatched the cards and threw them in the fire. George was stunned. He grabbed for the cards, too late. They were already burning brightly in the flames.

Before he could recover from this disaster, Sufei tore into him with pummelling fists. Though he outweighed her by twenty pounds, the fury of her assault sent him staggering. Finally, he managed to grasp her wrists and pin her down backwards on the bed. Both of them were breathing hard. She refused to accept his apology. For several days after she wouldn't speak to him. Again the bridge games halted, temporarily.

During 1947 the Central Committee and Mao Zedong

moved to Xibaipo in Hebei province. There, they were joined
by Liu Shaoqi and his wife Wang Guangmei. Her English was
very good, and she went to work in the Foreign Affairs Section,
which was further enlarged. George, too, spent almost all of his
time there. He doctored only occasionally.

The vastly superior Kuomintang military machine was beginning to crumble. Communist headquarters advanced further east in 1948. With it marched civilian personnel, women and
children. Donkeys driven by local peasants carried supplies,
the sick and wounded, and youngsters sitting in wicker baskets.
All along the road they were strafed by American planes—gifts
to dictator Chiang Kai-shek. Sweeping in low over the Hebei
mountains, the planes spewed a deadly hail of machine gun
fire. The driver of You Ma's donkey was instantly killed. Little
You Ma himself miraculously escaped being hit. At the front
the Generalissimo's armies were equipped with American
tanks and were guided by American "advisors". The goodwill
the Chinese had felt toward America dissipated rapidly. China's sons and daughters were being slaughtered by lethal weapons marked "Made in USA".

But the PLA pushed on and captured the city of Shijiazhuang, abandoned by hurrriedly retreating Kuomintang
troops. This was the first big city the PLA had ever occupied. They took over what had formerly been a Kuomintang-
controlled UNRRA office. Several foreigners had been participating in its operation. George met famous American lung
surgeon Dr. Leo Eloesser, then representing UNICEF. Many
of the relief supplies had slipped into private hands when the
KMT was running the city, and showed up for sale in shops
and marketplaces. George saw to it that a rightful share of the
supplies, especially medicines, went to the civilians in the
liberated areas and to the PLA.

You Ma had never seen a bed with a spring mattress before.
During their first night in Shijiazhuang he lay in the middle,
with George and Sufei reading on either side. The five-year-old
was too excited to sleep. All he wanted was to bounce up and
down, shouting and laughing. He thought it was great fun.
Afraid he would disturb their neighbors, Sufei turned off the
light. You Ma began to cry. She had to turn it on again, and
You Ma resumed his happy bouncing. After a few days the
novelty wore off, and they all were able to get some rest.

Chiang Kai-shek's armies were sustaining extremely heavy

losses, with troops surrendering or joining the PLA by the hundreds of thousands. But his forces were still strong in the air, and launched intensive bombing assaults. During one raid on Shijiazhuang with American block-busters, George held You Ma in his arms and tried to scrounge deeper into a shallow ditch.

"*Baba*, I'm scared," the child whimpered.

"You've got nothing on me, kid," George replied.

The city had just been cleaned up and the factories put back into operation. There wasn't a military objective in the place. Dr. Eloesser was highly indignant.

The next time the bombers came over, You Ma was home alone, except for a fourteen-year-old army "imp" who looked after him. The older boy rushed down with You Ma on his back and leaped into an air raid trench in the courtyard. He covered You Ma with his body as bombs shook the earth. Some fell so close they could actually see them spiralling down. Shock waves flattened everything within a hundred yard radius of the terrified children.

You Ma was deafened by the blasts. Sufei and George were worried the condition would be permanent. He gradually recovered his hearing, but it took nearly two years.

Three major battles shattered the bulk of Chiang Kai-shek's armies. In fifty-two days the PLA put 470,000 KMT troops out of action while liberating the whole of northeast China. Its own forces had grown to five million men, attaining numerical superiority for the first time. Next, in Jiangsu province, it defeated another half million of the Generalissimo's effectives, including his best armored units, and conquered all of east China north of the Yangtse. One million PLA men were now poised on the north bank of the river, threatening Nanjing, Shanghai, and the heart of Kuomintang rule.

Then, in January 1949, the PLA took Tianjin and Beijing in rapid succession, the first after an assault lasting only 48 hours, the second when warlord Fu Zuoyi, realizing the hopelessness of his position, peacefully surrendered. This enabled the people's forces to absorb another half million former enemy soldiers. All of China north of the Yangtse was now under Communist control.

The collapse of Chiang Kai-shek's seemingly invincible armies could not be blamed, despite the cries of the China Lobby in the U.S., on any deficiency in American support. In the

Top of his class, first year primary school, 1917, Buffalo, N.Y.

Shanghai, 1933, child laborers.

Medical School, Beirut, 1930.

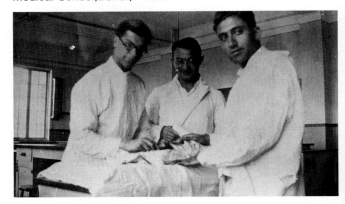

Clinic on Kiukiang Road, Shanghai, 1934, shared with doctors Levinson and Katz, classmates in Geneva med school.

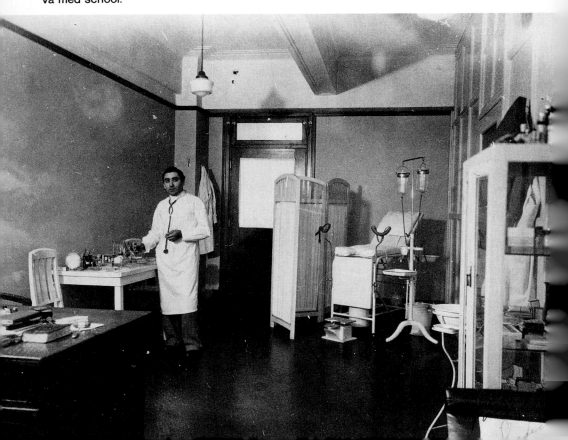

A wild welcome by the Red Army for George Hatem and Edgar Snow at Bao An, Shaanxi, 1936.

Snow loaned his "eight-pointed" hat to Mao, who was bare-headed, when he took this picture of him in 1936 because George thought it would look "more dignified".

After Snow returned to Beijing, Mao sent this note to "Dr. Ma Haide" in 1937 requesting him to forward to Snow another photo of himself, which he enclosed.

The International Peace Hospital, Yanan. Ma Haide served here, and with the army. Between 1944 and 1946 he treated some 40,000 patients.

Little son You Ma was two years old in 1945.

An autographed picture from Madame Soong Ching Ling, 1944, with a note thanking him for his work in the Hospital.

To Dr Ma Hai-teh

with warm appreciation for your donation to our IPH

Soong Ching Ling

Aug. 28, 1944

Yanan, 1945, with a US Airforce crew from Chengdu.

American special envoy Patrick Hurley talking with Ma Haide in Yanan, November, 1944. Hurley astounded the Chinese on his arrival with an Indian war whoop. "They thought he was a screwball," said Ma Haide.

March, 1947. Ma Haide was in charge of evacuating wounded soldiers and medical supplies from Yanan, attacked by KMT warlord Hu Zongnan.

The Chinese Communist Party delegation to the Tripartite Executive Headquarters in Beiping, with medical advisor Ma Haide and a Rockefeller Foundation delegation, June, 1946. Composed of Communist, Kuomintang, and American military representatives, Headquarters' function was to rush three-faction teams to quell any outbreaks of renewed fighting.

Qinghai. Demonstrating to Tibetans that giving blood samples is safe and painless.

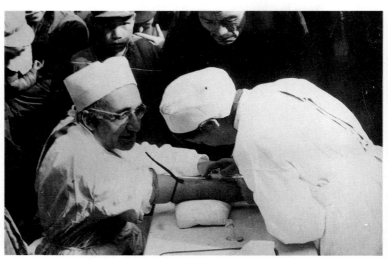

Kazak kids turn out to greet him in Xingjiang.

Examining a leprosy patient in Hebei. The man wept. "I have had this disease for 25 years," he said, "and no one has ever touched me with his bare hands!"

Travel this way was easier and more reliable.

At the Chinese Embassy in Washington in October, 1983, with Henry Kissinger, Ambassador Zhang Wenjing, and Leonard Woodcock - first American ambassador to the People's Republic.

At a reception in 1983 in the Great Hall of the People honoring Ma Haide for 50 years of service. He is congratulated by Deng Xiaoping. A beaming Rewi Alley and Wan Li look on.

U.S. Ambassador Arthur W. Hummel, Jr., presents Dr. Ma Haide with the Daimien-Dutton Leprosy Award for 1982.

With Prime Minister Indira Gandhi at the 12th International Leprosy Congress in India, 1984.

In 1986, on behalf of Lebanon's President Amin Gemayel, Lebanese Ambassador Frida Sahama presents Dr. Ma with the Ordre de Cedre-Commander for his medical contributions to China and mankind.

With Mrs. Mary Lasker, president of the Albert and Mary Lasker Foundation. Dr. Ma received the prestigious Albert Lasker Award for Public Service for his work in venereal diseases, leprosy and public health. New York, 1986.

From Eppie Lederer (Ann Landers), noted "Dear Abby" columnest.

Hans Muller and Rewi Alley at the "Mutton Joint".

Dr. Sam Rosen at the UN in New York.

Tokyo, 1985, with shipping magnate Ryoichi Sasakawa, activist in the fight against leprosy.

Sidney Shapiro, at the beach in Sanya, Hainan Island.

The North Carolina family, 1982.

His 77th birthday. With grand-daughter Ma Lan, wife Su Fei, son You Ma, daughter-in-law Luo Guifu, and grandson Ma Jun. The last family photo, 1987.

At the Great Wall.

Still entranced by China's ancient culture.

words of General David Barr, head of the U.S. Military
Advisory Group in China bolstering the dictator's regime:

> No battle has been lost since my arrival due to lack of
> ammunition or equipment. (And he added bluntly) The
> Kuomintang military debacles, in my opinion, can be at-
> tributed to the world's worst leadership and many other
> morale-destroying factors that led to a complete loss of will
> to fight.

Large quantities of American tanks, artillery and other
military hardware fell into the hands of the people's forces. As
Mao Zedong earlier noted, "We rely on the war industries of
the imperialist countries and of our enemy.... Equipment is
delivered to us by the enemy's own transport."

On January 31, 1949, the first units of clean, smiling young
PLA men marched smartly into Beijing through Xizhi Men,
the Northwest Gate. Contingents of artillery cassions, trucks
and white-wall-tired jeeps—all made in the USA, rolled
through the streets. No wonder the PLA ironically called
Chiang Kai-shek their "Quartermaster General".

George and Sufei were still in Shijiazhuang, but living
separately. You Ma remained with George. Sufei had become
part of a small theatrical troupe learning songs and skits which
they would perform in the streets of Beijing to explain to the
public how a new society would improve their lives. Suddenly
the troupe was ordered to move out. They went by truck to
Shijingshan, a mountainous suburb of Beijing. They found the
iron and steel mill in ruins. The next few days were spent
preparing to enter the city proper.

In mid-February the troupe shifted to an abandoned school
building outside the Northwest Gate, arriving at midnight. It
was very cold. They slept, badly, on a cement floor. The next
morning the truck took them into the city, where they sang
their songs and put on their skits before large crowds, drawn
by pounding drums and crashing cymbals. At night they
returned to the school.

George came into Beijing with Army Headquarters a few
days later, after putting up for a delightful week in the Summer Palace, once an imperial park of the Qing dynasty Empress Dowager. He was able to tour the scenic spots in the
Western Hills and visit the already liberated universities of
Yenching and Tsinghua. He ate better than he had in years.

But it was back to the spartan life when he entered the city, although given rooms above "Shikins", a White Russian restaurant and provisions store frequented by the Old China Hands in their halcyon days during the Kuomintang regime. Food supplies were scarce everywhere, and Shikins was no exception. Besides, none of the newcomers had any money. All military and civil personnel were "paid" on a subsistence basis. That is, food, clothing and lodging were issued, and a little cash for carfares and the like. There were no wages.

The first thing George did was to go with You Ma to the school outside Xizhimen, looking for Sufei. But she was not in. George left his address with the gatekeeper.

A few hours later, Sufei came hurrying to Shikins. She ran up the stairs, knocked on the first door, and tried to enter. The door could only open a fraction because Wang the orderly and the army "imp" who lived in that room had occupied most of the floor space with their bedding. They said they couldn't sleep in the soft "foreign" bed provided. "It puts your feet higher than your head," they complained. The wooden floor was nice and even. They told her George lived next door.

She walked in and was greeted by husband and little son with exultant shouts. George enfolded her in a bear hug that lifted her off her feet. When they had all calmed down a bit Sufei said what she wanted most at the moment was to use his precious tub and hot water to take a bath and wash her hair. You Ma got into the tub with her.

Sufei was tired, and the water was too warm. A few minutes soak and she grew dizzy and nauseous. She weakly called George. He lifted her and You Ma out, dripping wet, and dried them off. He put Sufei into bed and covered her. After half an hour's rest, she recovered. The three of them had lunch together in the room, and Sufei returned to her unit about four o'clock that afternoon.

They were re-united as a family a few weeks later when they were allocated a house in Gongxian Hutong (Bowstring Lane). It had belonged to Du Yuming, a Kuomintang general convicted and imprisoned as a war criminal. Commandeered, along with some excellent hardwood furniture, by the Ministry of Health, it was not a bad building. But the neighborhood was noisy.

Their next move was to a beautiful area on the north shore of Hou Hai (Rear Lake). They were allowed to bring the hardwood furniture with them and buy it very cheaply from the Ministry. The compound they were given, at one time the residence of a Manchu aristocrat, had also become the property of the Ministry of Health. It contained traditional single-storied tiled-roof buildings set in hollow squares around flower garden courtyards.

But it was filthy and very run-down. The whole family, with help of young Wang their orderly, got to work sweeping, washing and cleaning. Repairs were made a few years later when General Ye Jianying was appointed mayor of Beijing. Ye ordered that the place be made suitable for receiving foreign visitors who had already begun calling on George with some frequency.

BEIJING BEGINNINGS

In 1949 when the Ba Lu first marched in, Beijing was in a
sorry state. Hills of uncollected garbage reached the top of the
city wall along which it had been piled. There were few toilets,
and children relieved themselves in the city's hundreds of
unpaved lanes. Everything was in short supply, black market-
eers flourished, crime was rampant.

Within a few months miracles occurred. 200,000 tons of
refuse were removed in ninety days. Courtyards were swept,
housewives organized to keep lanes clean. Foreign names of
streets were converted into Chinese.

On Wangfujing, formerly Morrison Street, the main shop-
ping thoroughfare, for a time black market dealers in currency
continued to stand openly on street corners, jingling stacks of
silver dollars. Security police informed them that this was no
longer allowed. A few days later, those still at it had their
money confiscaterd. If, after another week, they persisted, they
were arrested.

A new currency was issued, pegged to the value of a few
essential commodities like grain, edible oil and cotton goods,
whose prices were strictly controlled. Gradually the inflation
subsided and prices stabilized.

The fabulous Beijing of old began to re-emerge. George was
enchanted. The only Chinese city in which he had lived for any
time was Shanghai, with its European architecture and office
buildings, its cars, its bustling go-getters in Western business
suits.

Beijing was something else. No city could have been more
Chinese. It breathed antiquity, power and refinement. It had
first become the capital when the Mongol emperor Kublai

Khan took the throne in 1280, and was built into its present magnificence in the 15th century by the emperors of Ming.

The bulk of the population lived in traditional hollow square compounds of tiled-roof one-storey structures in a wide network of earthen lanes. In many places stood princely residences guarded by stone lions. Arches of stone and wood painted in beautiful and intricate designs spanned major street intersections.

Situated in the exact center of Beijing was the Palace, also known as the Forbidden City, a huge complex of courts, compounds, terraces and tiers, all paved with stone and surrounded by ornately carved marble balustrades. A series of great halls rose gradually to a height overlooking the entire city, each with massive pillars supporting gleaming tile roofs of imperial yellow.

From here the city extended in the four directions of the compass with geometric precision. Ancient places of worship —Buddhist, Taoist, Confucian, Tibetan, Moslem and Catholic —temples, cathedrals, nunneries, monasteries... attested to Beijing's diversified religious and cultural influences. The whole city was encased in a thick crenallated wall punctuated at regular intervals by heavy brass-studded gates topped with tiled-roof forts.

To George it was a story-book world, the like of which he had never seen. After the miseries of Shanghai, the battles and hardships in the Northwest, Beijing seemed to symbolize the enduring solidity and beauty of Chinese culture, to promise that the new concepts would strengthen and take hold. He was convinced that the Chinese people, freed of their shackles, would create a China not just equal to but better than the China of the past.

In 1950 he was the first foreigner to apply for and be granted citizenship in the People's Republic of China. George now considered himself thoroughly Chinese in every sense of the word. But not all Chinese agreed with him.

The new government faced tremendous problems. After a hundred years of foreign aggression and internal disorder the nation's economy was in a shambles. Production of coal, iron and steel had fallen drastically from the pre-liberation peak year of 1943. Grain output had declined by one quarter and cotton by nearly half. Years of runaway inflation and Kuomintang indifference to natural disasters had reduced the great majority of the people to abject misery and desperation. The big Western powers, America in particular, considered the new government a fleeting chimera and refused even to consider diplomatic recognition. Chiang Kai-shek, installed on the island of Taiwan, declared he would strike back within two years.

As a start Beijing confiscated the holdings of the "Big Four" —Chiang Kai-shek, his wife's brother T.V Soong, H. H. Kung who was married to Madame Chiang's sister Ai-ling, and the "C.C. Clique". They were known as "bureaucrat-capitalists" because they used their official positions as high bureaucrats to convert government property and income into their own private capital. This included formerly Japanese-owned industrial and commercial complexes they had appropriated after the Japanese defeat.

On the eve of liberation the bureaucrat capitalists controlled two-thirds of China's industrial assets, 90 percent of iron and steel production, 67 percent of electric power, 33 percent of coal production, and all petroleum and nonferrous metal industries. The major banks, railroads, airlines, and the dozen largest trading companies were also in their grip. By the end of 1949 the new government had confiscated over 2,800 "Big Four" holdings employing 750,000 workers. Their conversion into state-owned enterprises laid the foundation for the socialist industrialization of China.

Extra-territoriality and most of the imperialist privileges extorted from China through the unequal treaties had been nominally abolished during World War II, and Japanese property had been taken over after V-J Day. Following liberation the roughly 1,000 non-Japanese foreign business concerns were encouraged to continue operations under Chinese law. But this they were unwilling or unable to do, more so after the U.S. embargo was imposed in 1951. Many closed shop and left. Some transferred ownership to the people's government by way of payment of taxes and debts.

Fundamental to the solution of the country's ills was a reform of the rural economy. Eighty percent of China's inhabitants were engaged in farming or in agriculture-related activities. Landlords and rich peasants, who constituted only ten percent of the rural population, owned seventy percent of the land. Ninety percent of the tillers—the poor peasants—had to scratch out a living from the thirty percent of the fields which remained. Rents were a killing half the yield, or higher. This kept the poor majority eternally in debt to the landlords —the backbone throughout Chinese history of all repressive regimes, of which the Kuomintang had been the latest.

A Land Reform Law proclaimed in June 1950, was implemented nation-wide. All land owned by the landlords, as well as their farm implements, draft animals, surplus grain and surplus houses were confiscated and redistributed to the tillers. The landlords and their families received an equal share. Whatever industrial and commercial enterprises they owned in the towns and cities remained theirs. Three hundred million landless and land-poor peasants received land, tools, animals and seed grain. Exhorbitant rents and uxurious interest rates were abolished. Economically, China's millions had a chance to survive and grow, at last.

But to truly liberate China, feudalism had to be extirpated from Chinese soil. Based on control by a landlord minority class, it rationalized its depredations with self-serving Confucian concepts which allowed, and even praised, contemptuous oppression of the population. Women, at the bottom of the male chauvinist social ladder, were the worst sufferers.

The Marriage Law of 1950 announced a new era for women. It stipulated that marriages should be monogamous, with partners freely chosen. Both sexes should enjoy equal rights, and the lawful rights of women and children be protected. It prohibited bigamy, concubinage, child betrothal, interference with the remarriage of widows, the exaction of fees and gifts in connection with marriages—all long-standing evils.... Custom, and continuing poverty in many regions hindered a full enforcement of the law.

One area which could be and was successfully attacked was prostitution—considered a medical as well as a social problem. Plans for its elimination were drawn up before the PLA entered Beijing. George had been appointed a consultant to the Ministry of Health, where his job was to help organize a campaign to wipe out venereal disease. Since the prostitutes were the main source of its spread, it was inevitable that he should take part in the great raid on Ba Da Hutong—Eight Big Emporiums Lane—center of Beijing's red light district.

The plan was top secret. As highly disciplined in such matters as he was free and easy in his personal affairs, George said not a word to anyone—even Sufei. In essence it was a

military operation, staged by the PLA. None of the troops of
Fu Zuoyi, the warlord who had peacefully surrendered Beijing,
were used, although they had been absorbed into the ranks of
the regular army. They were too recently a part of the old
society, too deeply imbued with the mentality which endorsed
prostitution. To prevent any involvement, they were moved
temporarily to the suburb of Wu Ke Song (Five Pines), southwest of the city.

Around midnight PLA soldiers, fully armed, surrounded Ba
Da Lane and burst into the brothels, followed by doctors and
medical personnel. Pimps, madams, customers and prostitutes
were rounded up. The girls wept and ranted. Some banged their
heads against the walls, some threatened suicide. In the past
these were the tactics used to get out of difficult situations.
Kuomintang police often arrived suddenly to extort money
from the brothel keepers. The girls would raise a fuss and they
would be let go, since they were not the objects of the raid in
the first place.

The customers were mainly well-to-do merchants, plus ras-
cals and gangsters from the Tianqiao district—a center for
criminal organizations. This time the girls and their "guests"
were very frightened. They knew little about the "Ba Lu Reds",
and had been deluged with horror stories by the Kuomintang.
To them all men in uniform were to be hated and feared.

George spoke soothingly to the girls. Taking their hands, he
told them not to be afraid. "We're only doctors," he said.
"We've come to treat your diseases. As soon as you are cured,
you can leave." The girls quieted down.

Everyone was registered. Lists were made of the girls, customers, pimps, madams, and attendants. The names and ad-
dresses of the establishments had been known in advance. All
were hit simultaneously. Many of the girls resided in the
houses, some lived outside and worked part time. The attendants were called *da cha hu*—"Big Tea Kettles" because part of
their job was to pour tea from the big bronze kettles and serve
food to the guests.

The girls were loaded on to trucks and moved to a hostel
outside the city, taking their belongings. The customers were
allowed to go home. The operators were placed under detention
in an army center for investigation. Later, the worst of them
were handed over to the judicial authorities for trial and
prosecution. Many of the girls testified against them. Those

convicted were sent to prison. A few of the most vicious were publicly shot.

"They ought to shoot more of those guys," George growled. "Most of those girls are practically children."

He spent several days at the hostel, examining the girls. The doctors and nurses took blood samples to test for venereal disease. Many of the girls were infected. While receiving a course of treatment it was carefully explained to them that the government regarded them not as criminals but as victims. Although the girls could not leave until they were cured, members of their families were allowed to visit. Meanwhile, they were educated and taught a trade. A large number later went to work in textile mills in other parts of the country. Their histories were kept secret from all except the factory heads. Those who wished to return to their native villages were sent off with their fares paid. The marriage rate among the rehabilitated girls was high.

The day after the raid George brought Sufei to see the former brothels. Except for broken furniture and smashed crockery, they were empty, tawdry-looking in the light of day. Only then did Sufei learn what had happened. George had kept the secret well. As a Communist he was often privy to inside information which he was not able to tell his wife. It was hard sometimes, but it helped that she never objected or raised any fuss if she subsequently found out.

He had always been a conscientious doctor, and now, having assumed the duties of consultant to the Ministry of Health, he felt an added sense of responsibility. He insisted on continuing to examine patients in the skin clinic in Gan Mian Lane two days a week.

"A medical consultant without constant practical experience isn't qualified to 'consult' on anything," George said.

Still the unbuttoned joker among his friends, he had grown more serious professionally, weighing his words carefully when discussing medical questions with his colleagues, or political questions with anyone. The arrival of the medical "experts" from the Soviet Union confronted him with a dilemma on both scores.

Beijing's adulation for all things emanating from Moscow seemed entirely natural and reasonable to China's intellectuals and to the Chinese public in general. The Soviet Union was then the one country which apparently had managed a transition from a society with many feudal remnants, similar to those plaguing China, to a fledgling socialist state without having to go through a developed capitalist stage. It had established state-run heavy industry and commerce, created a collectivized agriculture, and built a defense structure which had smashed the most formidable war machine the world had ever seen—Hitler's military juggernaut. It claimed impressive strides in health, culture, education and science. All this despite the hatred of the Western powers and their unrelenting efforts to impede Soviet progress.

Moscow had taken the philosophy and political precepts of Marx and Engels, with subsequent permutations by Lenin and Stalin, as its guide to action. The results, though not without flaws, seemed on the whole positive. Mao Zedong had been adapting this same guide to Chinese realities, also with considerable success. Moreover the Soviet Union had encouraged and helped the Chinese Communist Party from its inception, and had given China invaluable support in her fight against Japanese aggression.

The attitude of the West stood in sharp contrast. When, after years of bitter sacrifice and struggle, China was finally able to form a new government, President Truman proclaimed his "containment of communism" doctrine, and Winston Churchill warned against the "Iron Curtain" and the "menace of the Asiatic hordes". The West could have found no more effective means of thrusting China into the arms of the Soviet Union. Later moves only increased the impetus.

It was in this atmosphere that Mao went to Moscow in December 1949. Several weeks of negotiation with Stalin and other Soviet leaders produced a "Treaty of Friendship, Alliance and Mutual Assistance", plus several subsidiary agreements. China gained little materially from the pacts (a credit of $500 million was less than what defeated enemy Austria received from the United States after the war), but politically Mao's trip was important. China now had a powerful ally in the Soviet Union and friends in Eastern Europe. Moscow further endeared itself to Beijing by denouncing tsarist attempts to establish Russian spheres of influence on Chinese territory.

Washington's hostility, the friendliness of Moscow, the affinities the Chinese found in the Soviet Union to their approach to political and cultural affairs, the seeming success of

Moscow's bold social experiment... strongly slanted China toward the Soviet Union.

Now the Russians were helping China build industrial and engineering projects, and sending experts and advisors. While the Chinese had to pay stiff prices and high salaries, they were pleased for the most part with what they got, inclined to accept on faith almost anything coming out of Moscow.

There were some reservations. A few of the big engineering projects did not come up to standard, or failed completely, because Soviet engineers insisted on mechanically transposing copies of their own projects in disregard of Chinese materials and conditions. While many of the experts were sincere hard-working individuals, some were not. You used to see them tooling up to the Friendship Store that caters to foreigners in big Zis and Zim limousines and walking in with large suitcases. These they would cram with purchases of Chinese furs and silks for re-sale in the Soviet Union at several times the Beijing price. People began to suspect that by no means all were genuine "selfless proletarian internationalists". Even the kids in the lanes had a jingle they used to chant while skipping rope:

Soviet Big Brother in a big car goes to town,
Soviet Big Sister wears a fancy gown.

Still, Moscow's prestige was high. Russian was taught in the schools, lessons were broadcast over the radio. Soviet movies and dramas played in Chinese theatres, Soviet directors showed how to put them on, taught the Stanislavsky acting method. George and Sufei went to see a Chinese version of *Twelfth Night*, not exactly one of Shakespeare's most immortal dramas, put on with the aid of a Soviet *regisseur*. They were struck by the large putty noses on the Chinese actors, yards of lace at the cuffs, and splendid plumed hats.

A month or so later they sampled the version of *La Traviata* contrived by a Soviet impresario for a Chinese opera company. The troupe must have spent a fortune getting the costumes and scenery rigidly correct. Everything was sung, including the *recitatives*. This tickled the Chinese, whose opera *recitatives* are always spoken. The night George and Sufei went, when rich papa came to plead with Violetta to release his darling son from her wiles, even before papa entered the parlor the maid began to warble, in Chinese, of course:

"A gentleman to see you."

"Who is it?" trilled Violetta.
"Monsieur So-and so," in dainty staccato.
"Ask him to come in," Violetta chimed.

The audience collapsed into helpless laughter. George had tears running down his cheeks. It was several minutes before the show could go on.

Yet much of the Soviet art that came to China was excellent —Oistrakh, Richter, Ulanova, the Bolshoi.... Several new novels, translated into Chinese, reached millions of readers. The Soviet impact on Chinese culture was considerable. For that matter in every field of the social and natural sciences the trend was to emulate Big Brother.

This was very apparent in medicine. George did not approve of what he felt was an over-emphasis on Soviet experience and methods in treating ailments. He had nothing against Soviet medicine, but it seemed to him unwise to place complete reliance on the medical lore of any single country. In the prevailing atmosphere of pro-Soviet euphoria, however, it was impossible for him to say so, particularly since he was an American. Some of his colleagues would surely ascribe it to chauvinist prejudice.

What is more, the love fest with Moscow was clearly Party policy. As a loyal Communist he had no choice but to go along with it. Since reference materials and the names of medicines were now all in Russian, he had to learn them anew and take up a study of the language. Where he strenuously disagreed with the Soviet doctors on a specific question he did speak up. But invariably his superiors in the Ministry of Health ruled against him.

George found the heavily Russian flavor in which China's health work was then steeped hard to take. Fortunately, he was able to get away from it. In 1953 he was named advisor to and deputy director of the Institute of Dermatology and Venereology, which was concentrating especially on syphilis.

Syphilis was brought into China by colonial incursions in the 16th century. By the 20th, thanks to poverty, prostitution and severe exploitation of the bulk of the population, it had become widespread. Marauding Kuomintang and Japanese armies greatly increased its proliferation. In pre-liberation China families were often compelled to sell their children just to keep them alive. Daughters of the poor were forced into slavery or prostitution. Most people were ignorant, superstitious, barely able to survive.

There were no public medical services. The poor could not pay private practitioners even when they were available. An injection of neosalvarsan for syphilis in 1940 would have cost an ethnic herdsman a cow or a horse, which was much more than he could afford. At the time of liberation distribution of syphilis varied in direct proportion to the extent that women were sexually exploited in a given area. The lowest rate was in the farming countryside—3 to 5 percent. Next came the cities and urban areas with 5 to 10 percent. The highest rate—10 to 50 percent, was in the ethnic minority regions.

The Tibetans and the Mongolians were the worst off. In many of their monasteries George personally investigated he found anywhere from 80 to 90 percent of the lamas infected with syphilis.

Conditions were primitive. The people were mainly nomads who travelled with their flocks and herds to the grazing grounds. They were very promiscuous, the men in particular. Because they lived in temporary encampments scattered over vast empty plains, they warmly welcomed any rare guest, offering him their wives or daughters to sleep with as a matter of courtesy. If the visitor was a lama monk and he consented to lie with one of the women, the host considered himself honored. Although the nomads loved children, the women were so heavily infected they could not give birth.

Kuomintang officials used to say, "Fine. No need for us to fight these people. Disease will wipe them out in a few decades." Of course Chiang Kai-shek's government provided little or no free medical treatment.

While the root causes of venereal disease nationwide were poverty and prostitution, in the ethnic regions the problem was compounded by backwardness and ignorance. How could small health teams composed of educated medical people from the cities teach primitive nomads to recognize their ailments and persuade them to come forward for strange and unfamiliar treatment? It had never been done before, but this was precisely what George and his colleagues were determined to do.

The Soviets kept saying that blood tests were the only reliable method for the detection of venereal disease. But the Chinese knew it was not possible to test thousands of people spread over a huge area. They didn't have the facilities or the personnel. George proposed that the Institute send medical teams into the ethnic areas and train local groups in each community to recognize symptoms of venereal disease, pass this knowledge on to the local people and persuade them to submit to examination and treatment. That was the only way the Chinese medics would have a fighting chance to cure the disease. The Institute agreed with this course of action.

Among the first duties as deputy director George allocated was to appoint himself leader of the teams sent into China's outlying regions to attack the venereal diseases prevalent among the ethnic minorities. He headed the team that went to Inner Mongolia. They started at the capital, Hohhot, where they agreed upon which banner (county) they would visit first. Discussions with local authorities at banner headquarters enabled them to draw up a list of encampments to call at, and an order of precedence.

As they approached the first encampment in their jeeps, men on horseback raced forward to meet them. It was like a scene from a Wild West movie. They even looked like cowboys —broad-brimmed felt hats, boots, high pommelled work saddles, and riding tough pinto ponies. Instead of lariats, they carried long poles with a rope loop at the end. Later George saw them cutting horses out of a herd with those pole-loops, fast and effective.

A group of elders and a headman welcomed the Chinese medical team at the settlement, and they and the team ceremoniously exchanged *hatas*—special silk scarves always presented on formal occasions. After an interval of polite conversation, they settled down to business. The team would begin by organizing the traditional practitioners. *Mengu daifu* (Mongol doctor) used to be a term of contempt for any inept Chinese physician. The scorn was unjustified, since the local practitioners obtained good results for many ailments. But they were unable to explain the reasons for their cures, and generally they were quite unsanitary.

Their attempts at treatment of venereal disease were often calamitous. For syphilis they used over-powerful drugs, including arsenic compounds which killed many patients. In twenty-day training periods the Chinese taught them to recognize symptoms of VD, bring the patients in for treatment, and administer "606", that is, penicillin. Training and treatment went on at the same time.

Most encampments contained about one hundred adults.

The aim was to give a blood test to every adult. Local people were superstitious about losing blood, and some were just plain scared. George encouraged them by demonstrating on himself.

"See, there's nothing to it," he would say, stabbing a hypodermic needle into his forearm and producing a drop of the precious fluid. "Which of you bold heroes will be the first to try?"

Under the interested gaze of the local girls, one of the young men would stride forward to prove his courage. Others would quickly follow. Still, many would not come to the clinic. How could cases among them be discovered?

The answer was a promotion campaign by local activists urging all adults to fill out a ten-point questionnaire prepared by the health teams. The questions covered every possible symptom which might lead a person to suspect that he or she had syphilis or had been exposed to it. If they now or previously had skin lesions, falling hair, genital sores... they were invited to come in for an examination and blood test.

These questionnaires had to be introduced at public meetings. In China, as in any other country, there is a stigma attached to having a venereal disease. How could you persuade people to admit to being infected? The key was the local activists. The Chinese doctors would gather the villagers around and explain the matter clearly and simply.

"Venereal disease was a scourge of the old society," George would say. "We've got rid of the old society, but remnants of the scourge are still hanging on. The old society is to blame if you have syphilis. You needn't be ashamed. It's not your fault. We have a paper here. It asks ten questions, and you should answer them honestly. If you can't read, tell us, and we will help you. If you find you have any of the symptoms, come in for a check-up. Treatment is free, and we guarantee to cure you. Comrades, we can't take syphilis with us into socialism."

Before long people began pouring into the clinics for examination. Blood tests showed that one in twenty of those who had answered "yes" to any of the questions had venereal disease.

The questionnaire method reduced the problem of case-finding to at least manageable proportions. The strategy against venereal disease was to treat the whole community —not just individual patients—by mobilizing the activists and educating the entire population. It was what an application of what the Chinese Communists call the "mass line". It did not find acceptance easily or all at once. Some "experts" and conservatives who thought in the old way did not believe in it. They said a lot of cases would be missed, that the methods were too crude and unscientific. But the "mass line", under qualified medical supervision, worked like a charm as a means of detecting venereal disease.

A couple of the doctors on George's team had been to school in the States. When they sat around with George at night summing up the day's work they used to speculate on whether the system they were using could be applied to the v.d. problem in the West. George maintained it couldn't.

"Why not?" the doctors demanded.

Well, (George said,) suppose you took a bunch of Americans on Fifth Avenue in New York and said, "Now, boys, let's go through this questionnaire together." Maybe their wives are standing next to them. You wouldn't get to first base. It wouldn't work. Each country has to develop its own methods, develop a social system wherein your public, your personnel, your medical people are more intensely motivated than they are now. Maybe you need block wardens or people who go from door to door collecting for various charities, maybe these people could be induced to serve as health volunteers. America has to evolve its own method for treating its own society. That's for sure....

Tours of the medical teams into the ethnic regions were conducted all through the fifties and for the first two or three years of the sixties, twice a year, each tour lasting three months. The medics went to every autonomous ethnic province in China, except Taiwan and Tibet. They did, however, treat thousands of Tibetans living in other provinces. Qinghai, for example, has more Tibetans than Tibet.

Each team was composed of about twenty persons—doctors, nurses, lab technicians. The treatments they gave were quick and effective. Patients were allowed to work, but were urged not to have sex until they were cured. The health team would move on to the next encampment after the twenty-day training period, leaving medicines and equipment, including a microscope, with the local traditional doctors who continued the treatments.

George disagreed with the Soviet approach. Their specialists favored the use of penicillin combined with arsenic and bismuth compounds over a long period of time. This was not good for China. George and the Chinese specialists advocated penicillin alone, administered for just ten days.

To prove the efficacy of this method, starting in 1954 George led medical research teams every year to ethnic minority agricultural and pastoral regions in provinces like Inner Mongolia, Qinghai and Gansu, and checked on the results of the short penicillin treatments which had been given there in 1950 and 1951. On the vast grasslands it was extremely difficult to find and re-examine every nomad who had been treated before. They often had to travel miles to locate a single former patient.

In some places the water was impure, so that they couldn't guarantee the reliability of their plasma tests. Or there was no electricity for the dark background electronic microscopes they used to check for the presence of syphilis spirochetes. George wasn't fazed a bit. He showed the medics how to make sand precipitant filters for the water, and rigged up batteries for their microscopes. He utilized whatever was at hand, but was strict in his demands for accuracy.

Because of the hardships he had endured in Yanan days, he developed stomach ulcers and bad teeth. But he didn't complain. He slept with the men on crude brick beds, and ate the same coarse food. Whenever they moved he was always there to load and unload the trucks, and help the women carry their luggage. At the end of the day, when the exhausted young medics were deep in dreamland, George would be discussing with the local officials what the next steps should be, or summing up their work to date. If anything had been left undone, he did it himself. He never awakened any of the staff. Some nights he didn't sleep at all. But the next morning he was up with the rest of them, cheerfully bustling about.

George led all of the tours. It was tough work, but he revelled in it. The nurses didn't share his joy. They were changed every year. Although delighted in the beginning with the beautiful scenery, and being able to dress up and have their pictures taken in colorful native costumes, they couldn't stomach the local food. Welcoming banquets in the Mongol areas of boiled mutton, unsalted, and fatty sheep tails, soon wilted their high spirits. Beautiful Mongol girls would kneel on one knee and present the honored guests with choice bits of sheep liver. George enjoyed looking at the girls and consuming their offerings. The nurses, mostly southerners who generally eat little meat anyway, would decline, and George would gladly accept their portions in addition to his own.

Food in Mongolia is mainly mutton, milk (cow, horse, or camel), cheese, fermented mare's milk (koumiss), roasted millet, but no vegetables. Although the rivers and lakes teem with fish, the Mongols don't eat them. From their point of view fish are useful only to be "set free", thereby earning the liberator a merit on his Buddhist scorecard. Han members of the health teams asked their hosts whether it would be alright if they caught and ate the fish.

"Sure," said the Mongols. "Go ahead."

The Hans made nets and simply scooped them up—they were so plentiful. This provided a welcome addition to the health team's diet. Still, one tour was usually enough for the nurses. They rarely volunteered for a second.

George happily immersed himself in the life on the rolling plains. He wore Mongol felt boots, rode the wiry Mongol ponies, and participated vigorously in the Mongol dances held around a campfire almost every evening. His energy and cheerfulness made him a great favorite with the out-going Mongol girls.

His passion for dancing struck a responsive chord among his Han colleagues. While on the road with George one night, their truck broke down. They couldn't repair it in the dark, and the weather was bitterly cold. To keep warm they, and George of course, danced until dawn. Then they repaired the truck and went on.

A herdsman's wife came in for an examination during George's first trip to the Mongol grasslands. She was longing to have a child but could not conceive. She wept. He gave her a blood test which revealed that she had syphilis. He treated her, and in a few weeks she was cured.

It was the practice of the venereologists to periodically re-check infected areas visited earlier. George returned with another health team five years later. The same woman called, and she wept again. She had given birth to five children, all healthy and growing lustily. She and her husband couldn't afford any more. Would the doctor please tell her how to stop this cornucopia of offsprings?

George recommended a falliopian tubal ligature. It was a simple procedure which could easily be undone later if the couple changed their minds and decided to further enlarge their family. As distinguished from the Han majority, at that time ethnic minority couples were encouraged to have as many children as they wished. The result was a big increase in China's ethnic population, so severely depleted by the hardship and exploitation suffered under Kuomintang rule.

Careful records were kept of every person treated in every settlement and encampment. Local traditional doctors continued the medication after the health teams departed. When George came again with a team to check a few years later, he insisted on seeing all previous patients, regardless of their present place of abode. There could be no exceptions. Some had to be brought in from many miles away. Though he didn't often lose his temper, any negligence enraged him. He knew how quickly venereal contagion could spread.

GUIDE AND MENTOR

In a way it was easier for foreigners helping with the Chinese revolution before victory than after. It was simpler, then. You were confronted with a clearly defined, easily recognizable enemy who was openly out to destroy your Chinese friends, and you along with them, and you were obliged to defend yourself and defeat the enemy. There were, certainly, currents and counter-currents within the ranks, but these were generally muted while everyone, Chinese and foreigners alike, made common cause for common goals.

With victory and the establishment of a government, a bewildering array of new problems arose. Hard work and camraderie alone were no longer enough. How did a foreigner join in the effort to pull the country up by its bootstraps and wrench it from something called "feudalism" into something called "socialism"? How did one adjust to Chinese colleagues who were themselves struggling to adjust? In a word, how did a foreign supporter understand and go forward with a constantly changing environment?

Problems surfaced in their profesional lives, in their private lives, they were puzzled by some policy decisions, certain actions they found difficult to comprehend.... Where could they talk these questions out? It wasn't always possible to find solutions among themselves, or among their Chinese friends. And so, they turned to George. He could recognize what was troubling them, and why. He and they spoke the same language, could talk together calmly, reasonably. While George didn't necessarily have all the answers, he could at least explain to them the Chinese point of view, as seen by a person with a Western background.

124

That doesn't mean he sat around placidly like some oracle waiting to be consulted. He felt this was an area where he could be of direct and immediate use. If he heard that a friend was perplexed about anything, or having some sort of difficulty, or medical problems, he would drop by of his own accord to see what he could do. It got to be a kind of joke in their small foreign community. One man said George's Chinese name shouldn't be Horse (Ma), but Firehorse because he was off and running at the first sound of an alarm bell. Another fellow joked that if there hadn't been the phrase "let George do it" someone would have had to invent it.

These were people he knew and liked, people who were supporting China. George knew more than they about the political tactics and the inner workings of the Communist Party, and could enlighten them on that. As a doctor he also could and did look after their health. To most he was cordial, with a few he was intimate friends. Rewi he knew from the Shanghai days. Hans Muller he had met in Yanan. With these two he was very close, and saw them regularly once or twice a week.

Hans had two children—a boy and a girl a few years younger than George's son You Ma. His wife Dongcun was Japanese, but spoke quite good Chinese enabling her to converse easily with Sufei. They lived in a more or less Chinese style as George and his family did. But the strongest ties between the Hans and George were their medical professions and their similar views on Chinese affairs.

An internist and a first-rate diagnostician, Hans was the director of the military hospital in Shenyang—formerly Mukden—for a number of years after Liberation. He also doubled in a dozen important other jobs which so exhausted him that he suffered a heart attack. George moved him and his family down to Beijing on the train and nursed him back to health. Hans was then appointed Vice Chancellor of Beijing Medical Institute. Through the years he and George had frequent discussions on the state of China's medical and health work.

Politically, they saw pretty much eye to eye. Their Yanan background, their Chinese citizenship, their membership in the Chinese Communist Party, made them privy to inside information, brought them into proximity with the country's leaders, and gave them an understanding of the personalities involved. Foreigners within China and visitors from abroad, if not always convinced by their interpretations of the China scene, found them lucid.

Rewi had made an important contribution to defeating the Japanese during World War II by organizing and enlisting international support for the Chinese Industrial Cooperatives. The co-ops were mainly little workshops in rural areas, providing local employment and turning out everything from blankets to bomb casings. Rewi also headed the Baillie school in the wilds of Gansu. There he created technicians and accountants out of peasant and famine refugee children, many of whom are engineers and administrators today. His ideas of combining practical work with study were new to most Chinese educators, and are only now beginning to take hold.

Rewi, moreover, was a poet and a journalist. Writing with passion and sensitivity he produced hundreds of poems and dozens of books and articles, nearly every one about China and the Chinese. In his later years, when he lived in a large frame building in the spacious tree-lined compound of the Chinese Friendship Association, he was a font of China learning to which foreign visitors gravitated. These ranged from New Zealand Maoris, sticking their tongues out as they stomped ancient tribal war dances on his living room floor, to prime ministers and heads of state, sipping tea and nibbling little sandwiches.

Rewi never became a Chinese citizen, nor did he join the Chinese Communist Party. But he was remarkably knowledgeable about China, thanks mainly to his own wide experience and partly to the information he gained from George. In the Shanghai days Rewi had been George's teacher. Now George, because of his activities in the Communist Party and participation in Chinese practical affairs, was able to provide Rewi with a broader understanding than most foreign residents could attain.

Every Monday and Friday evening George went to Rewi's for dinner and a two or three hour chat, usually accompanied by Hans. Sometimes Rewi would pick George up in the afternoon in his car and take him out for a walk in the park. More often than not, when Rewi was receiving visitors from abroad, he would ask George to help out in the discussions. George was a very useful adjunct. The foreigners frequently directed their questions at him, taking some of the strain off Rewi, who was already in his eighties.

The relationship between the two was particularly close. As a friend and a doctor George accompanied Rewi on his summer vacations at the mountain and beach resort in Beidaihe and during his few weeks every winter on the tropical island of Hainan. In both places they swam, wandered through the surrounding villages and talked with the locals. In both places they held informal salons with foreign dignitaries and scholars who managed to track them down.

George had a great respect for Rewi's knowledge of Chinese history and archeology. Often their "walks in the park" turned into visits to antique shops in the old city outside Beijing's Qian Men (Front Gate). Watching Rewi sort through bronze artifacts and ancient pottery and hearing his colloquies with the shopkeepers, George acquired a good bit of information, and soon grew completely hooked on antiques. China is the happy hunting ground for collectors. Its history is so long, its culture so rich, that you can't sink a spade into the ground anywhere without digging up some priceless relic from ancient times.

George started a modest collection of his own, limited by his very limited finances. Most of his pieces came from Chinese friends who, when they learned of his infatuation, presented him with things they picked up on their travels. Due to the meaning of his name "Ma" in Chinese, it was perhaps inevitable that before long he should acquire a whole herd of horses —Tang dynasty tri-color pottery replicas. Lining the shelves around his living room walls, they brightened the decor nicely.

Among the foreigners helping China George was everybody's doctor. People got sick, their kids came down with something... George dropped in. Or they were seriously ill in the hospital, were dying.... They asked to see him. When Edgar Snow was in the last stage of terminal cancer in Switzerland, George flew out to be by his bedside. He doctored veteran American journalist Anna Lousie Strong and was her frequent companion for several years, until her death in Beijing in 1970 at the age of eight-four.

He discovered early on that patients recovered more quickly if the doctor was comforting and reassuring. Huang Zongjiang, prominent Chinese dramatist, called him "the world's greatest calmer-downer." Huang had a bit of high blood pressure a few years back, but whenever George took it, it was normal. Huang claimed George had the same cheering effect even on those spending their last moments on earth.

"My brother-in-law Zhao Dan, pioneer film star, was dying of terminal cancer in the Beijing Hospital," Huang recalled. "I was with him when Lao Ma 'dropped by'. In any hospital he acted as if he were casually visiting around. He chatted and joked with patients in such a relaxed, conversational manner that the dying felt they weren't really going to die. Or that even if they were, it wasn't anything very drastic—simply a move to some other, no doubt more interesting, locale."

Surgeon Wu Weiran was also there that day. Zhao Dan had been in a critical stage several times, but each time had pulled through. As they came out of the room Dr. Wu commented on it to George.

"A remarkable will to live. If he doesn't want to go, he just won't go!"

George agreed. "A remarkable will to live."

He and Huang left the building together. Huang knew that George too, not long before, had also been critically ill. His abdomen had been cut open, and had been stitched closed with great difficulty. Huang asked him about it. George replied with a smile.

"It's a fact," he said. "They were all set to see me off. The funeral oration was already written. But old Marx up in Heaven wouldn't have me. '*Lao* Ma,' he said, 'you're doing pretty well down in China. Why don't you stick around a while longer....'"

Huang's laugh was somewhat forced. "You have a 'remarkable will to live' yourself. So that's the reason. You want to 'stick around a while longer' so that you can do more for mankind."

George shrugged. "There's no use in brooding on the inevitable. It only cuts down on your ability to function in the time you have left. If I can last another couple of years, we may be able to knock out venereal disease. And no man wants to leave his family and his friends."

George had friends from many different countries. Of the long-term foreign residents, I was his closest American friend. We first met early in 1949, when George called on me in Beijing after Fengzi, Joan and I had failed in an abortive attempt to get to the liberated areas.

He introduced himself. "I'm Dr. George Hatem. My Chinese name is Ma Haide."

"Hi. I'm Sidney Shapiro. This is Fengzi, my wife. And this

is Joan Hinton."

"Hello." George shook hands all around. "I've come to tell Joan it's all set for her to join Engst in the interior."

I was then a good looking young man of thirty-two with light brown hair and hazel eyes gazing through thick glasses. My wife Fengzi, effervescent and very pretty, was a veteran of the legitimate stage. George's Sufei was also an actress, and so the wives, chatting in Chinese, had similar interests. George's son You Ma was about six years older than our daughter Yamei. He became her Big Brother, and when she was still an infant, used to pull her, screaming delightedly, along our carpeted floor. George and I, it turned out, had a lot to say to each other, in English.

I told George that my presence in Beijing, or for that matter in China, was the result of a series of absurd quirks of fate. In 1942 I had been a member of an anti-aircraft gun crew in the "Jersey Meadows", guarding the nearby Westinghouse and General Electric plants against possible attacks by German bombers.

In view of our marksmanship it was fortunate for the war effort that they never came. Our only assailants were rats and mosquitoes and the fragrance of the Secaucus pig-slaughtering establishment, wafted in on every breeze.

And so when the call came for volunteers to the ASTP—the Army Specialized Training Program, I jumped at the chance. Crash courses were given at various colleges in everything from dentistry and veterinary science to foreign languages. Having studied a few years of French in high school and college, I applied for the French course. I passed the qualifying exam, but when I appeared before a board of professors and army officers for formal assignment I was told that they had entirely too many French students, and it was therefore decided that I had "volunteered" to learn Chinese.

This was a bolt from the blue, but I recovered rapidly when I found myself on the gentle slopes of Cornell University, surrounded by trees and lovely co-eds. After being crammed for nine months with spoken Chinese, I and my classmates were ready to take off for the exotic East.

But the projected landing of American forces on the China mainland—if one was ever contemplated, was called off. We were put into Signal Intelligence and given a cryptanalysis course, in Virginia, and taught to break Japanese code. From there we were shipped to MIDPAC—Middle Pacific Army Command, in Honolulu, where we finished the war deciphering three-month-old messages from Japanese control towers to departing pilots on the state of the weather. In our spare time a few of us audited Chinese courses at the University of Hawaii.

By then I was thoroughly entranced with the language and what I was beginning to learn of China's history and culture. When I returned to civilian life in 1946 I had no interest in being a young lawyer again, as I had been before the war. Instead I took Chinese language courses, first at Columbia, then at Yale, and in 1947 booked passage on a freighter and sailed for China.

I landed in Shanghai a month later on April 1, 1947, April Fools Day, and had cause later to wonder whether the date wasn't significant. I had two hundred dollars in my pocket, and a letter from *Variety* saying that if I ever wrote anything and they ever published it, they might pay me. My money soon ran out, and I was reduced to doing what I had travelled 12,000 miles to escape. Again I was an attorney at law—in the offices of an American practitioner looking desperately for a junior partner.

But all was not dark. I met and, a year later, married Fengzi —meaning Phoenix. Formerly a famous actress and journalist, she was editing a left-wing magazine. Most of her friends were progressive, a few were in the Communist underground. Through them, and through witnessing daily the horrors of Kuomintang rule, I began quickly to acquire a knowledge of the realities of China.

Rumor had it that Fengzi was moving up on the KMT hit list. Friends advised us to leave. We had heard intriguing tales about bold social experiments in the interior, and decided we would like to see for ourselves, and perhaps to stay. I invented the story that I had to go to Jinan, in Shandong province, to get certain American clients out. From there it was just a few miles to the "liberated areas". When Fengzi and I departed from Shanghai we took Joan Hinton with us, at the request of the underground. She was hoping to join Irwin Engst, the man she was engaged to, who was then working as an agricultural expert in Communist territory.

Our underground guide escorted us to Tianjin, which was to be our jumping off place. But we were stopped at a military

police check point on the outskirts and refused passage. Our
guide sent us back to Beijing, with instructions to keep a low
profile. Our cover had been blown, and the Kuomintang would
be watching. He assured us the city would soon fall. We found
shelter in the College of Chinese Studies, where a few of my
professors at Yale had been teaching. The profs had decamped
as the siege net around Beijing tightened. I was left holding the
baby. Henry Fenn, chancellor of the college had asked me to
look after the property. It was here George found me when he
came calling on us a few days after the city was liberated.

George and I had a special relationship. We were, in a way,
echoes of each other's past. In common was our American
background, and our American ways and tastes, many of
which we never lost. With each other we spoke our native
patois, complete with slang and vulgar expressions. It was a
relief to feel completely understood without having to choose
our words, particularly since it turned out we were in accord
on the world's major issues. We talked about what was happening in America, the possibility of a rapproachment with China,
the trade deals being explored. We collected jazz records and
went to dances, with our wives.

I was working as translator of Chinese fiction into English
for Foreign Languages Press, which put out books in several
languages and circulated them all over the world. I travelled
to various parts of China, individually and in small groups,
and read extensively in Chinese novels and short stories. It is
an excellent way to get into the lives of the many diverse
Chinese persons and onto the places depicted in the fiction I
was translating.

It also gave me a "feel" for the realities of China. Having a
Chinese wife and Chinese friends no doubt helped considerably. I often went to George with questions about the old
Liberated Areas, which George knew from first-hand experience. Fengzi and I saw George and Sufei frequently. And we
mixed socially with like-minded Westerners.

Social life among the foreigners at first was limited. George
and I were members of a small amorphous group which met
every week or two at a bar and grill we rudely christened "The
Dump". It was rickety, the walls tilting slightly beneath the
weight of years, and had sawdust on the floor. But it had beer
on tap, and served steak and French fried potatoes which could
have held their own in any high-class American emporium.

During the course of the evening flashily dressed young ladies would escort gentlemen friends to rooms upstairs.

Most of the time our little quorum consisted of George, Rewi, "Yap" and me, a select if varied gathering. "Yap" was Ye Chu-pei, an American-born Chinese of Fukienese ancestry, and "Yap" was how they pronounced the name which would be "Ye" in any other part of China. The dialects they speak in Fukien have been compared to the "twittering of birds", and are understood only *in situ* and in Fukienese neighborhoods of the Chinatowns of the world.

Yap spoke no Chinese of any sort, and was just beginning to learn "Mandarin", or *putong hua*—the Common Speech used by most of China's population. He was married to an American girl he had met in the States and brought back with him. She taught English at Peking University. They had three kids—a boy and two younger girls. Yap was one hundred and ten percent American. He could quote the batting average of every important player in the major baseball leagues, and tell you which shortstop stole how many bases in any given year.

He was also one of the world's leading experts in the science of steel making. But he was not appreciated and could not get along with his Chinese colleagues in the Steel Institute. They clashed frequently. He was a rugged individualist who wanted to do everything himself and in his own way. The Chinese socialist approach was collective, working as a team. Yap was always taking his troubles and complaints to George, who did his best to explain to this very un-Chinese Chinese how the Chinese in China functioned, but with little success. Relations in the Steel Institute were so bad that when the Cultural Revolution erupted in 1966, Yap was attacked as a "bourgeois reactionary" and virtually hounded to death.

George was father confessor and guide to innumerable members of the foreign community. Those who had been neither communists nor activists in their own countries had particular difficulties in adjusting to a society and code of conduct which often seemed to them rigid and doctrinaire. They came to George because he was familiar with both worlds and able to talk about their respective pluses and minuses in terms they could understand.

Beijing was then graced by a distinguished British literary figure. William Empson, author of *Seven Types of Ambiguity*, was lecturing on Shakespeare at Peking University's Hong Lou, or Red Building, Division, where Mao Zedong had once served as librarian. Since Empson was drunk a good deal of the time and mumbled through a heavy growth of beard, his Chinese students, whose level of English comprehension was generally low, were confused by more than seven types of ambiguity whenever they attended his lectures. Fortunately, they were able to copy, in keeping with the traditional Chinese method of learning by rote, the words he scribbled on the blackboard.

His wife Hedda, a robust attractive sculptress of Boer Dutch descent, gave frequent parties in the garden of their large compound. They were lively affairs, for the punch the Empsons served consisted of one part orange juice and four parts *Er Guo Tou*—a fiery sorghum liquor closely resembling Missouri's notorious White Mule. This tended to bring out aggressive qualities in some of the guests, who were of varied backgrounds and professions.

At one party Michael Shapiro, a newly arrived Communist from the Stepney district of London, earned himself the sobriquet of "The Horizontal Shapiro" by madly pursuing a Dutch diplomat's wife through the rose garden. (I demanded to be called "The Vertical Shapiro" as a means of confirming my own unblemished virtue.) Alan Winnington, who wrote for the British *Daily Worker*, after generously sampling the punch, belligerently demanded of the British ambassador, "When are you bloody sods going to get out of Suez!" George and I occasionally attended, as much to keep class warfare among the foreigners from breaking out as to banter and dance with the charming young ladies present.

Hedda, between parties, had periods of depression, and she would consult with George. Her family life was not happy, she felt she was not getting anywhere with her sculpting. Her two little boys were growing up wild. They spoke flawless Chinese, enriched by the colorful profanity they acquired from the pedicab drivers with whom they spent most of their time.

George advised her to go home. Not long thereafter, the Empsons returned to England.

Bob and Jane Hodes, Americans, also had a big garden in the early fifties. He worked as a biology specialist in one of the medical institutes. They had two small children, a boy and girl. The boy, Peter, went to nursery school with my daughter Yamei. The Hodes ran an open house at which all sorts of people dropped in.

Among their more frequent visitors were half a dozen young Americans who had been POWs in a Chinese camp in Korea. They had signed strong statements against the "UN police action" and had requested permission to attend school in China. Since they were of different educational levels, special classes were set up for them in which they learned Chinese and various ordinary subjects. The Red Cross provided them with comfortable quarters, gave them spending money, and even engaged a cook who could make delicious steaks and chops and apple pie.

Long-term residents like George and me envied their diet. We were eating much more modestly. We never missed the outdoor barbecue the Hodes threw every Fourth of July. In addition to charcoal grilled goodies, somewhere the Hodes managed to find root beer! However much George and I disagreed with Washington's foreign policy, gastronomically we remained loyal Americans.

Needless to say, George was the POWs' favorite mentor. They were a pretty confused bunch. George was kept busy trying to hold them on an even keel. While they had genuinely disapproved of US intervention in Korea, they felt uncomfortable with having gone against their government. They didn't know what they wanted to do with their lives. Several wanted to go home, but were afraid of being prosecuted. The majority did finally return, and were amnestied. Two or three found jobs in China, married Chinese girls and settled down permanently.

Bob Hodes was a solid, careful scientist. Wife Jane was erratic and highly strung. She had frequent clashes with her Chinese colleagues, resulting in emotional blow-offs on her part. She would come to George in steaming indignation at what she considered Chinese arbitrariness, and he would vainly attempt to cool her down. Jane's fury became such that the Hodes decided to leave. One more instance of the inability of individualistic Western personalities to adjust to the calm, and at times irritatingly slow, pace of the traditional Chinese collective approach.

George shook his head wryly. "Americans say 'Do It Now', but the Chinese slogan is 'Make Haste Slowly'."

A favorite gathering place, as the English-speaking foreign colony grew in number, was a restaurant we named "The Mutton Joint". Housed in an ancient frame building, with balconies on the upper storey overlooking the beautiful Shi Sha Hai, or Lake of the Ten Monasteries, it was three hundred years old. Once it had been the haunt of young Manchu nobles, sneaking out at night from the palace in the Forbidden City. They would bring their girl friends to drink and dine while they recited poetry to the moonlight shimmering on the water.

The prime attraction was the strips of mutton or beef, first soaked in soysauce and ginger water, then grilled on huge iron griddles heated from below by glowing fragrant pine logs. The end product stuffed into toasted sesame seed rolls made delicious Manchu sandwiches, consumed at the dining tables and washed down with mugs of beer.

George loved to eat meat, and the Mutton Joint was only a ten minute walk from his home on Rear Lake. Every couple of months he would invent some excuse for convening a gathering of convivial Westerners, with their Chinese husbands or wives, around the festive board—often his "birthday", which he contrived to occur four or five times in the course of a year. They were hilarious affairs. George would appoint himself Master of Ceremonies and deliver what he hoped was a funny opening address, and then call on others to speak. Many preferred to sing. Americans would render ditties like *The Wiffenpoof Song*, or *Clementine*. The Brits sometimes injected a note of class struggle with immortal lyrics reminding everyone that *It's the rich wot gets the pleasure, it's the poor wot gets the blime*....

The Mutton Joint bashes rarely were more serious than that. They were a chance for Westerners, engaged in various jobs and living in different parts of the city, to get together, joke and gossip. With George presiding and the beer flowing freely there was little likelihood that the gatherings would be anything but festive.

One winter night George and I and Alan Winnington decided to go skating on the Lake of the Ten Monasteries. To fortify ourselves against the cold we first had some grilled beef at the Mutton Joint and too many snifters of *Er Guo Tou*. We walked unsteadily down to the lake, but when we put our skates on we skimmed like snow flakes across the ice. Anyhow, we thought we did, all inhibitions gone. Even our falls seemed light and graceful.

George liked Alan. Not only was he a good drinking companion—he gave the best parties of anyone George knew. The

Xinhua News Agency, where Alan and Michael Shapiro worked, put him up in a handsome two-storey house. There he lived in style with his newly acquired beautiful wife Esther, also from England, where she was born of a Chinese father and —according to Esther—a Jewish "gypsy" mother. Alan's Saturday night get-togethers were prized social functions. He served good food, plenty of booze, and had a large parquet floor and the latest jazz records for dancing. Since George was not averse to a drink or two and inordinately fond of dancing, he was there whenever Alan entertained.

But these were not the only qualities which won George's admiration. Alan was a first-rate journalist, and did fine work for what George considered the side of the angels. During the Korean War Alan Winnington and left-wing Australian reporter Wilfred Burchett, evolved an ingenious way of helping the Western media at Panmunjom. The foreign correspondents were dissatisfied with the handouts they were receiving from the U.S. press officer on the progress of the battles. These usually proved to be glowingly triumphant fabrications, or were so vague as to be useless.

The two periodically lured them to quiet meetings at a bar with bottles of Korean ginseng liquor—guaranteed foolproof male virility stimulators, in exchange for vintage PX scotch and bourbon. At the same time they passed on the real news, which they had obtained from the Chinese, to their brother gentlemen of the press, who then incorporated it into their dispatches.

Michael "the Horizontal" Shapiro, with his plebeian London wit and humor, early joined the ranks of George's Jewish friends. In the late fifties George and I attended Mike's wedding luncheon at the home of his bride, Liu Qinghe, a charming Chinese child psychologist who hailed from Fujian (Fukien) province, opposite Taiwan. The meal was cooked by Qinghe's mother, who served what we were told were typical Fujian dishes. Finally, mama brought out the *pièce de resistance*—balls of finely chopped fish, wrapped in its own skin and garnished with slices of carrot. George recognized it immediately.

"Gefilte fish!" he chortled.

And indeed it was, though the fish balls were smaller than the traditional Jewish favorite. The guests were astonished by the similarity, and wondered if Qinghe's ancestors might not have included one or two of the Jewish traders who came on Arab and Persian merchant vessels to Fujian seaports during the Tang and Song dynasties. In any event, the question of whether gefilte fish travelled from Jewish to Chinese tables, or the other way around, remains open for further academic study.

Between George and me there was a strong rapport. Though we were both pro-China, we wanted very much for America to be liked—or to put it more accurately, to behave in a manner which would win China's liking.

For a year or two after the formation of the People's Republic in 1949 a residue of affection for the U.S. still lingered. American boys had fought and died to defeat the Japanese, and the Chinese had never been stripped of parts of their territory by the Americans as they had by the Western colonial powers. Shortly after the new government was formed there was some American interest in doing business with China. George and I entertained David Drucker who came on behalf of a large U.S. enterprise to explore the possibility of a sale of steel to China.

But then in 1950 American and Chinese soldiers began killing each other in Korea, and American planes started bombing Chinese cities—allegedly with germ cannisters as well as conventional explosives. By the time the fighting ended in 1953, Chinese attitudes toward the U.S. had changed drastically.

Although our Chinese friends and colleagues repeatedly assured us that they blamed Washington, not the American people, George and I could not help feeling distressed. All the more so because we were treated with the same kindness and friendliness as ever. We were as unhappy about the destruction of U.S. youngsters as we were about the slaughter of young Chinese.

"What a waste," George fumed. This was when Eisenhower was castigating what he called the "military-industrial complex". I agreed that the leaders of this powerful financial combine were the villains of the piece.

"Those are the bastards who ought to be shot, not a lot of innocent kids," George said. "America wouldn't be in Korea in the first place if it wasn't a chance for Big Business to make more big money."

He viewed the U.S. incursion into Vietnam in much the

same light. It was a constant topic of conversation between George and me. Washington's attempt to play policeman to the world, we felt, was pure arrogance. When General William C. Westmoreland howled "We'll blast them back into the Stone Ages!", George hit the ceiling.

"Pea-brains like Westmoreland have never left the Stone Ages," he raged. "They've got the mentality of ape-men!"

George and I had no disagreements on the communes and the calamitous Big Leap Forward of 1958. If George had any reservations, he never expressed them to me. I was not a Communist, but we both accepted the Communist Party "line" and Party statements at face value.

Members of the foreign community, myself included, became confused at rumors that all was not well in relations between the Chinese Communist Party and the party of the Soviet Union.

The first signs of malaise between the two parties surfaced in 1956, after Khrushchov made his dramatic "secret" exposure of Stalin at the 20th Congress of the Soviet Party, which somehow immediately found its way to the pages of the *New York Times*. Khrushchov alleged that Stalin had a "persecution mania", that he indulged in "mass repressions and terror", that he was a "criminal... bandit... idiot... fool...."

The Chinese, in two newspaper editorials, politely but firmly expressed doubts about this appraisal. They said Stalin had committed serious errors and it was correct to criticise him. But they felt his accomplishments outweighed his failings. After all, it was under his leadership that the Soviet Union built up a solid economy and defeated Hitler's Nazi hordes. Stalin also made some contributions to Marxist theory and stood for working class rule. Why try to negate him completely? In Beijing, Stalin's portrait continued to be prominently displayed, and translations of his writings remained on sale throughout China.

In 1957 the next clash occurred when a world conference of Communist parties met in Moscow. China obviously thought the meeting important. Mao Zedong personally led the Chinese delegation. The Soviet members with characteristic modesty touted the "majestic results" of their just concluded "splendid" 20th Party Congress, reiterated their attack on Stalin and tried to steamroller through a Declaration confirming their brand of "peaceful transition" which had been plugged by Krushchov at the Congress.

According to Krushchov the world had changed and it was now possible to go from capitalism to socialism by following the "parliamentary road". In other words, muster enough votes against capitalism, and the country's rulers would meekly and docilely let it fade out of existence.

Absurd, said the Chinese. Even if in a particular country the majority of voters favored socialism, those in power would simply blast them away if they tried to take office. It was naive to think fundamental changes could be effected in a social system through the ballot box.

As for the attack on Stalin and the 20th Congress, Beijing continued, one of its "majestic results" was to delight the enemies of communism. The director of the US Information Agency said Khrushchov's speech had "never so suited our purposes". A *New York Times* editorial acclaimed it as a "weapon with which to destroy the prestige and influence of the communist movement". And John Foster Dulles had mused thoughtfully that it might help to bring about a "peaceful transition" of the Soviet Union.

Though irked by Chinese criticism Krushchov doggedly pushed ahead. In September 1959 he had his talks at Camp David. "A turning point in history", he called them. Gromyko said they marked "a new era in international relations". The Soviet leaders praised the "sensibleness" and "good will" of American presidents. They foresaw "a world without wars", and dreamed of a universal disarmament which would "open up literally a new epoch in the economic developments of Asia, Africa and Latin America".

To their Chinese friends and allies they were not quite so kind. In 1958 they put forward demands "designed to bring China under Soviet military control", as the Chinese cryptically described them. Beijing coolly declined.

They proposed that China join Comecon—an economic grouping of socialist states serving mainly as suppliers to the Soviet Union of raw materials and semi-finished products at lower than world market prices in exchange for Soviet manufactures at higher than world market prices. The Chinese said they preferred self-reliance.

In June 1959 Moscow unilaterally abrogated a treaty with China on technical military assistance concluded less than two years before, and refused to provide a sample atom bomb or any data concerning its construction, as stipulated in the agreement.

At a meeting of Communist parties in Bucharest in June 1960 Khrushchov fulminated that the Chinese were "madmen" who "wanted to unleash war", that they were "picking up the banner of imperialist monopoly capitalists", that they had behaved in a "purely nationalist" manner in the Sino-India border clash, and that their attitude toward the Soviet Party was "Trotskyite".

The Chinese would not be cowed. They issued a calm, reasoned statement, sticking to their guns. So far as they were concerned the era of "Big Brother knows best" was over.

Khrushchov blew up. In July he abruptly broke all 343 contracts under the "Sino-Soviet Treaty of Friendship, Alliance and Mutual Assistance", cancelled 257 programs of scientific and technical cooperation, and called home all 1,390 Soviet experts, instructing them to bring the blueprints with them. Suddenly there were incidents on the Soviet border and unrest fomented in the province of Sinkiang.

At the same time, he couldn't do enough to fawn on and win favor with the West. The Soviet Union supplied transport for UN troops to suppress revolutionaries in the Congo, it agreed —without consulting the Cuban government—to "inspection" in Cuba during the missle crisis, it called the bloody slaughter of the Algerian people an "internal affair" of France, it announced that it would "stand aloof" when the US invented an "incident" in the Gulf of Bac Bo as an excuse for escalation in Vietnam....

In America, Khrushchov was a hero. "Nikita Khrushchov has destroyed irrevocably, the unified bloc of Stalin's day. That is perhaps Khrushchov's greatest service—not to communism, but to the Western world," said *Newsweek*.... "We ought to be grateful for his mishandling of his relationship with the Chinese," *US News and World Report* declared. "We should be grateful for his introducing disarray into international communism by a lot of quite bumptious and sudden initiatives".... And *Newsweek* again: "The administration is now convinced that the US should offer Khrushchov maximum support in his dispute with Red China".

The measures which brought America such joy were a cause in China of severe suffering and privation. Reactions among Chinese friends and colleagues went from incredulity to anger.

George was furious.

"With friends like that, who needs enemies!" he cried.

The Soviet betrayal left China with newly started or half-finished projects which, in a way, were worse than none at all. For they were being built according to Soviet plans and specifications, were designed to be equipped with Soviet machinery, and the plans had been taken away and delivery of the machinery cancelled. There were empty silent plants and factories all over China. Only two and a half of the six planned rolling mills of the Wuhan steel complex had been finished. Such projects either had to be abandoned, or completely redesigned and equipped.

There wasn't enough to eat. Rationing tightened. Protein was in short supply. (This was thought by some doctors to be a factor in the hepatitis epidemic which followed a few years later.) Young people in offices in Beijing swelled with edema. Large vats were set up in backyards. They were raising algae, served in daily soup to fill in the protein deficiency. Calesthenics and sports were out. Everyone was advised to rest when possible and go to bed early. There were cases of mass starvation in hard-hit parts of the country, and relief supplies had to be rushed.

Meanwhile Chinese freight cars continued rolling toward the Soviet border, in keeping with contracts earlier made. Moscow refused to permit any delays of shipments by so much as a single day.

These hardships came at time when China was stricken with three years—from 1959 to 1961—of unprecedented natural disasters. Floods, draught, insect plagues, followed in spate. The Chinese fought back, turning out in huge well-organized forces of men and women who built dams and dug canals to bring water to their parched fields. Or drained off floods and replanted quickly and extensively. Or came out in the thousands and flailed locusts to death. Great floppy bags containing methane gas (we called them zeppelins) were attached to the tops of buses to supplant the shortage of gasoline.

It was slow hard work, but China made a virtue of necessity. The Soviet squeeze coupled with the American boycott (the US prohibited any trade with China) were converted into blessings in disguise. Chinese machines, Chinese industrial processes were born. There were new and original approaches in science and technology. Unity among the people and support of the government hardened rock-solid. In the end China survived, but the Chinese would never forget the cruel and callous treatment the Soviet Communist Party inflicted upon them.

George and I were both shocked by the Soviet's cruelty and callousness, but I was the more surprised of the two. George's inner-Party information made him aware of the pressure the Soviet Union had been putting on the Chinese to accept Soviet control, and of Khrushchov's fury over Mao's refusal to knuckle under. We both approved of Beijing's *Nine Polemics* —a series of articles criticising Soviet "revisionist" economic methods. Some of these same methods are being practised by China today. And we had to admit there was merit in Khrushchov's lampoon of China's communes and our "Big Leap Forward".

I consulted George when I began what I called my "meteoric rise as a film star" in 1962. Actually, it was only a bit role in a Chinese motion picture entitled *After the Armistice*. The film centered around the "Executive Headquarters" which had been organized to settle, with U.S. intervention, clashes between KMT and Communist troops after the Japanese surrendered in 1945. Since George had been actively involved in the Executive Headquarters on the Communist side, his recollections provided useful insight.

Secretary of State Dean Acheson in his White Paper had proposed, in the hope of salvaging the collapsing Chiang Kaishek power structure, that the new government to be formed in China should be neither Left (Communist) nor Right (KMT) oriented, but be ruled by a "middle force". To this end Washington wooed those it believed were middle-of-the-roaders in the intellectual community. American ambassador Leighton Stuart, a respected educator who formerly had been president of Yenching University, did his best to win them over. In the film I played the role of an American professor presumably representing the spirit of this endeavor. I amused George with a recital of my difficulties to look the part.

No one had told me what my make-up would be, and I sat dreamily while various adornments were being affixed. When it was over I looked into the mirror and saw staring back at me a gentleman with a bald head, a mustache and a goatee —Vladimir Ilich Ulyanov Lenin! The make-up artist had been instructed to bring forth "a foreign intellectual", and he had recreated me as the foreign intellectual with whose face, in those days of pro-Soviet enchantment, he was most familiar. I went screaming to the director, and was soon restored to my normal visage, except that my hair was parted in the middle and I wore horn-rimmed glasses.

"You should have been flattered," George grinned. "Though I don't think Leighton Stuart would have been pleased."

Audience reaction to my performance was mixed. Chinese friends said politely I "looked just like an American". Fengzi, who had been a leading lady in theatre, told me with wifely candor, "As an actor you make a perfect talking prop." I put that down to professional jealousy. But I vowed I would never cavort before a camera again.

In the summer of 1962 George was floating peacefully on his back in the sea at Beidaihe, popular beach resort some 200 miles east of Beijing, when a strident voice hailed him from the shore.

"Ma Diafu, Ma Daifu, ni baba laile, kuai chulai!"

"What's he saying? I can't hear him," George yelled to Sufei, who was standing next to the man who was calling.

"He says come out, quick. Your father has come!" Sufei shouted back.

"The devil he has." George swam to shore. "Impossible."

Finally, he got the story straight. His father had indeed come—to the Chinese embassy in Syria. George's mother had died some years before. The old man—he was eighty—had seen a piece in a North Carolina newspaper saying that his son George Hatem was an important man in China, a friend of Mao Zedong and Zhou Enlai. This confirmed earlier reports that George was alive and well. The old man wanted to see him, meet his family. He had travelled from North Carolina to Lebanon, where he stayed with relatives. Since China then had no embassy in Beirut, he drove over, alone, in his car to the Chinese embassy in Damascus, Syria.

The ambassador and his wife knew George. Mr Hatem's resemblance was uncanny. A further check on the old man's identity firmly established the connection. The ambassador offered to send him to China for a visit. Mr. Hatem regretfully declined. He had already travelled so far. He wouldn't be up to another long journey at his age.... The ambassador consulted with Beijing, after which he said, "In that case, we'll bring George and his family here." The old man was overjoyed.

And so it was arranged. Within one week passports were

issued to George, Sufei and You Ma. They were fitted with new clothes. Plane tickets were purchased. All expenses were paid by the Chinese government. They flew to Moscow, the next day to Prague. The following day, August 2, they arrived in Damascus. The entire trip had been made in one of China's first jet-engine passenger planes. A suite of rooms was provided for them in the embassy, another for Mr. Hatem. They had their own cook and kitchen, a car and a driver. It was agreed they would stay until the end of September.

The reunion was an emotional one. George and his father hadn't seen each other since 1928 when George had left the States to study medicine in the American School in Beirut. George presented Sufei and You ma to the old man, who hugged and kissed them delightedly.

"Dad", as George called him, quickly recovered his aplomb. He was quite a kibitzer, and still had an eye for the ladies. Sufei could see where George got his sense of humor. George offered to introduce him to Sufei's 84-year-old aunt. He said they'd make a fine match. Dad replied that twenty years ago he would have married Sufei if George hadn't nabbed her first.

They talked in English. After many years in America, the old man spoke it quite well. George couldn't speak Arabic, he knew only the names of a few tasty Lebanese dishes. Dad insisted on buying them expensive imported gifts. He seemed to have plenty of money. He dressed smartly. His luggage and all of his clothes were monogrammed.

Dad asked George whether he owned much real estate. He couldn't understand it when George confessed to very modest worldly possessions. How could that be, if George was such an important man in China?

Every afternoon, Mr. Hatem and You Ma, then 14, played the pinball machine in the embassy's game room. You Ma always lost. The old man jokingly would demand payment. You Ma would pull out his pants pockets to show that they were empty. "Just like your Uncle Joe," Mr. Hatem would laugh. Clearly, pranksters ran in the family.

Near the end of their stay the embassy gave a party for some of George's Lebanese relatives. Thirty were invited, nearly three hundred showed up. They drove over into Damascus in cars loaded with husbands, wives and children. George drew a list and a chart to help him remember who was related to whom. Everyone wanted to kiss Sufei. The men's bristly beards scratched her face so badly it hurt for days. But it was a great party, one that all would long remember.

After a warm farewell, Dad departed with the relatives for Lebanon. George, Sufei and You ma flew to Prague, where they again stayed at the Chinese embassy. Otto Braun came specially from the Democratic Republic of Germany to see them. He invited them out to dinner. He and George talked of the many changes in the world and in their own lives since they shared a cave in Yanan twenty-five years before.

The next day an embassy aide took them to the beautiful hot springs resort in Karlovy Vary (Carlsbad). They had lunch there. The menu was very poetic. They could only guess at the meaning of the names of the dishes. The aide, although he spoke Czech, didn't know either. They decided to take a chance on "Pearls in the Empress's Diadem". Fortunately, they turned out to be very good meatballs.

From Prague they went on to Moscow, where they spent October First—China's National Day, living here too at the embassy. The ambassador gave an afternoon tea party, after which he and his wife, the embassy staff, George, Sufei and You Ma washed the dishes and cleaned up. Then they all sat down to a family style dinner. The next day the ambassador took them to see his dacha in the wooded outskirts of the city. It had been built for Mao Zedong's 1949 visit, and was quite luxurious.

For the next few days they wandered around Moscow. They admired the subway stations and visited Lenin's tomb in Red Square. A long line of people were waiting. The guards were very polite, and escorted them right to the front of the line. In spite of the bad official relations between China and the Soviet Union, the Russian people were warm and friendly.

The embassy gave them some spending money, but there wasn't much to buy. Shelves in the stores were half empty. With George hitting top score, they consumed many cones of Moscow's delicious ice cream and a large number of local hotdogs and pickles, which Sufei and You Ma agreed were excellent. Even so, most of the money was left over, and they returned it to the embassy.

An aide saw them off at the airport. They handed out cartons of Chinese cigarettes judiciously, and were able to depart with their overweight luggage free of any extra charge.

The following year, 1963, when I became a Chinese citizen,

George was very pleased. "Welcome to the club," he jested. "We need all the good American know-how we can get." George was at the Beijing railroad station when Phoenix and I arrived with my mother.

At the age of seventy she had flown, alone, from New York to Hong Kong. It was a brave venture for a lady who used to get seasick on the Staten Island ferry and had never been on a plane in her life. During our summer family tours when I was a child she was accustomed to giving invaluable admonitions from the back seat to my father as he drove the Buick through the New England mountains. On the plane, after an uneasy first half-hour, she had no choice but to relax and let the pilot fly the aircraft himself. To her surprise, they reached Anchorage in one piece. By the time they arrived in Tokyo she was such a veteran traveller that she didn't trouble to stay over and rest a few hours but boarded the next available shuttle to Hong Kong. There, a China Travel Service man met her and took charge. The next day he delivered her to the border at Shenzhen, where Fengzi and I were waiting. After a few days' rest, we took her with us by train to Beijing.

She was bewildered by so many rapid changes in so short a time. George spoke warm words of welcome in her native American, and presented her with a bouquet of flowers. Mom was touched. Their mutual fondness was instantaneous. It grew deeper during her month's stay, since George was a constant caller at our house, and an active participant in banquets in her honor. In later years during visits to the States he never failed to telephone her and give her glowing reports of how marvellously well I and the family were doing.

FAITH UNDER FIRE

In twentieth century China the word "liberation" has come to mean national independence, the overthrow of the old repressive forces and the formation of a new order which gives the people full opportunity to exercise their creativity in a free and democratic environment. Thus, October 1, 1949, when the People's Republic was formally proclaimed, is known as the day of China's "Liberation". To George personally "Liberation" brought two important developments. On the one hand it enabled him to engage in medical and public health work on a scale and in a manner never possible before. On the other it marked the beginning of a long period in which he was the victim of political discrimination and mistreatment.

The first clear indication came in 1953, when he was assigned as Advisor and Vice Director to the newly formed Institute of Dermatology and Venereology, a national body under the Ministry of Health. He was introduced to the young Director of the Institute, Dai Zhengqi. Dai was embarrassed. When they got to know each other better, he told George why.

He said they had met in 1936 when George came to Gansu with Edgar Snow to visit the Red Army troops. It wasn't easy for the young Americans to reach there. The Red Army soldiers were fighting far out in the wilderness, and the Kuomintang had them blockaded on all sides. Their slogan was "We have friends all over the world", but this was the first time foreign friends had ever come to see them.

"It was proof that the slogan 'we have friends all over the world' was true," said Dai, "that people in other countries really cared. It gave us a big boost."

Dai was then with the medics, not a doctor, just a general

helper. George inspected the field hospital. Dai remembered that although George could scarcely speak any Chinese, he asked concrete professional questions through an interpreter.

By 1953 Dai had graduated medical school and become a full-fledged doctor. For a while he had served in the China Soviet Friendship Hospital as a Vice Superintendant, working jointly with a Soviet medical expert who was also a Vice Superintendant. The hospital was staffed by Soviet doctors and nurses. When the Institute was established under the Health Ministry in 1953, Dai was transferred there to be its Director.

George had been working in the Ministry as only a consultant. Dai thought a man with his qualifications and record in the Liberated Areas should have been at least an Advisor in the Ministry, not merely an Advisor in the Institute. He called it a case of *da cai, xiao yong*—little use of a large talent. Clearly, something was wrong. Dai, at first, didn't know what, though George had a pretty good idea.

He could sense Dai's awkwardness, and quickly tried to put him at ease.

"Aren't I welcome?" George asked with a laugh.

"Of course. It's just that I'm afraid our temple is too small for a big spirit like you," Dai replied lamely.

"There's nothing small about the job we've got ahead of us," George smiled. "It won't be any picnic."

Dai later told him he had been very concerned. Dai was only thirty-two. They also had a Soviet Advisor on their staff. How was he going to work with two experienced doctors and get everyone operating as a harmonious team? At that time China tended to worship the Soviet Union and look at America disparagingly. The pro-Soviet atmosphere was intense.

But Dai wasn't afraid. He had the greatest respect for George, and his job was to eliminate syphilis. He would do whatever was necessary to get results. The Soviet treatment was to give injections of penicillin, in combination with other medications, over a long period of time. The cost per patient was high.

George favored treatment in clinics, with penicillin taken orally. He didn't insist, but he did explain the advantages in a poor country like China of a shorter period and limited expense.

Observing Dai's hesitation, he said, "We should of course go along with the prevailing policy. But in specific cases we should also consider the particular circumstances. 'In stormy seas keep an eye peeled for whirlpools', as the saying goes."

Dai understood. George was hinting they should be flexible within the general parameters of policy. Dai made up his mind —they would try both methods. That would be the scientific approach.

And so in the ethnic areas they gave both the Soviet course of treatment and the one recommended by George. The results indicated that while there was nothing wrong with the Soviet method of treatment—it included penicillin and worked eventually—it required more personnel and money than China could afford for a broad campaign.

George and his colleagues evolved basic medical principles for both the detection and treatment of syphilis, strengthened the leadership of the local health units, and set up a prevention network throughout the region. He brought in specialists to treat the patients. He launched programs to educate the public on the need to wipe out VD and control leprosy.

These measures were decisive factors in the efforts to eliminate VD nationwide. They also provided the Chinese health people with a medical theory and mental attitude, to say nothing of an organizational structure, materials and methods, which proved invaluable in their subsequent attack on leprosy. The Institute therefore adopted the approach George favored.

In the next few years it was used successfully in the ethnic regions of Inner Mongolia, Hainan Island, Yunnan and Xinjiang, and throughout the China mainland. By 1966 George stated in a formal report to the Institute of Dermatology and Venereology of the Chinese Academy of Medical Sciences: "Veneral disease is no longer a public health problem in China".

Dai had made many Russian friends in the China-Soviet Friendship Hospital. Dozens of them had come down to attend the opening ceremony of the Institute. But the Chinese had to do what was best for China where the treatment of syphilis was concerned. Their Soviet advisor had a home leave every year. He saw how things were going, and when he went back to Moscow he did not return, and no other advisor came to replace him.

In spite of the unfair way in which George was being treated politically, all the Institute people knew that medically he deserved the credit. There were a few Soviet doctors in various clinics run by the Institute, but George was the sole advisor for the entire Institute from then on. The Chinese staff liked his objective approach and his constant study of research materials in English coming in from abroad.

Dai and he talked almost every day in Dai's office for two hours or more, discussing all manner of things, voicing their opinions, agreeing and disagreeing. Dai told George he thought in view of his experience he ought to be working on a higher level, dealing with matters of China's medical problems nation-wide.

George raised one dark eyebrow quizzically. "You're a clever fellow. Can't you see the kind of period we're in? Although I'm a Communist and have to follow Party policy, that doesn't mean I don't have ideas of my own. If they're not accepted now, maybe they'll be accepted later. What's the hurry? We've a long future ahead. I as an individual don't matter."

He knew he was being discriminated against. There were political reports Dai could hear and George couldn't, documents Dai could read and George couldn't. It was all because in Yanan Kang Sheng had said he didn't trust him. But George didn't sulk and he didn't shirk.

"Kang Sheng suspects me," he told Dai. "I'm cut off from some political activities, I'm not fully trusted. But never mind. I just do my job. Investigation is bound to prove I'm clean."

Dai was impressed. He knew George must have been very unhappy. But the position George took, his outward behavior, were always perfectly normal. He was hard-working, yet humorous and relaxed.

George rarely lost his temper, but sometimes, in private, he spoke angrily to Dai about things he considered wrong. For instance, officials would provide a big feast when he came to check on health conditions in their locality. The splurging of public funds infuriated him. George wouldn't say anything, but he wouldn't eat much either.

"I won't go to any more of those meals," he told Dai hotly. "You ought to order local health units to quit doing that sort of thing."

"Look," Dai said, "I don't approve either. But Chinese feel obliged to show their guests hospitality. That's the way they've been behaving for centuries. The next time you run into it you can say, 'Let's split the cost. Please, no more lavish meals in the future.' Give them a little face, a graceful way out."

George nodded. "Good. That's how I'll do it."

But he couldn't learn to be diplomatic with smarmy gluttons. Sure enough, when he visited the same place again, they put on the same elaborate spread. George forgot all about the polite formula Dai had suggested.

"If you want to stuff yourselves at the people's expense, go ahead," he snapped. "I don't want any part of it." He got up and stalked out of the room.

George never got over being a blunt American, shooting straight from the hip if he thought a principle was being violated and the public was being harmed. It was one of his failings, for in China much better results are attained by circumlocution—pussy-footing around a point of contention, using a softer touch. George knew that, but he just couldn't do it.

His individual interests—his status, his salary—to him were matters of small concern. But he was very unhappy at being treated as a semi-pariah politically, as a second-rate Communist. It made him miserable to be excluded from, or be allowed only limited participation in, Party activities. From the day he began working in the Institute in 1953 until the Cultural Revolution ended in 1976, he was continually "given small shoes to wear"—that is, constrained, restricted and discriminated against. His professional duties were also affected.

Dai formally proposed to their superiors that Ma Haide be made head of the Institute of Dermatology and Venereology. The reply came back: "No foreigner can be put in charge of a government unit."

"Foreigner, indeed!" Dai said to George angrily. "You're not only a Chinese citizen but a member of the Chinese Communist Party. It's just a flimsy excuse to avoid ruffling Kang Sheng's feathers."

Interestingly, none of George's colleagues in the Institute looked down on him. He was warm, helpful, and entirely democratic in his relations with them. That is not to say there was absolutely no back-biting and petty jealousies. This is common enough among intellectuals in China. But they saw the respect with which Dai treated George. After all Dai was the Institute's Communist Party Secretary. At that time the prestige of the Party was high.

Dai admired George's attitude as a revolutionary and considered him his teacher, not only medically, but in domestic and international political affairs, as well. They used to talk about the things George read in foreign newspapers and journals. They were good friends, and played bridge together. George liked Dai for his no-nonsense, practical approach.

"The devil take these so-called doubts about you," Dai said. "You're doing a great job. Go out into the border lands among the ethnic minority folk. Clean up their venereal disease. I'll go with you."

And that was what they did. They were in the field, away from Beijing, six months of every year. It was a wonderful tonic for George. He was being eaten up inside at the unjust treatment he was receiving in the Communist Party, literally —he developed stomach ulcers. But he wouldn't complain. He kept his feelings bottled up inside, maintaining a cheerful front, joking, helping the young medics, doing his best to be a good doctor and researcher.

George decided that in addition to checking on syphilis cases, they should examine and treat any local resident who came in with any ailment whatsoever. Of course nearly everyone wanted to be treated by the "foreign specialist", and this took up most of what little remained of his rest time. At the end of a tour when they got back to Beijing George would be thin and burned dark. He would usually have to go into the hospital for his stomach ulcer, and have one or two infected teeth pulled.

One night when they were travelling in a jeep in Gansu they ran head-on into a truck coming the other way. Dr. Wang Hongshen suffered a bad concussion and a rupture of part of the spinal membrane. Their driver's ribs were broken in nine places. Fortunately, George was sitting on a pile of luggage, or the metal floor board, as it split, surely would have fractured his thigh. Some of the other passengers were also hurt, though not seriously.

Worried and upset, he rushed around giving emergency treatment. Finally, the team was able to go on and reach its destination. Dr. Wang was confined to bed. Aside from continuing to direct their check on syphilis cases, George spent every spare moment looking after Wang.

"I'm afraid I was a rather rebellious patient," Dr. Wang recalled, smiling, "and added to *Lao* Ma's burdens. He lost quite a few teeth as a result of that trip."

His family and his friends were as affectionate as ever, and this emotional support, plus his own determination to take the broad view, enabled him to carry on. What helped most was getting away from the city. Out in the field he was in fine fettle. There he felt the warmth and respect of the Chinese people—responding to his own enthusiasm, dedication, and care. He had the same response from the local officials. In the evenings he danced and joked around at impromptu parties.

George seemed to blossom whenever he went on a field trip. His health improved, he had more bounce to his step. Colleagues attributed this to fresh air and exercise.

But the moment he got back to Beijing his spirits drooped. He was quieter, more subdued. Friends could see it. This was where he was "suspected" by higher authorities, where he was restricted in his political participation, where even his professional abilities were not allowed full scope. Only his immediate family and very close Chinese associates like Dai, and old friends Rewi Alley and Hans Muller, knew how he suffered over being held at arms length by the Party and government to which he was so completely devoted.

He certainly was no Pagliacco—clowning though his heart was breaking. His jocular manner, his efforts always to put the best possible face on China's actions when talking to foreigners, were genuinely cheerful and optimistic. But that didn't prevent him from being gnawed by an inward grief.

"I suppose you could say my life as a Communist can be divided roughly into four periods," George mused. "The first lasted from when I joined the Party in 1937 till our entry into Beijing in 1949. It was a satisfying, happy time, though conditions were spartan and dangerous. I did important work and was treated with respect."

The second period, from when he became advisor to the Institute of Dermatology and Venereology in 1953 to the start of the Cultural Revolution in 1966, was a big come-down. Few of the top leaders had any time for him. Zhou Enlai and Ye Jianying used to drop around once in a while, but they were very busy. There were no more special missions for him, like the Executive Headquarters assignment. In his work at the Institute he had to swim in a sea of veneration for Soviet Russian medical experience, and a tendency to write off everything American as bourgeois and backward.

Worst of all, he was being given the cold shoulder politically. Although still a Communist Party member, he was limited in the reports he could hear and the documents he could read. Kang Sheng had poisoned his life. In Yanan Kang had said —privately, though word got around—that he couldn't believe a foreigner would give up the "comforts" of his own country to suffer the hardships of China's revolution.

"He was an ignorant, bigoted son-of-a-bitch who thought everyone was as selfish as he was," George grated. "As if that wasn't enough, he had that lying smear written into my record."

George heard the details of the rest, and worst part, of the slander against him only in 1978, after the Gang of Four was overthrown and the Cultural Revolution ended, when someone finally came around from the higher-ups to explain.

It seems that when George first flew into Beijing in 1946 as medical advisor to CLARA and to help the Chinese Communist representatives at the Executive Headquarters, he was questioned for a few minutes by the Americans, who had taken over control of the airport. Word of this got back to Kang Sheng and he wrote it into George's Party record—only he expanded the few minutes into "several hours", and added that Ma Haide should be suspected as a "foreign spy". For thirty years George suffered under that cloud.

"And I really suffered," George said. "There's nothing worse than not being trusted by your own people."

During the long years of being silently held at arm's length George talked with his doctor colleagues as equals, young and old, as if he hadn't a care in the world. He favored analysing all problems together.

"Three stinking tanners pooling their brains are as smart as wise man Zhuge Liang," he would quote the old saw with a laugh.

He played and worked as hard as the circumstances would permit. Dai, director of the Institute of Dermatology and Venereology was one of his constant card-playing cronies. Once they played bridge very late, and decided to make a night of it, rather than disturb people at home.

Sufei charged into Dai's office the next morning, very angry, and bawled him out. The men played once or twice a week in the Institute office, and George often came home late. She always waited up. It disturbed her rest and affected her work the next day. She said it was Dai's fault for permitting all that bridge playing. He contritely apologized.

George was still bridge crazy, but he loved dancing best. He also liked collecting antiques, and used to haunt the shops. Sometimes Dai went with him, and had difficulty in dragging his away.

But they were much more involved in work than in play. George and Dai went to many leprosy hospitals—in villages, in ethnic regions, travelling by donkey, small boats, climbing many a mountain. Days and nights, they lived, ate, and worked together.

"The third tough period, from 1966 to 1976, was the Cultural Revolution. I was completely in the dog-house," George recalled. "Nevertheless we continued doing stints on the farms in the suburbs of Beijing, harvesting wheat during the day, sleeping on the same *kang* at night. I was kept busy every minute. Wherever we went, I was surrounded by welcoming villagers and local officials. Patients, while being examined, asked me all sorts of questions: what was happening in Beijing, what was the government doing to solve the farmers' problems?..."

In a village which had leprosy he would go to the afflicted section immediately upon arrival, and talk with the patients and the health personnel. If people were afraid to give blood samples, he would demonstrate on himself. If health workers were afraid of being infected, he would make a point of shaking hands with the lepers and conducting examinations without either gloves, or gauze face mask, or any of the usual protective clothing. He would comfort the patients, and teach the local doctors and health personnel, and encourage them by his own behavior to follow his example.

Unfortunately, all of their work was vitiated by the Cultural Revolution. The Leprosy Research Center they were about to open in Pingzhou in Guangdong province was labelled a "nest of revisionism". Their Leprosy Prevention and Cure Brigade was disbanded and its members scattered. The gains for which George had given his heart's blood were snuffed out. Veiled criticism was directed against him. In 1970 the Dermatology and Venereology Institute moved down to Pingzhou. George was left behind. He was assigned as an ordinary doctor to the skin clinic in Beijing's Fuwai Hospital.

George didn't indicate his disappointment, but went on with his work, serving his patients with his usual diligence and warmth. In Fuwai he encountered an old comrade, Jiang

Yizhen, a former medical administrator who had been forced from office by the Gang of Four.

Jiang had been imprisoned by the "revolutionaries" and developed a serious heart condition. In March of 1972 he was transferred to Fuwai Hospital for "treatment in isolation". At that time George had been "moved down" and was working in the skin clinic. A guard was posted at Jiang's door, and kept all visitors out. George induced the nurses to sneak in Chinese and foreign pictorials and reading materials which put Jiang back in touch with what was going on in the world. He had been held incommunicado for nearly seven years. Jiang was deeply moved by the understanding and trust which George demonstrated.

In August the guard was removed, and George promptly appeared at Jiang's bedside. From then on, he paid him long visits every Sunday.

One day Jiang received word that Liu Shaoqi, Chen Yi, and Fu Lianzhang had all died as a result of the torments they endured. He was devastated. When George came by, Jiang wept as he told him about it. George spoke words of comfort, and urged Jiang to take care of his health. They reminisced about the great contributions those old comrades had made. George expressed confidence in the revolution in spite of the existing chaotic situation.

"Our Party committed many mistakes before victory," he said. "The worst one wiped out ninety percent of our members in the 'Soviet' areas. In the enemy-controlled zones we lost one hundred percent. Today, we're again taking huge, heart-breaking losses. But I'm sure the Party will correct its errors and put our country back on the right track."

George was referring to the early thirties, when the Communist Party was under the control of Li Lisan and Wang Ming, and other "super-Left" leaders. Although the country was being bled white by imperialist and feudal exploitation, they called on the workers in the cities to overthrow all capitalists, including the small shopkeepers. This antagonized large sections of the urban populace. Without their protection and cooperation, Communist activists were easily caught by Chiang Kai-shek's dragnet of secret agents, operating in tandem with foreign police in the concessions.

In the countryside, the Red Army, following a similar rash and unrealistic policy, adopted the tactics proposed by Li De

(Otto Braun), military representative of the Comintern, (and later George's "cave-mate" in Yanan), and waged positional warfare against a much stronger and better equipped foe. As a result, the Red Army and all the rural revolutionary forces suffered crushing losses. The Soviet Areas had to be abandoned.

Finally, in January 1935, at an enlarged meeting of the Political Bureau in Zunyi, in the province of Guizhou, the Party recognized its mistakes and created a new leadership under the joint command of Mao Zedong, Zhou Enlai and Zhu De. The Red Army set out on the famous Long March with 300,000 troops. Only ten percent reached their destination in northwest China at the end of the year. Yet little more than a decade later, the Communist Party and its revitalized Red Army had liberated the entire mainland and established the People's Republic of China.

That the Party had been able to correct such deadly errors and climb relatively quickly to unprecedented heights, George said, convinced him there was no blunder, however serious, it could not overcome.

Jiang agreed, and he complimented George for his stand.

"A foreigner who devotes himself to the Chinese revolution pays a much higher price than the ordinary person," Jiang said. "For a long time you were continually slandered by Kang Sheng. You were labelled a 'suspected agent' and even a 'foreign spy'. Politically you were looked down upon and kept apart. In your work you were limited to 'controlled use'. But you never wavered in your love for China and the Chinese people, your enthusiasm for the revolution never waned. During this so-called Cultural Revolution you have been severely harassed. People urged you to leave the country, or to openly criticise the units which had discriminated against you. But you never gave such ideas any consideration. You have remained steadfast in your faith in the Party, and are optimistic about the fate of the revolution. You are still fully confident of the Party's future and your own."

George was embarrassed by Jiang's praise. While he felt sure the Party would straighten itself out as it had done before, in his heart of hearts he wasn't terribly optimistic about his personal prospects. With all of the crazy nonsense Jiang Qing and her Gang of Four were pushing, George was very worried. The radicals were persecuting the best and most dedicated leaders.

His own house had been ransacked. Sufei and he had been lured away by an invented "meeting" at the Beijing Film Studio where Sufei worked. "Revolutionaries" from the Studio, pretending to be looking for "reactionary" material in her possesssion, went through George's papers and took off loads of books and magazines. George scoffed when they came home and saw what had happened.

"They can have them," he said. "Most of that stuff is in English. It will take them years to go through it all."

A few of his foreign friends were also having difficulties. Rewi was being smeared as a "revisionist". Cloak and dagger type agents tailed Hans wherever he went. I was distressed because my wife Fengzi was under detention in a kind of adult camp in the country her office had moved to, and was not allowed to come home. Most of the "foreign experts" working in Beijing were confused by the erratic path of the Cultural Revolution, but were trying with misplaced zeal to involve themselves in its developments.

This was understandable. It was a very complicated situation of a kind none of them had ever experienced. There were only one or two whom George utterly despised—the "super-revolutionaries". He considered them poseurs and hypocrites.

In this latter category fell one smooth and affable American whom we shall call "Munchhausen". Eighteenth century German baron Karl Friedrich Hieronymus von Munchhausen was notorious as a teller of absurdly exaggerated stories. A U.S. radio comedy series inspired by his adventures brought "Munchhausen" into the American lexicon as a popular term for bald fabricators.

Our Munchhausen appeared on the scene in 1946 in Shanghai where he met American journalist Anna Louise Strong. She was about to leave for Yanan and was looking for an interpreter. Munchhausen, who spoke fluent Chinese, volunteered. He was with her when she interviewed the greats of the Communist Party, remaining on after she departed in 1947. While in Moscow in 1949, preparing to return to China, Anna Louis was arrested as a spy on trumped up charges and deported. She had no choice but to return to the United States. In 1955 the Soviet Union admitted that the accusation of espionage was without foundation.

But in China in 1949, because of his close association with

her, Munchhausen was put under house arrest pending investigation. The "investigation" lasted eight years, until after Anna Louise was cleared, by which time it was obvious that Munchhausen was not a spy either. He was released with profound apologies. The Chinese were very embarrassed at having wronged this sincere friend of the revolution.

From then on, they bent over backwards to make amends. Because of this, and because of Munchhausen's unquestioned talents, he rose quickly in rank. When the Cultural Revolution started in 1966 he was the director of all the foreign language broadcasts on Radio Beijing. Leaping into the forefront of the Chinese factional squabbles, he became active in several sectors. As part of a trio consisting of a girl, a very young man and himself, he seized control of Radio Beijing—the government's official broadcasting station, beamed to every corner of the globe.

Another of his accomplishments was to bring a play and its author from Tianjin to Beijing and have it performed on the stage of the Friendship Hotel, where most of the foreign experts stayed, for their edification as well as for the enlightenment of members of the diplomatic community, whom he also invited. The play was called *A New Madman's Diary*, and was written by a man who later turned out to be genuinely insane. Ostensibly an attack on Liu Shaoqi, it was thought by many to be a diatribe against Mao, and was the subject of hot debate among the warring factions.

Munchhausen had the play translated into English, French and Spanish, and mailed abroad. Its first performance in the Friendship Hotel's theatre was also its last, because it provoked a punch-out and wild melee on the stage between two hostile Chinese factions, much to the amusement of the diplomats in the audience. This did little to enhance China's image overseas.

On his trip to Tianjin he had brought with him as part of his entourage two Western foreign experts. Young Chinese dizzy with "revolutionary" fervor conceivably could have been impressed by a foreigner who could intone the slogans in their own language, smile and back-slap. But it is surprising that any Westerner could have been taken in by him. He was an obvious hustler, a typical high-pressure salesman who would have been spotted immediately on the streets of New York or London. Their naivete was another reflection of the heady influence the euphoric atmosphere had even on politically mature foreigners living in Beijing.

Nevertheless, despite the "Madman's Diary" fiasco, Munchhausen's prestige among the foreign experts was unimpaired. He was able to induce some of them to sit on the podiums of meetings called by one or another of the factions in various organizations, and maybe even say a few words of support, although they hadn't the faintest idea of what the issues were or where the factions stood. Encouraged by the stamp of approval received from "international friends", the host faction would then go out and attack their opponents, sometimes physically.

Manoeuvring slickly from one clique to another, he strove always to be on the winning side. But finally the tide turned. The "outs" in Radio Peking, his home base, became the "ins". They seized power and proceeded to demolish their opponents. Munchhausen, as leader of the former ruling triumverate, was the ideal target. They put him on trial at a mass meeting for a number of crimes, not the least of which was the usurping of control of Radio Peking—a sensitive government organization, and the furore he created with the public performance of *A New Madman's Diary*. The leader of the Gang of Four, Mao's wife Jiang Qing, who Munchhausen proudly proclaimed had invited him to breakfast eight times, threw him to the wolves when he came under attack, even adding a few accusations of her own. He was again cast into prison for an indefinite term. Incarcerated with him were the two foreign innocents who had helped him bring the play to Beijing.

Munchhausen was a shockingly inept and transparent spinner of tall tales. He had one yarn which he told gravely when they let him out of jail in the late seventies after the Cultural Revolution had ended. He loved Zhou Enlai, he asserted. When he heard about his death in January 1976, he clipped Zhou's picture out of the newspaper and pasted it on the wall of his cell, and tied around his arm a black strip from some garment which he just happened to have been wearing!

Zhou Enlai did not reciprocate his "love". On March 8, 1973, at a celebration of International Womens' Day, which I attended, in the Great Hall of the People, the Premier addressed a group of foreign experts. A few had just been released from incarceration. They had taken part in the complicated factional struggles. The Premier apologized to them for the investigation of their alleged "crimes" having taken so long.

Munchhausen was then still in prison. His case, the Premier said, was entirely different. Zhou Enlai described Munchhausen as a "rotten egg".

George detested him. He called him "the operator", and did whatever he could to undo the mischief Munchhausen was spreading among the foreign experts. It wasn't easy, and George had difficulties of his own to contend with. Although he didn't approve of imprisonment without a proper legal trial, he was not unhappy that Munchhausen was put out of circulation for a while.

"It couldn't have happened to a better man," George said privately to Rewi, who also scorned the fellow.

In any event George didn't think phonies like Munchhausen and the Gang of Four, plus all the innocents they had deluded, could prevent China from moving forward. When the Cultural Revolution was at its height, several Chinese who had returned from abroad, and many foreigners, left. Sufei wondered about George, though she should have known him better.

"Things are in such a mess. Are you wavering?" she asked.

"In what respect?" he countered.

"In your belief in the Party."

"Absolutely not," George said firmly. "Any party which is able to openly admit its own mistakes and corrrect them is a great party. The present methods are wrong, but wait and see, they'll be changed."

When some foreigners they knew were detained in the name of being "protected", a Chinese friend suggested that George take Sufei and the children and get out.

"What for?" George retorted. "I love this land, and I love its people."

"You may love China," replied the friend. "But China doesn't love you."

George was incensed. He glared.

"Who says so? That's a lot of crap. This is all the work of a small bunch of bastards. They're the ones who don't love China. But they're not going to win."

Later George called Sufei aside. "If I'm ever put under 'protection'," he said, "don't be upset. You can rest assured I've never done the slightest thing to harm the people or the Party. Sooner or later I'll be back."

He continued to maintain a positive view. And he kept his sense of humor. During the ten years of turmoil it was the practice to put up posters with the names of people labelled "traitors" written upside down and covered with big red crosses.

One afternoon he returned home and announced with a grin, "My Chinese is getting better. Even when my name is stood on it head and crossed with a big 'X' I can still read it!" And he added sarcastically, "In a Communist Party which has led the country to victory, how come there are so many 'traitors'?"

While he refused to join any of the factions contending for power, he stood firmly on the side of those old comrades being unjustly attacked. He gave them medical treatment, sent them money, food—all in secret. At times he hid in his home people from other parts of China on the run from persecution.

George was nauseated by the rituals established by the "revolutionaries". Whether in schools, offices or factories, everyone had to line up before large pictures of Mao Zedong and Lin Biao the first thing in the morning and "request instructions"—which meant intoning quotations from Mao, and being told how the witch hunts would be conducted that day. In late afternoon another convocation would be assembled, where all would chant in unison, "Long life to Chairman Mao, a long, long life!" and "Good health to Vice Chairman Lin Biao!"

"What's the difference between this rigmarole and religious ceremony?" George snorted.

He thought it was a disgusting violation of Marxist principles. But if ever he was tempted to give way to despair, he was sustained by the knowledge that thousands of good honest comrades were still around, fighting for the same goals he was. Several were quite vocal in their opposition to what the Gang of Four were doing.

Old friend and colleague Dr. Wang Hongshen, today a prominent dermatologist in Beijing's PUMC Hospital (formerly the Peking Union Medical College, a Rockefeller institution), said openly the raid by "rebels" from the Beijing Film Studio on George's house was a disgrace.

"Imagine them harrassing a man who has devoted his life to China's revolution and health work!" cried Wang.

He knew George since 1953, and had been with him through every medical campaign thereafter. He remembered their first meeting. George had been serving as a consultant in the Ministry of Health, and came to check on their preparations for setting up the Dermatology and Venereology Institute. He was wearing a faded grey padded tunic and old cloth shoes, and spoke fluent Chinese, but with a heavy northwest accent.

"If I hadn't seen your large luminous eyes and your prominent nose I would have taken you for a typical *Ba Lu* veteran," Wang said.

"Hardly that," George laughed.

The American had been affable enough on a personal level, but very serious where work was concerned. He had questioned every item of their preparations, discussed them in detail, then made a final determination on each. Wang had been impressed by his meticulousness. Subsequently George had been appointed the Institute's Advisor, and put in charge of their work and research on the elimination of venereal diseases and the control of leprosy. The Chinese medics called him "Ma *Daifu*", Dr. Ma.

At that time Wang and George were in the same Communist Party group. Wang was a young new member. Because the American was warm-hearted and direct, treating everyone as an equal, whenever there was some political decision that didn't seem to make sense to Wang, he would come to George about it. George would patiently explain the reasoning behind Party policy, in the light of Marxist theory.

"When we discussed ideological matters, I never had the feeling that he was a 'foreigner'," said Wang. "To me he was just a good comrade, a good leader. We all liked and respected him very much."

When the fanatics acclaiming the mad Cultural Revolution as "unprecedented" forced intellectuals to do "voluntary labor", George insisted on working with the rest of the Institute staff. Sweating with his shirt off in the broiling sun, he fitted pipe and laid it in underground culverts, in a clear demonstration of whose side he was on.

But he kept a cool head, participating only in normal political activities, and refusing to join any of the factions contending for power. At the same time he displayed support and sympathy for those being persecuted.

One afternoon he saw Dr. Wang being marched under the grim surveillance of scowling Red Guards. He hailed the prisoner with a big smile.

"How are you, Dr. Wang," he called "It's good to see you!"

George's open support sent a current of warmth and strength

surging through Wang at a time when he needed it badly.

"Though it may not sound like much now," Wang recalled, "in those days of hysterical venom against persons labelled pariahs, to address me so cordially, and by my professional title, required considerable courage."

In 1970 Wang was sent to serve in a commune in Gansu as a "barefoot doctor"—a kind of first-aid dispenser not permitted to handle any serious medical procedures. When Wang returned to the capital in 1974 he went to see George in Beijing's Fuwai Hospital where he was then working as an ordinary doctor in the skin clinic. George had developed a bad heart condition. His lips and fingernails were purple. But he still attended the clinic every day and made rounds of the wards. At noon he would lie on the examination couch in the skin clinic and have the nurse give his a plasma transfusion.

Throughout the Cultural Revolution George made his position plain in every way possible. He invited Dr. Zheng, a leprosy specialist colleague, to a performance of the Vienna Philharmonic. Jiang Qing, Mao's wife, was then imposing "Eight Model Operas", revised by her, on the hapless public, and maintaining that these were the only "pure and true" musical fare. At such a time the attendance of a prominent person like Dr. Ma Haide at a concert featuring the waltzes of "bourgeois" composer Johann Strauss was a defiant gesture gladdening the hearts of all who favored the artistic freedom of an intelligent socialist society.

There was still some film making, but all under the benificent guidance of Jiang Qing. I had kept my resolve for thirteen years never to set foot before a camera again, but in 1975 I succumbed to pleas to be an American movie villain once more. I reported my adventures to George.

The Changchun Motion Picture Studio in Northeast China had asked me to play the Commanding General of the U.S. Airforce in Korea. Phoenix went with me to Changchun, and rehearsed me every night in our hotel room. What I liked best about my role was that it required me to wear smartly tailored uniforms and smoke excellent Cuban perfectos.

Film makers at that time were faced with an insurmountable problem. Jiang Qing was a mad egocentric. She dreamed up the principle of what she called "The Three Emphases". This demanded that in any artistic creation the positive be stressed, and within that the heroic, and within that the most heroic.

The net effect was a hero or heroine of sheer cardboard who, already at the pinnacle of heroism, had no room for development. All the other characters could serve only as foils and echoes, and under no circumstances surpass the main protagonist.

Villains got the opposite treatment. On stage they often wore make-up of bilious green. For the cinema, the camera usually panned down on them from a height to make them look smaller. To stress their murky natures they were filmed in such dim light it was difficult to discern their features. They skulked around in the sinister manner of baddies in old-fashioned melodramas, their wickedness immediately apparent to everyone in the audience. But it took the "most heroic character" a full three or four acts to see through them, which made viewers wonder whether the author was trying to equate nobility of soul with thickness of wit.

Despite my sterling performance, I had to confess to George that *Eagles of the Sky* did not qualify for any Chinese Oscars. The high point of my stay in Changchun was not the film-making however, but a mass meeting of the entire studio, which Fengzi and I were invited to attend, celebrating a statement Mao had issued criticising the arbitrary banning of another film by the much-hated Jiang Qing. We returned to Beijing expecting to find our friends savoring what seemed to us a sure sign that the tide was turning against the Gang of Four.

But when we told this to George, he knew nothing about it. Neither did any of our colleagues. Jiang Qing had prevented the statement from being circulated. She was still riding high. It would be another year before she and the Gang could be brought down. I asked George how could she have so much power? Why, if Mao didn't approve of the things she did, couldn't he control her better?

George had heard from inner-Party sources that Mao had criticised her severely several times at high Party meetings, and warned her that she was heading for trouble. But also that Mao had underestimated her strength and the group behind her. Since George had no solid confirmation of this story he said only it was because Mao was old and couldn't go to the grassroots any more to check things out, that he was being misinformed by some of the people who surrounded him, which was true enough.

Why, I demanded, should the fate of a huge complicated country like China depend on the physical condition of a single man, and why should all major decisions rest with him? Where had the Chinese Communist Party's principles of democratic discussion and collective leadership gone?

George admitted that these principles had been neglected, and that this was partly responsible for the current chaos. But he was sure, he said, that the Party would once again correct its mistakes, as it had in the past.

The fourth period of his life in the Chinese Communist Party began after the Cultural Revolution ended in 1976.

"I was really 'born again' in 1978 with the complete clearing of my name and record," George said. "Once more I was respected—honored, even. I was selected for membership in the Chinese People's Political Consultative Council, travelled to many countries, received awards for my work in leprosy.... And, most satisfying, I was able to help organize an all-out campaign against the disease in China and coordinate efforts worldwide."

Though his confidence was shaken by the rampant graft and moral deterioration in Chinese society which appeared in the eighties, George clung to his faith in China's Communist Party. To his mind the problem was that the country had a history of 2,000 years of feudalism. Veneration of the patriarch, the elder statesman, was deeply embedded in Chinese tradition. Even where there was rule by committee, the tendency was to look to its most venerable member for the final word. The Party did not approve of this, and was trying to change it, George said. It would take time, but he was convinced change definitely would come.

GOODWILL AMBASSADOR

George was one of the best PR men China ever had. He loved to talk, his language was colorful and colloquial, his mind was orderly, logical, he spoke eloquently with obvious sincerity and conviction. George enjoyed one-on-one conversations, group discussions, lecturing before an audience—anything that allowed a maximum of intellectual exchange. While he revelled in the mental stimulation for its own sake, at the same time he felt he was fulfilling an obligation, namely, to tell as much of the world he could reach everything he knew about China, his China, answer their questions, make them understand.

He did this extremely well, a fact testified to by a whole series of foreign visitors and persons he spoke to on trips abroad. Journalists, doctors, diplomats, scholars, ordinary bread-and-butter tourists—he charmed most of them and intrigued them all. They remembered what he said, wrote about him in their books and articles, quoted him to their friends and associates. Cumulatively, his influence on what people outside thought about China was enormous.

It started early, in Yanan, and continued almost till the day he died. The list of those with whom he spoke, or heard him talk, in China and abroad, is long. Prominent among the writers were several who were themselves molders of public opinion.

Han Suyin, for one, never failed to pick George's brains during her frequent trips to China. The daughter of a Chinese father and a Belgian mother, she was raised in China, but spent most of her career in Southeast Asia and Europe. She has turned out an impressive number of best-selling novels, most of them centered on China. As a much sought after public speaker she was able to reach audiences in countries closed to friendly Sinologues in the hate-China era. A good deal of the interpretations in her novels and lectures was based on her discussions with George.

Edgar Snow, famous American author whose books on China have had perhaps the most lasting impact on the Western reading public of all the foreign journalists, warmly acknowledged his debt to George Hatem.

"He helped me understand the logic of some things that had puzzled me in China," Ed wrote in *Red China Today*, published by Random House in 1960. Snow told why their friendship was of such importance to him.

> He knew the faults and failures of the regime but he also knew the misery of Old China and the enormity of the problems it presented. Because he was the one American who had for twenty-five years intimately shared the ordeals of the men and women who fought for the responsiblity to bring China to her feet, his continuing faith in what they are doing merits attention.

When Snow asked him whether some of the bitter fighting and bloodshed could have been avoided, George replied, "China simply could never have stood up in any other way. Nearly everything done has been necessary and nearly everything necessary has been done. And all in all it's been a success."

Ed noted that in the West China's failures seemed more evident than its successes.

> It was seen abroad as a nation of starvation, overwork, commune blunders, cultism, belief in "inevitable war", shrill propaganda reflecting the fears and tensions of a harassed leadership, forced labor, brain washing and persecution of individualism.

But if that were so, how can one account for China's undoubted gains? Snow queried. He found the answer to this, too, during a visit to Beijing, "...in the quiet of Dr. Hatem's tiny garden beside the still lake".

As Snow understood it what George told him was this:

> Behind all the propaganda stood millions of unknown and unsung men and women who had successfully and devotedly carried out the real work of releasing half a billion people

from a heritage of dense ignorance and superstition, widespread disease, illiteracy and universal poverty. The task was far from accomplished, but the foundations of a modern civilization had been laid, with little outside help, and against handicaps to which America had made heavy contributions. These foundations would last regardless of what government ruled in the future—unless, of course, it was destroyed by war and all the people perished with it. China is bigger than any government. Because this government had been doing things for China it had been able to command support even from many who were opposed to communism.

George Hatem's summary was accepted by Snow as reasonable and accurate. Although other factors were involved, it is entirely possible that George's analyses, as filtered through Ed's brilliant exposition, penetrated the mists of Foggy Bottom and prodded some of the more obtuse minds toward changing their perceptions of China. Unquestionably, Snow's interview with Mao that year and the articles he published were instrumental in hastening America's rapproachment with China, expressed in the Shanghai Declaration in 1972.

George had accompanied Ed when he was entertained by Mao during visits in 1960 and 1965. In 1965 the Chairman gave them a small private lunch in his residence, including his favorite throat-searing peppers. Snow's *The Other Side of the River* resulted from the 1960 visit, the film script *One Fourth of Humanity* from the trip in 1965.

George went to Geneva as head of a Chinese medical team when word of Ed's terminal illness from cancer reached Beijing in January 1972. He worked with smooth efficiency—as liaison between the Chinese and the Swiss doctors, coping with the press, meeting visitors, doing a million and one things. Ed and his wife Lois had always called George by his old nickname "Shag". In her book *Death With Dignity* (Random House, 1974, New York City), Lois tells how "Shag" managed to maintain some semblance of order in the chaotic grueling last few weeks of Ed's life, after he moved into the Snow's converted farmhouse home in Eysins, in the outskirts of Geneva:

Soon his room turned into a miniature pharmacy, the bookshelves cleared to accomodate a jumble of jars, bottles liquids and pills—Chinese calligraphy mixed with Latin inscriptions.... Shag's fluency in French and Chinese the means of communication. He dressed Western style, usually in slacks and sweater. On a rare visit to Geneva one evening, he donned the sports jacket he had worn on arrival in Switzerland. It was eye-catching, a thick, handsome, multi-colored tweed, different from any I had seen in China.

"Where in the world did you get that, Shag?" Lois teased.

"From Chou En-lai," he replied seriously. "When I saw him the day before we left Peking, he asked me what I was going to wear in Europe. I had on my nice old padded jacket and I told him that that was what I was going to wear. 'You are not!' said the Premier. 'You'll disgrace us all in that.' He called a tailor and I had this the next morning."

George turned around for inspection. A black beret perched on his head added French zest to the general effect.

But George had little time for play. According to Lois:

> Shag hardly ever left the house; he was the last to go to bed, the first of us up in the morning. In his easy way he was available to everyone, yet always ready in a corner of the room whenever Ed wanted to talk, to turn, to get out of bed.... He was constant and so was his strength and wit. It was clear what a perfect companion he had made in those far-ago days when he had gone with Ed in search of the "Red bandits" in China's forbidding northwest.

Word spread that George Hatem had come with the Chinese doctors. He would have been deluged by callers if he had responded to all of the telephoned messages. He answered a few from old friends of Geneva days and finally, after special pleading, he agreed to talk at a special meeting with the medical personnel of the local hospital.

That month in Eysins was heart-wrenching for George. Though Ed was older than he, George loved him like a father loves a son, and Ed looked up to him with almost a filial admiration. In those final few weeks the bond between them was all the more poignant because both knew this was the end. But they carefully avoided mentioning the implacable menace waiting grimly in the shadows of the room. They talked about everything else—their past adventures together, the Cultural Revolution, U.S.—China relations, the state of the world.... George watched in silent misery as Ed's voice faded and his brilliant mind grew dim. He was with Ed when he died on February 14, 1972, just as Nixon was preparing to visit China.

I arrived in Eysins a few days later. I had been in London,

on my way back to China from my first trip to the States in twenty-five years. The Chinese Charge d'Affaires Office told me of Ed's passing and, at my request, quickly got me a Swiss visa so that I could attend the funeral. I helped George prepare the short oration he delivered.

It was a moving ceremony. The Chinese ambassador read condolence messages from Mao Zedong, Zhou Enlai and Madame Soong Ching Ling. Friends from several countries also spoke.

When it was over I agreed with George it would be good to take Lois' mind off things a bit now that the tension had eased. And so we gladly accepted her invitation two weeks later to go with her and her children, Xian and Chris, and her sister Kashin, to a chalet her friend Lee Ambrose had borrowed in the Swiss Alps.

We spent about ten days high amid magnificent mountains covered with snow. It was rugged country, but the accomodations weren't exactly austere. Our two-level house, beneath its cuckoo clock trim, was steam heated by an oil burner furnace and had piping hot water all day long. In the nearby "center" shops sold all the blessings of civilization at prices to suit the altitude. The kids skied every day, while we older folks went staggering through the drifts or rode to the tops of impossible peaks in cable cars. Everyone was glad to collapse before the fireplace in the evening and muse on world affairs.

In Geneva we had watched on TV Mr. Nixon's almost silent entry into Beijing on February 21. The visit and its significance was the main topic of conversation. There was a division of opinion as to where this move was leading. Lois was afraid that receiving Nixon in the Chinese capital would improve his chances of re-election and hurt the anti-war forces in the West.

"Keep your shirt on," George advised. "There's more than one way to skin a cat."

He went on to explain that the Chinese attitude, as he saw it, was this: In Asia the underlying long-term contradiction was between the drive toward socialism—as represented by the socialist countries and the people's movements there—and the attempts of the imperialists to maintain and extend their hold. But there was also an acute global contradiction between the two major imperialist powers—America and the Soviet Union, the last having earned the label by its foreign military and economic incursions. A dialogue was possible between China and the U.S. because people's war had made the American position in Asia untenable, and it was the Americans who had to make the concessions.

These, said George, were mainly an acceptance of the inevitable. The U.S. military had to get out of Vietnam, Laos and Cambodia as rapidly and with as much grace as they could muster. This had first priority. Taiwan and the Chiang Kai-shek crowd had gradually to be abandoned. No further impediments should be placed in the way of trade and diplomatic relations between China and Japan. Sato and his *bushido* warriors had to go.

The months which followed saw China continuing adamant in her support of the three small Indo-Chinese countries. American planes were no longer able to attack from the convenient proximity of Taiwan. Korean troops began withdrawing from Vietnam. The fall of Sato and his war gang sparked large public demonstrations in Japan against the manufacture of arms for the U.S. forces in Indo-China and interference with their shipment. The new Japanese government placed restrictions on American use of bases and port facilities.

Japan established diplomatic relations with China. Australia and New Zealand elected labor governments which did the same. Since calm fruitful discussions were obviously possible with Beijing, America's main theoretical prop for the invasion of Southeast Asia—"the need to contain China"—was knocked out from under.

All this followed Nixon's Beijing visit, and was of considerable encouragement to the anti-Vietnam-war forces the world over. It could hardly have helped Nixon's chances in any future election campaign, since his trip to China was recognized as an admission of failure of U.S. Far Eastern policy under his leadership. Moreover, the American people were judging him on how quickly he ended the war in Vietnam, and this he showed no signs of doing, merely switching from ground attacks to massive bombings.

Most of these events had not yet transpired when we American armchair strategists were batting around the possible effects of the Beijing meeting in our Swiss chalet. Arguments waxed hot and heavy, neither side able to convince the other.

Lois was in fairly good spirits. She was talking about going to New York later in the year to put the finishing touches on a book Ed had been writing and getting out one of her own

—on the Chinese theatre. George and Kashin and the kids were staying on for a while, but I had to get back. I was already several weeks over my planned leave. George returned to China in March, laden with Swiss chocolates and a shower attachment for the antiquated plumbing of his Beijing bathtub. Brother Joe, who had arrived after the funeral from his home in Roanoke Rapids, North Carolina, bought the contraption for him.

Thereafter, George travelled more frequently to foreign lands. In 1974 he was able to visit his relatives in Lebanon at the invitation of President Frangie. Sufei went with him. They also met Amine Gemayel in southern Lebanon.

In 1978 he and Sufei flew to the U.S., his first trip home in fifty years. It would also, George believed, be his last. They had come to my place two years before for a roast duck dinner prepared in our Dutch oven. On the twenty minute walk back to the house on Rear Lake, George vomited. He and Sufei assumed it was from overeating. When the condition persisted, George went to the hospital for a check. Nothing serious was found wrong with his digestive system, but he did have an enlarged prostate. Surgery in March 1976 successfully removed the distended portion, which proved to be non-cancerous.

He was rushed to the hospital again in October 1977, with a severe bout of jaundice. An exploratory operation revealed that a large lump in the head of the pancreas was blocking the flow of bile from the gall bladder, thereby causing the jaundice. A smear test for cytology study from a needle probed into the pancreas suggested possible cancer of that organ. It was already too late to operate. George was put under intensive irradiation to delay the inevitably fatal progress of the disease. As a doctor, he believed he had six months to a year to live. He spent many months in the hospital.

Early in 1978 George was made a member of the Chinese People's Political Consulatative Council—an extremely high honor, and joined in a grand reunion in Beijing of the old Dixie Mission. These were happy occasions, but his health was clearly failing. George decided in April 1978 it was "now or never", and took off with Sufei for the States. The Chinese government provided $20,000 for fares and expenses. They said to come right back if he got worse.

Brother Joe and a few other relatives and friends were

waiting at Dulles Airport in Washington with a wheelchair. To their surprise George, though forty pounds thinner than when Joe had seen him in Geneva in 1972, walked firmly and was mentally alert. He and Sufei flew down with Joe in a private plane to Roanoke Rapids, North Carolina, where Joe and sister Shafia lived with their families. They spent a pleasant few weeks together, and met a number of George's old Chapel Hill classmates.

They also went to Greenville for a "fiftieth reunion" of his high school graduation class. It was held a second time especially for him because he had not been able to attend the gathering in 1977, which was the actual date of the 50th anniversary. Most of his old schoolmates it seemed to George were living a circumscribed kind of life, with their interests focused on local matters, religion and hometown politics. Though some were lawyers none had become doctors. Only one, who had climbed high in the tobacco industry, was considered a real "success".

After a few days' stop-over in Washington, where they were hosted by officials and medical authorities in and out of government, George and Sufei went on to New York City. They were the guests of Dr. Sam Rosen and his wife Helen, whom they had met during the Rosens' first visit to China in 1971. Sam was a famous ear surgeon who had invented the stapes operation. He learned ear acupuncture in Beijing as a treatment for deafness, and experimented with it on a group of afflicted children at Mount Sinai Hospital in New York City. Because he had reported an almost complete lack of success, he had been attacked by other American doctor "friends" of China. George admired Sam and respected him for his honesty.

In New York City he had a joyous reunion with Rob Levinson, his medical school classmate, and one of the two colleagues he had opened a clinic with in Shanghai when he first arrived in China. Rob was married to Doris Weston, a prominent designer of women's clothes. She and Sufei hit if off immediately, and the two old friends reminisced.

From there George proceeded with Sufei to Buffalo, where they met cousin Theresa and more family, then on to Cape Cod and the summer cottage of Manny Granich, who had encouraged George to explore Marxism in Shanghai in the thirties. Among Manny's guests were TV personalities Walter Cronkite and Barbara Walters. George fascinated them, and their stimulating arguments seemed to improve his appetite. For a dying man he put away a healthy number of hot dogs.

In San Francisco, the next stop, George spoke at the national convention of the US-China People's Friendship Association. Americans still bemused by the Cultural Revolution, and other "super-Left" afficionados, gave him a hard time, denouncing the Chinese as having abandoned Marxism and gone "revisionist". George agreed with the majority of the Friendship Association membership, who felt that China was right to break away from its former doctrinaire approach.

Next, George and Sufei went to Tucson, Arizona. They stayed with Dr. Herbert Abrams and his wife Sophie. While serving as a doctor in WHO after the Japanese surrender in the forties, Herb had delivered UN medical supplies to Chinese guerillas in Shandong.

George's health was miraculously improving. He had put on weight by the time he and Sufei arrived in Kansas City, Missouri, as the guests of Dr. and Mrs. Grey Dimond. Edgar Snow had been born and raised in Kansas City, and the University of Missouri Library housed the Edgar Snow Memorial Collection. It included the famous picture of Mao, at forty-two, wearing the hat Ed had loaned him. Dimond, who had known Snow, had been to China several times, endeavoring to increase the flow of medical information and personnel between China and America. His book *Inside China Today*; *A Western View* (Norton & Co., New York), setting forth his recollection of conversations with George plus his own personal interpretations, is interesting, if slightly contrived.

When George returned to Beijing from his "farewell journey", he made some notes for his private records. Apparently, from the conversational tone and careless grammar, they are a transcription of a tape of a talk he gave in the States:

> People there kept asking me whether I was experiencing any culture shock, (George wrote.) No, I told them, though I feel a bit stupid saying so, since everyone obviously expects the opposite answer. I said in Beijing I used to listen to the Voice of America shortwave broadcasts. Some of the things they thought up during the time of John Foster Dulles and his like were really comic—mostly hate-China propaganda —but they did provide a lot of information. Besides, I knew the basics of American society from before, and later came to understand them in a Marxist way. I also read U.S.

newspapers and magazines, and had some personal contacts with American visitors. What I hadn't previously seen I knew enough about not to be surprised, or shocked.

But George was both surprised and shocked in his own field, medicine.

Some things struck me pretty hard, (he said to the American doctors.) On the surface it sounds reasonable that it's better to use a plastic syringe and throw it away than hire a nurse to spend time sterilizing a re-usable one. You people measure everything by cost, and labor is more expensive than a little waste of material. U.S. medical services are very well developed—you have local peaks of achievement. Provided a person has the money, he or she can get what's probably the best treatment in the world.

But your medical services really have no way of delivering preventive medicine. This is what shocked me most. We in China are used to saying, "Prevention first". We do mass surveys, test entire populations, for this and that. In cancer prevention, for instance, we check for early signs of breast, cervical and esophageal cancer. But in America, where the doctor works for fees, he can't go to a patient and say: "I'm going to observe you for ten years to prevent breast cancer, so pay me 3,000 dollars". Yet preventive medicine means, first of all, the distribution of prevention.

Sure, there is a public health service, and a health office in every county. You put up posters and give away pamphlets explaining, let's say, that smoking is bad for you, and what you should watch out for, and the nutrition in foods. But that's only a small part of the job—there's nobody to actually carry out the prevention. Yet the amount America spends on prevention is tremendous. If China had only the tail end of it we could run our medical services affluently.

This, George alleged, underscored for him the key role of the social system in medicine. As he told his American counterparts:

Even with all that money and all those resources you still may not be providing what's most needed. A capitalist country also needs to provide some health for the workers, because if they were all sick who would work for you? So sewage disposal, clean water and the like are ensured, more or less. But the elimination and prevention of diseases de-

pends most of all on the social system. Only the integration
of natural science and social science gets results. That ex-
plains why we in China could eradicate venereal diseases,
but the U.S. still can't. You have many more doctors, much
more knowledge and research, and for VD a patient can get
treated free of charge. Yet VD is still around. Why? The
answer, I think, is a good concrete example of the advantages of socialism.

Today, one is impelled to ask whether the renewed spread of
venereal disease in China contradicts the efficacy of socialism,
or is it that Chinese socialism has changed?

But socialism, as George understood it in 1978, did indeed
seem to him to be the answer to national medical problems. He
continued in the same vein, citing by way of example the
differences between China and India in their methods of
coping with leprosy:

India has world-renowned scientists in the field, good
research, backed with funds and equipment and a network
for free treatment (he said to his American doctor audience.) But their leprosy rate doesn't seem to go down. We
talked this question over with our Indian colleagues. The
answer is simple, it's in the social condition of the leprosy
victim. He can't afford even one bar of soap a year, so
where's the hygiene? He can't find a doctor, perhaps for
many years. He can't read and write, so education doesn't
get to him. He has no living space—a lot of such people sleep
literally crowded on top of each other, in three shifts. Many
of them have only 1200 calories a day in food. We in China
have an average of 2500 to 3000. Food, shelter, clothing,
education, hygiene are very important.

If your leprosy patient lacks all these things, and has in
addition malaria, worms, anemia, and so on, no matter how
good an anti-leprosy drug you give, it doesn't help much. He
has very low resistance, he catches any infection that's
around. That's why we say leprosy is a poverty disease, a
social disease.

In China we have 5.5 square meters of living space, on
the average, for each person, 65-70 percent literacy, between
two and three thousand calories a day, the means to buy
soap, enough clothing, some ideas of hygiene—plus medical
services for all diseases. Our anti-leprosy campaigns and
treatments are much more effective because we're dealing

with a healthy population.

So the problems of both VD and leprosy, two fields I am familiar with, show the extreme importance of the social system.

Functional literacy in China was probably only around thirty percent in the late seventies, when George was speaking. But there is no reason to doubt his medical and health statistics.

In an interview George gave to John Gittings of the British *Guardian*, for the science page of a special issue concerning Third World countries, Gittings asked him, "What lessons has China for the Third World?"

China's main lesson is that a country with a billion people can provide health and medical service for this vast number by working together with the population, (George replied.) Although our medical facilities are still only moderate, we get results through such means as co-operative medicine and paramedics—we call them "Barefoot Doctors". China has proved that with proper social organization you don't have to wait till you are affluent before you can provide health for your people, regardless of how large your population may be.

Even before such things as clean running water and a sewage system are generally available, a Third World country like China can control food quality, flies and feces, dig better wells, compost its manure for safe fertilizer—in other words, create hygiene. If you gain the support of the people, they will help you. You don't have to wait till you have a lot of money. Of course, it's better to have the money than not. But things can be done with surprisingly little if you have the will, a government that works for the health of the people, along with the efficiency a better social system brings.

George complained to Gittings that some of his Chinese medical colleagues are dazzled by what they see when they go abroad:

They get fascinated by the tremendous medical centers in California or New York, and start thinking in those terms rather than those of our own conditions and tasks, he said. If they only thought a bit more, they'd realize that if Beijing had a big medical center like the one, say, in Duke Univer-

sity in North Carolina, the amount of electricity it would
have to use per year would be roughly enough to supply a
whole municipal district for all purposes. Rich countries can
do many things artificially. In China we have to rely heavily
on acupuncture and other traditional remedies, get warmth
and light from the sun by building houses with southern
exposures, and so on.

Well, our medical people go abroad, visit a hospital, see
the luxurious private bedrooms with TV, telephone and
whatnot and forget that's why the charges are $200 a day. Is
that a lesson for the Third World? No, the lesson is that even
without affluence the people's health can be largely provided for—if you have the right organization of a people's
society. It was the contrast I saw in America in my own
field, medicine, that taught me the advantages of our system
in China.

In short, I wasn't awestruck by America's present day
wealth. If there was "culture shock" it was at how poor the
medical service there is, in spite of all the money that's spent
on it.

George addressed a meeting of Chinese health and medical
personnel on returning from his 1978 visit to the States. He
said that doctors abroad are very interested in the preventive
medical care and in the combination of traditional Chinese and
modern Western medicine.

I told the American doctors that China's experience with
acupuncture anesthesia and the treatment of burns and
abdominal emergencies is of general significance. And that
we have eradicated some once common diseases. When we
came to Beijing in 1949, cardiovascular diseases were the
tenth most frequent cause of death, and cancer was the
eleventh. Now they are first and second on the list—because
we've got rid of most of the ones that used to be ahead of
them.

Everyone realizes by now that China has a fairly well
developed public health system. When we say we'll wipe out
leprosy, we're believed—we have a scientific reputation.
Some people don't understand that you can be behind in
some fields of science, but that if a country can actually
eradicate VD it's well up in front and not backward at all
in the general sense, for how many countries have managed
that?

What is scientific level? If you know about the spirochete only through an electronic microscope and can count its every hair, but you can't wipe out syphilis, your scientific level isn't all that great. So in some cases we can be justly proud of what we've done—it can't be belittled.

At the same time George was very conscious of the failings in China's medical and health work. "We must develop along lines suitable to China," he said. "We can't just copy from abroad, though some people here and there find that hard to understand."

Modernization can be of two kinds. For instance, we shouldn't blindly copy the Western type medical center. It's not suitable for us, it needs a basis we lack. Medical work in China should keep prevention as its guiding idea, and have schools to develop and train people for it hand in hand with curative medicine. Recently we had a meeting to establish a Chinese-style preventive medical center—by combining older institutes into a single organization for research and training in the prevention of various diseases. This is China's road. In a socialist country if you give knowledge about hygiene to the people and they act upon it, they become immune to many ailments.

In the old Red Army days we used to tell every fighter, "Boil water, never drink it unboiled." Once we put that across we got collective immunity to diarrheal diseases. This, in simple form, is socialist epidemiology as developed here. Now after several decades, our experience must be raised to the theoretical level—in both epidemiology and preventive medicine. They're different from their counterparts in capitalist countries.

George believed that China and the West should learn from each other in medicine and hygiene. China would surely gain a great deal, he said. But he thought it unlikely the West would be able to utilize much of the Chinese experience.

He explained:

In their social system they can't call a meeting of a residents' street committee and say, "Get all the men together in one group and the women in another to discuss eradication of VD, and ask everyone: Have you these symptoms or have you noticed them in others—if so come in for an examination...." We've held many such meetings in

China, mobilized such people, obtained their cooperation. But can you imagine a block of apartment houses in America where you could get anyone with symptoms to sign up on the board? Theirs is a highly individualist society. We can work the way we do here because ours is a different, cooperative type.

While in Buffalo George had his cytology smear, obtained from pancreas needle aspiration during his abdominal operation the previous year, analysed again at the Roswell Park Memorial Institute, famed division of the Department of Health of the State of New York. Although the result also indicated the possible presence of cancer, its location could not be pin-pointed. Roswell said that George was otherwise in good health.

Encouraged by this report, and a feeling of general well-being, he went with Sufei on a tour of England and France, with Switzerland as a last stop. They spent ten days with Lois Snow in the converted farmhouse in Eysins, another ten days in the Chinese Consulate in Geneva, then back to Lois for a final ten days. The big old house was draughty and poorly heated, and George caught cold. They decided it was time to return to China.

When Dr. Wu Weiran, famous abdominal surgeon, had examined George in Beijing at the end of 1978, he found his health favorable on the whole. Under the circumstances, Dr. Wu tended to doubt cancer, and was cautiously optimistic.

Then suddenly in the spring of 1979 George was gripped by intense stomach pains, and bleeding from the mouth and rectum. He was taken to the Beijing Hospital, where Dr. Wu was Chief Surgeon. The majority of the team of doctors in attendance now believed that George was in the last stages of an inoperable pancreatic cancer. Sufei refused to accept this. She said in the U.S. George had been devouring steaks with a gusto no terminal cancer sufferer could have mustered.

An argument arose on whether or not to operate. Some said, "He's going to die anyway. Why torment him?" The dissenting opinion—held by Sufei, Wu Weiran, and friend and doctor Hans Muller—was, "He'll surely die from the internal bleeding if we don't operate. Suppose it isn't cancer? Even if there's only one chance in a hundred, we've got to take it."

The next morning the whole family gathered at George's bedside. They asked him to decide. "Operate," said George. If he died, there should be no autopsy, no memorial meeting, just a simple funeral. He urged the children to carry on and work hard for China.

Immediately after, the operation began. The doctors had been up all night, consulting and preparing. Dr. Wu performed the surgery. Hans Muller remained present in the operating room throughout the entire procedure. It lasted nine hours. They phoned down to Sufei periodically, reporting on how it was progressing.

Finally came the long awaited call from Wu Weiran. The bleeding had come from a large duodenal ulcer near the pancreas, caused by the heavy irradiation George had been receiving. There were some gallstones, which were removed together with the gall bladder. The ulcer and part of the stomach and intestine were cut away. The formerly swollen head of the pancreas had actually shrunk. From this Wu concluded that the pancreas had only been inflamed, not distended by malignancy.

Everyone was overjoyed. George had been granted a new lease on life. Although his recovery was long and at times "stormy", as Dr. Wu put it, he did gradually recover. Because of the large size of the incision George had to wear an abdominal corset, but otherwise he could function normally. In fact he regained his strength and spirits to such an extent that he was able to lead a Chinese delegation to Canada in November of the same year, 1979, to attend a memorial meeting in honor of Dr. Norman Bethune. Sufei went with him. They took the opportunity to again visit family in the States.

LAST BATTLE

During his 1979 visit to the States, George launched his global drive for funds to fight leprosy in China.

He had started tackling the disease in the early sixties. The Chinese had made such huge inroads against venereal disease that they decided to switch to leprosy as the main dermatology target. For nearly three decades George Hatem played a leading role in the campaign.

Warm-hearted, emotional George reacted sensitively to the suffering of his patients. He felt a special sympathy for leprosy victims.

"People with leprosy are doubly unfortunate because society looks down on them," he said. "It's very unfair."

The age-old fear of the scourge, the shocking appearance of the lepers, aroused in otherwise humane individuals acts of savage cruelty. Persons who had leprosy, or even those believed to be afflicted with it, were driven from their villages. Their entire families, although usually free of the disease, were expelled with them. Their homes and possessions were burned. If they were lucky, they were permitted to eke out an existence on some high mountain top, or in a remote wilderness. It they were not so lucky, and panic gripped the community, they might be beaten or burned to death, drowned, buried alive.... In the few areas where health and medical units made attempts at treatment, the victims were congregated together and isolated from the rest of the population.

George's research and observations provided facts at variance with popular belief: Leprosy is only mildly infectious —much less so than tuberculosis, for instance. A person with the disease very rarely infects his or her spouse, although

183

eating, sleeping and living together for years. Medical treatment and cure are neither difficult nor expensive. Even in the late stages leprosy can be arrested, and the ravages repaired by corrective and cosmetic surgery. There is no need to isolate the patients. They can live and work normally among their neighbors without putting anyone at risk.

He concluded that leprosy is preventable and curable, and declared it could be wiped out in China by the year 2,000. Certain conditions, however, had to be met. First came the formidable job of educating the public. And before that could be done, the medical personnel themselves had to be educated. Many of these were as hag-ridden with fears and superstitious beliefs as were the ordinary citizens. Dr. He Daxun, one of China's leprosy specialists today, recalled how George helped him make the transition.

I came in contact with a leprosy patient for the first time in 1960 at a research project we conducted in conjunction with the Baoding Leprosy Hospital on the use of a combination of medicines. Although I was a doctor I was scared stiff of leprosy. At that time the practice was to cover ourselves with protective clothing from head to foot, so that we looked like members of the Ku Klux Klan. It created a hiatus between ourselves and the patients, but that was fine with me.

Ma *Daifu* came by to check on our work. He was very critical of our protective garb. He explained that leprosy is only slightly infectious, that treatment quickly destroys the virulence of the leprosy germs. Wearing only the usual white doctor's coat, he scorned the gauze masks with which we covered our faces up to the eyes, and laughed at our rubber boots and latex gloves. When he conducted an examination he always shook hands with the patient first, creating a warm bond between them. I'm ashamed to say that for a long time we still didn't change our ideas and follow Ma *Daifu's* example.

Apparently it was not only inexperienced doctors who were "scared stiff of leprosy". A young medical school graduate who once had leprosy and was preparing to go abroad for advanced studies came into the Dermatology and Venereology Institute for a check-up. The results confirmed that he was completely cured. He had recently married, and his wife, also a doctor, would be going with him. She too was examined, and pronounced free of the disease.

Nevertheless, the young man was refused permission to leave China. He was assigned to the Ministry of Health, but was instructed not to come to work, and simply stay at home. He received full pay. This went on for several years. It was a closely guarded office "secret".

One day, by chance, George found out about it. He stormed into the office of the Minister of Health. "I want this man as my secretary," George demanded. The minister, who had been unaware of the situation, hastily agreed, and so the matter was settled. But ignorance and fear of leprosy was by no means extinguished among medical people.

George threw himself into battle with his customary vigor. Besides absorbing as much written material as he could find in Chinese and English, as usual he sought practical problems and solutions at the grassroots level. Many doctors worked in the field with Ma *Daifu*, or *Lao* Ma as they more familiarly called him.

Ma *Daifu* never sought any special treatment when he was out in the countryside. He ate the same food as the rest of the medical personnel, travelled the same roads, climbed mountains and rode donkeys with them, sat in the same big wagons. On one trip he was issued a jeep. He let the girls and women use it, while he rode with the men in an open truck.

When they were on the tropical island of Hainan he got so hot he worked stripped down to a pair of shorts. His back was red and peeling after being exposed for hours to the sun.

He stayed with the leprosy teams in all kinds of accomodations—Mongol yurts, dilapidated village inns, abandoned temples.... One night they lay four under a single tattered quilt, with the mosquitoes biting so fiercely none of them could sleep. Ma *Daifu* put on his raincoat, buttoned it up to the neck, tied the openings of his sleeves and the bottoms of his trouser legs, snuggled under his work clothes, and slept.

Sometimes the leprosy teams lived like that for a month. But Ma *Daifu* wouldn't quit, even when he ran a high fever. Once he travelled all day with them on a horse-drawn wagon to reach a clinic in the wilds. It was very cold. When they got there his legs were so frozen he couldn't move. Only after a nurse bathed them in warm water was he able to climb down from the wagon.

Despite the harsh environment George continued to work cheerfully. After hours, he chatted with the medics, joined in the dancing. Or he might ask one of them to help him write a letter home. He would dictate and a medic would put it down. His written Chinese wasn't good enough, and Sufei couldn't read English.

Living and working together in adversity, he and the doctors and nurses became very good friends.

The Cultural Revolution, which began in 1966, brought the anti-leprosy program to a virtual standstill for a period of ten years. George was happy when the overthrow of the Gang of Four in 1976 was followed in 1978 by the Third Session of the Eleventh Chinese Communist Party Congress. The policies formulated at this landmark meeting ushered in a new era of initiative and creativity.

"I feel younger, stronger," George told Dai Zhengqi. "I can't wait to hit leprosy again." Dai was still head of the Institute of Dermatology and Venereology, though planning to retire.

Whenever Dai went to see him George started talking leprosy the moment Dai entered the door. Sometimes George got so warmed up he forgot to eat. Sufei would have to call him several times before he would come to the table, and he would drag Dai along so that he could continue his dissertation.

"Conditions are good for a drive against leprosy," he insisted. "The improved political conditions, the foundations we laid earlier, the demand of the victims for action, the interest aroused in the medical profession—they're all on our side. Of course we still have to persuade the Finance Ministry to give our Institute a substantial allocation for leprosy work in its next budget...."

Not only did the Institute get government approval of everything they asked for, but also an official statement calling for the essential elimination of leprosy by the year 2,000—just what George had proposed.

On hearing the news he excitedly telephoned Dai to come right over. George demanded that he join the campaign. Overwhelmed by George's enthusiasm and stirred by the prospect of expunging this scourge still rampant in many parts of the world, Dai agreed to head the administration of the newly formed Antibiotic Research Division, which would spearhead the Institute's drive against leprosy.

In 1978, at long last, George was named Advisor to the Ministry of Health—not just, as before, Advisor to the Institute of Dermatology and Venereology. Now able to utilize the full machinery and power of the Ministry, he organized extensive research on the nature, causes, treatment and prevention of leprosy, bringing all available medical resources into play. He pushed for earlier diagnoses, tight control on the spread of the disease, prevention of recurrences, and the correction of deformities in patients who had recovered. George was a strong advocate of combining traditional Chinese medical treatments with those of the West. He sent teams out on mass screening drives all over China, with the exception of Taiwan and Tibet. A few of them he led personally, ranging as far as the Burmese border at the southernmost edge of Yunnan province.

George contended that the leprosy colonies and villages favored by the West in the 19th century were no longer suitable for China. He proposed four basic principles: social prevention and treatment instead of hospital isolation; the combination of several kinds of medicine instead of a single medicine; equal emphasis on treatment and rehabilitation; and mobilization of the whole society for the effort instead of only the professionals.

These principles were adopted and greatly accelerated China's conquest of leprosy. Since the establishment of the People's Republic in 1949, half a million cases were diagnosed and over eighty percent cured. Occurrence and recurrence rates steadily declined. Many cities and counties either basically eliminated the disease or had it under control.

This is what George was able to tell medical people on his trips abroad. He provided them with detailed reports and analyses, coupled with a plea for financial and technical support. He remained in Beijing during 1980, but from 1981 on he travelled to many different countries every year, answering questions about China, about himself, but talking always of leprosy, and the real possibility of defeating it the world over, given global understanding and cooperation.

He attended the International Leprosy Congress in Australia, with Sufei, in 1981. They made friends with a kangaroo on a family farm in Brisbane and visited a leprosy hospital in Darwin before going on to New Zealand at the invitation of the New Zealand-China Friendship Association. They met and drank and dined with friends and relatives of native son Rewi Alley, who hadn't felt up to making the long journey to his old birthplace. In both countries George participated in conferences and lectured on leprosy.

Later that year he convened in Beijing China's first International Conference on the Exchange of Leprosy Technology.

Many foreign specialists took part. They provided broad international contacts which subsequently helped obtain foreign assistance for China's anti-leprosy drive.

In 1982 he led a Chinese leprosy delegation on a world tour, and won pledges of financial and technical aid. While in America he attended the fiftieth reunion of his North Carolina University graduating class. He persisted in swimming at Beidaihe that summer although his movements were hampered by a large ventral hernia.

Dr. Wu Weiran repaired this in October, inserting a Marlex Mesh webbing to bolster the weakened abdominal wall. Two months later, at the end of December, a chest x-ray taken as part of a routine physical examination revealed a small dense shadow on the left lung. A CT scan of the pelvic region showed an enlargement of the residual prostate gland. The lung lesion was excised in January 1983. Cellular study suggested that it was a metastatic cancer. A biopsy of the prostate confirmed this. Two weeks later a castration operation was performed. (Cutting the male hormone flow from the testes causes a subsiding of the prostate cancer.) George's reaction was characteristic.

"I've always wanted to sing soprano," he said.

The surgical procedure apparently was successful. I went to see him in the hospital as soon as he was able to receive visitors.

"All I want is another three years," George told me. "By then we can be sure of a firm foundation to destroy leprosy." As it turned out he was granted not just three more years of life, but five.

The conclusion reached at the Duke University Medical Center in Durham, North Carolina, after examination in May 1983, was that "...he is seemingly asymptomatic and responding well to conservative therapy." A diagnosis at the Roswell Park Memorial Institute in Buffalo, New York, in October 1983, found "...no evidence of prostatic cancer metastasis." A check at Roswell in August 1985, concluded, "Dr. Ma Haide seems to be doing extremely well and at present has no evidence of active prostatic cancer." A further check , also at Roswell in May 1986, brought the good news, "Dr. Hatem's present condition appears to be quite excellent."

Heartened by these periodic reports, George resumed travelling around China and the world with his old verve only slightly diminished. People formerly considerate of his uncertain health, no longer hesitated to make demands on his ever-generous assistance, or to engage him in a wide range of activities. In that respect the foreigners were bad enough, but Chinese friends were even worse. While Westerners are accustomed to writing or telephoning for appointments, most Chinese simply drop in, unheralded and unannounced. George, who could flare up over sloppy work or unprincipled behaviour, invariably received such callers with patient courtesy.

I confided to him that I was worried by the changes becoming evident in Mao. No longer was he exercising his earthy sense of humor to put across political points. In the fifties when voicing opposition to the wide-spread executions taking place during the drive against "counter-revolutionaries" Mao had quipped "People's heads aren't like scallions. They won't grow back if you lop them off." But in 1975 he seemed to be befuddled and losing control.

Mao had always been against killing his opponents. He preferred winning them over. A few who had been active enemies were enrolled in the Chinese People's Political Consultative Council, formed when the PRC was established in 1949. The Council consisted mainly of members of other political parties, various associations and organizations, and outstanding persons in every field of endeavor. It acted as an interim legislature. Its main task was to create a government organization and a Congress.

Once this was done the Council assumed its permanent function of watchdog and friendly gadfly. In addition to criticising legislation and policy, it can also propose amendments and alternatives. Its members, chosen by their colleagues, are usually tops in their particular sphere, and serve as a bridge between their own grassroots and the government. Although more or less of a rubber stamp for a time, in recent years the Council has played an increasingly important role in encouraging support from China's professionals.

George was the only foreign-born member until 1983, when it was decided to accept about a dozen other foreigners who had become Chinese citizens. I was one of them. Although our working sessions were in different committees, George being in "Medical" and I in "News and Publications", our membership in the Council and going off on periodic separate fact-finding junkets gave us more to discuss, and argue about, concerning China and the world. In the eighties I was starting to express more scepticism and worry, but George continued to maintain that ultimately all would be well in China.

I saw a great deal of George in the ensuing years. We had talked in hospital rooms before and after operations, when I brought him books and magazines and jazz cassettes. But I was always careful not to tire him, not to stay too long. Now that George seemed well again, we were able to chat frequently. We both went with our families to Beidaihe every summer, and for a few weeks each winter George would accompany Rewi Alley to *Lu Hui Tou*, a beach resort on Hainan Island, where Fengzi and I also vacationed. There we were able to talk with few interruptions.

George had been helpful when I was writing *An American In China* (NAL, New York, 1980). I had attempted to cover all major events between 1947 and 1979, and George knew an enormous amount about them. While he didn't know as much about the theme of my next effort—a history of the Chinese Jews, he was very supportive. George had a special affinity with Jews. He cared nothing about a person's race or religion. But, for whatever reason, his most intimate classmates and medical colleagues, as well as many friends who shared his political views, happened to be Jewish.

His family were Maronite Catholics, one of the largest religious sects in Buffalo. George attended church regularly as a child, and served for a time as altar boy. In "Father Baker's" reform school, according to his cousin Theresa, "...he learned to do what he was told...." She didn't know whether it was a resentment against the Maronite "discipline" or his own reasoning which turned him away from religion. In any event, by the time he was a young man he stopped going to church and became an agnostic. She recalled a friend asking him whether he believed in life after death, and George's reply: "There is no scientific proof."

But Theresa didn't give him up for lost. She came to China to visit him in the summer of 1973. He and Sufei and Fengzi and I were having dinner with her in Beidaihe, and I told them about a chance meeting I had in the park one Sunday with a pastor who was the head of the Baptist Church with the largest Black congregation in the state of Georgia. The cleric said he was amazed to find that the teachings of Mao Zedong were the same as those of Jesus Christ—except that "Mao doesn't believe in life after death."

George laughed. "There are a couple of hundred million of

us here in China who agree with those teachings. We feel it's our duty to love and cherish our fellow man."

"Why, George," said Theresa in pleased surprise, "you're a real Christian!"

George encouraged me to write a history of Jews in China, as seen by Chinese scholars, because he believed such a book, aside from displaying the quality of Chinese academic research, would testify to China's traditional freedom from racial and religious prejudice, a part of the heritage which Mao's concepts continued.

I must admit that my original motivation in starting the project was not so lofty. George was amused when I told him how it came about. Jewish vistors from the West would frequently seek me out, asking questions about the Jews they heard had settled in China centuries ago. They assumed because anyone named Shapiro was bound to be Jewish, and because by then I had lived in China for nearly forty years, that I knew all about the ancient Chinese Jews. The fact was I knew very little.

Partly out of embarrassment at my ignorance, and partly because I felt I had an obligation as an American-Chinese-Jew to help, I began to dig. I found that although much had been written on the subject by foreigners, virtually nothing of the works by the Chinese themselves had ever been published abroad. It seemed to me this was a gap just crying to be filled. And so, after considerable research and interviewing and running around, the book I was finally able to produce was called *Jews In Old China*; *Studies by Chinese Scholars* (Hippocrene, 1984, New York City), with particular emphasis on the latter half of the title.

It attracted considerable attention, and I basked in its reflected glory. When the Second Asian-Jewish Colloquium was about to be convened in Hong Kong in March 1987, its sponsors asked the Chinese Academy of Social Sciences whether it could recommend a Chinese scholar who could give a talk on the Jews of China. "We have just the man," said the Academy, and suggested me.

Eyebrows rose when I walked into the meeting hall. "You don't look very Chinese," joked one of the participants—all natives of various Asian countries. Which gave me the opportunity to retort with a grin, "And you don't look very Jewish!" The general laughter set us off on a genial footing.

Isi J. Leibler, C.B.E., Vice President of the World Jewish

Congress and Chairman of the Asia Pacific Jewish Association, had convened the conference. It was chaired in turn by Malcolm Fraser who had been Prime Minister of the Commonwealth of Australia, and Sir Zelman Cowen, formerly that country's Governor-General. Some excellent papers were read on the Jewish presence, currently and in earlier history, in the nations of Asia, and prospects of expanded cultural ties were explored.

"Did you find an answer to the question 'What is a Jew?'" George smilingly asked.

"He's a *sibuxiang*," I replied, straight-faced. *Sibuxiang*—literally "four not resembles"—is Chinese slang for the Pere David deer. It has the head of one animal, the ears of another, the hoofs of a third, and the tail of a fourth, but has no entity of its own. And so the term is jestingly applied to things amorphous.

"He can be a citizen of any land, nationalist or pro-Zionist, secular or religious, holder of any of the political creeds or philosophical tenets in the spectrum," I continued. "It's easier to say what he isn't than what he is, and I'm content to leave it at that."

"So am I," George laughed. "Here in China those things don't matter much. All we ask, really, is that a person be decent and law-abiding, and give a little thought to his fellow man once in while."

He was pleased with the results of the colloquium. Always sharply attuned to political implications, he urged me to be more active in the Jewish cultural field. "International relations on a people-to-people basis are very important, sometimes more important than official government relations," he said. "You've become a sort of 'authority' on the history of the Chinese Jews. That will give you opportunities to meet and talk to people involved in Jewish affairs. Appreciating each other's culture can do a lot to preserve world peace."

His prediction proved to be correct. Later in 1987, when I was on a lecture tour of the States, invited to talk about China by the US-China People's Friendship Association, there was almost as much audience interest in the history of the Chinese Jews as there was in the current situation in China. The Sadye Bronfman Centre in Montreal and the Royal Ontario Museum in Toronto—which had a number of relics from the old Kaifeng synagogue, also wanted to hear more about them, and persuaded me to speak in Canada as well.

The Asia-Pacific Jewish Asssociation, a division of the World Jewish Congress, hosted me and Fengzi in Australia in April 1988. Then in March 1989, we were guests of the Jerusalem International Book Fair, where I was happy to see *Jews In Old China* on display in Hebrew. We met Shamir and Peres and several other diplomatic and cultural personages, and initiated a few literary exchanges between Chinese and Israeli publishers. Because we were the first Chinese citizens to travel directly from China with government approval, the media gave our visit a big play. Unfortunately, George was already gone. These developments would surely have pleased him.

George's achievements in the field of leprosy brought him world renowned by 1983. In April he received the Damien-Dutton Award, presented to him by Ambassador Arthur W. Hummel Jr., at a ceremony in the U.S. embassy in Beijing. Ambassador Hummel's father was the late Arthur W. Hummel Sr., distinguished Sinologist and editor of the classic *Eminent Chinese of the Ch'ing Period*. The ambassador and his wife formed a warm liking for George, and he for them. They sometimes invited him and Sufei to small informal dinners. At one of them, which Fengzi and I also attended, Mrs. Hummel gave George a box of brownies she had baked for him herself.

The US-China People's Friendship Association asked him to be the keynote speaker at their 9th annual conference in Los Angeles. He went with Sufei in October 1983, after first calling at the Chinese embassy in Washington and meeting Henry Kissinger and other American notables who were attending China's National Day celebration on October First.

"At our National Day reception," Zhang Wenjin, then Chinese Ambassador to the United States, recalled, "Dr. Ma, a legendary figure to many Americans, became the center of attention. He talked tirelessly about his experiences in China. He also talked frankly about some of our country's problems. His humor aroused frequent laughter. Receptions like this lasted about three hours."

In November 1983, returning to China, he was elevated to membership in the Standing Committee of the Chinese People's Political Consultative Council. That same month he received a citation from the People's Republic of China, the Ministry of Public Health, the Chinese Association of Friendship with Foreign Countries, the Soong Ching Ling Memorial

Foundation, and the State Council's Foreign Experts Bureau, jointly, for fifty years of meritorious medical service. It was presented at a banquet held in his honor in the Great Hall of the People. China's highest leaders and several old comrades attended.

Deng Yingchao, friend from the Yanan days and widow of Zhou Enlai, and Deng Xiaoping, another old friend and leader of the Chinese Communist Party, both spoke and paid George glowing tribute.

"*Wushi nian. Bu rongyi.* Fifty years. Not easy," said Deng Xiaoping, meaning that George's accomplishments were commendable enough, but to have achieved them over a fifty-year period under what were often extremely difficult circumstances, was truly remarkable.

I made what I firmly insisted was my final appearance on the silver screen in 1984 when I was tapped to play W. H. Donald, Australian advisor to Chiang Kai-shek, in the feature film *The Xian Incident*. The Young Marshal, warlord of Manchuria and Chiang's ally, arrested the Generalissimo in Xian in 1936, to pressure him into taking a stand against the invading Japanese. Chiang's wife, the high-powered Soong Meiling, sent Donald hastily to Xian to mediate between the stubborn Genralissimo and the Young Marshall, who respected Donald because the Australian had been his English tutor when he was a boy.

I asked George what he knew about Donald. "Not much," George confessed. "I was already in Yanan in 1936 when Chiang was captured."

He took me to call on mutual friend, Rewi Alley. The New Zealander had known Donald well in Nanking and was able to give me a thorough briefing. Rewi said that Donald was a typical Down-Underer in his appearance and dress, yet able, in spite of his bluntness, to handle the Generalissimo beautifully.

Unfortunately, the costuming had gone ahead without consulting me, and they decked me out in pinstripe banker's grey. I wasn't able to rectify this until they were about to shoot a party and dance scene in Madame Chiang's Nanking residence. For the foreign guests they had corralled students at Nanking University from a dozen different countries. The visiting father of an Austrian girl came to watch. He was wearing a sports jacket with large checks. In response to my pleas he loaned me the jacket and smilingly joined, in my pinstripe, as one of the extras. A Viennese, he turned out to be the best waltzer on the floor.

In that same sequence Donald is interrupted while dancing with Madame Chiang by Foreign Minister T.V. Soong, who comes rushing in to tell her that the Generalissimo has been arrested in Xian. She announces to her guests that she must leave, and hurries out. A foreign young lady asks me (Donald), in English, what has happened. Most Chinese movie directors shoot and record separately. That is, the actors mouth their lines, and dub their voices in later. Chinese actors had dubbed me, in Chinese, in my two previous films. But in this one the director wanted me to speak English, and do my own dubbing.

Since I had exactly one line in the Nanking party scene and was in a hurry to get back to Beijing, I asked whether I could go immediately after the shooting, and have some English-speaking student dub the line in for me. The director agreed, and I left. Some months later, at the first screening of *The Xian Incident*, which George also attended, we heard me replying to the young lady's query with: "I haven't the faintest ideah," in flawless British upper class enunciation.

But the rest of my dialogue was delivered in my normal speech. As a consequence I was able to tell George I was confident my portayal of Donald would earn me the accolade of the only Australian character in Chinese cinema history with a Brooklyn accent.

George chuckled. What amused him more was something else which occurred during the filming. As Donald, I was sitting in the back of a car with the Young Marshall, after having been picked up by him at the Xian airport. We had to stop for a few minutes in the countryside in our 1930's limousine while the road ahead was cleared of 1980's vehicles. Local farm folk surrounded our car and peered in at the two actors, one in military uniform, the other, hatless, in civilian garb. Two old ladies discussed the verisimilitude of their make-up.

One pointed at me with pouted lips and chin. "What about him? Does he look like a foreigner?"

The other old dear looked me over, then shook her head. "Not really."

George roared with laughter. "Never underestimate the power of suggestion," he said. "I've had the same thing, in reverse, happen to me a dozen times. You go into some country village and ask a local granny a simple question in reasonably good Chinese, and she doesn't understand a word. Just stares at you blankly. Her mind flatly rejects the possibility that anything resembling her own language could emerge from beneath such a large foreign nose."

In 1984 George was off and running again. He attended the 12th International Leprosy Congress held in India, and was received by Prime Minister Indira Gandhi. He was in Tokyo in September for the inauguration of the Japanese division of the Soong Ching Ling Foundation. There he visited the State Leprosy Hospital, and examined patients at the National Leprosarium in Okinawa. October found him and Sufei in Manila, where he took part in a Conference of Western Pacific Leprosy Specialists, convened to discuss their experiences in their respective countries in the treatment of the disease using a multi-drug therapy.

He was back in Japan again in 1985, talking about the prevention and treatment of leprosy in China at a committee meeting of the National Leprosy Association. He also had discussions with Ryoichi Sasakawa, the ship-building magnate, and other members of the Sasakawa Memorial Health Foundation. In June he and Dr. Wu Weiran, on the way to Budapest for a peace conference held by the International Physicians for the Prevention of Nuclear War, stopped over in Moscow for three nights. A letter to Rewi Alley dated June 26, 1985, after their arrival in Hungary, reads:

> Three nights in Moscow. Saw all the sights and many changes in 24 years. Stalin now has a statue stele. His company are the ones who followed him—with some exceptions. Khrushchov is in another place.
>
> The city is in its most splendid late spring early summer. Green trees and flowers galore—and clean streets, not crowded (subways take the load), except in the Red Square —foreigners and Russians in equal quantities. We rode trams—Dr. Wu and I—subways and buses, travelled in Benz cars, and on foot.
>
> Now we have ended in the grand old city of Buda and Pest, living in a $45 a day Hilton, Room 404, waiting for the meeting to start. We came two days early! The Embassy received us. Ambassador Ma Li, former Secretary of Zhou Enlai. Very warm and capable.
>
> The rest of the day we—Wu and I—travelled all over Buda and Pest—the castles, the Danube, the ice cream and the horse buggies and churches.
>
> We also did some great tasting of various Hungarian

delicacies. We made two wonderful meals of them in our rooms. Wu Weiran is a great organizer and cook....

Returning to China via the U.S., George was honored by the W.K. Kellogg Foundation for his outstanding international contributions to the field of public health, and was elected to Distinguished Membership in the Lyman A. Brewer III International Surgical Society.

He gave me a list of some of his "spare-time" China activities in 1985. These included Director of the China Leprosy Control and Research Center, Chairman of the China Leprosy Association, President of the China Leprosy Foundation, Council Member of the China Medical Asociation, Council Member of the Soong Ching Ling Memorial Foundation, Honorary Council Member of the China Welfare Fund for the Handicapped, Honorary President of the China Cancer Foundation, Member of the Medical Research Council of the Ministry of Public Health, and Council Member of the China United Nations Association.

"Just to make sure," George said solemnly, "that time doesn't hang heavy on my hands."

He tended to laugh away the public acclaim he received. I asked him how he felt about one of his latest award certificates.

"It's very nice," he said. "With this and twenty-five cents I can get a good cup of coffee anywhere!"

The honors and the attendant media coverage spread his fame still further. He cared little about this. What did make him happy was the fact that he was known and loved by thousands of Chinese people—former patients, their families, friends, veterans of shared hardships and joys, colleagues, neighbors, ordinary folk....

He was tremendously busy. Sometimes, during an October First National Day holiday, he and I, with Sufei and Fengzi, would stroll in the Summer Palace Park, hoping for a chance to chat. But we couldn't walk ten steps without someone hailing "Ma *Daifu*!" and rushing over and grasping his arm and pouring out a stream of reminiscences. Of course he didn't really remember most of them—there were so many. But you could see him swell with pleasure as he responded warmly. To him they were "family", and he wanted nothing more than to give them his all.

1986 was a year of whirlwind tours. But first, in March, the Lebanese Ambassador to China, on behalf of President Amin

Gemayel, decorated him with the Ordre de Cedre-Commander for his medical contributions to China and the world. April found him in San Francisco attending the Annual Conference of American Physicians. During a visit to his birthplace on May 16, the mayor of Buffalo proclaimed that date Ma Haide Day, and named him an Honorary Citizen. In June he went to Belgium and the Federal Republic of Germany and discussed leprosy with the specialists there. Switzerland in November, and visits to Edgar Snow's widow Lois, and Hans Muller's daughter Mimi. Then, on to New York to receive the prestigious Albert Lasker Award for Public Service, the first ever presented to a Chinese citizen. Its citation said, in part:

> Dr. Ma's contributions can be compared in importance to the eradication of yellow fever and the bubonic plague, and, as model for the public health control of venereal diseases, they stand alone.

In New York in November he was interviewed on the TV program *The Open Mind*. The host asked him whether he thought China would be able to cope with AIDS, if it came to China, better than the United States, and if so why.

"AIDS and VD are both intertwined with the country's social fabric, its economic and cultural background," George replied. "That's why we call them social diseases. Our attempts to treat them medically have to be supported by social changes and understanding."

> After Liberation we were able to treat VD successfully because we had public support. Eighty percent of the population lived on the land. They strongly supported the government because the government freed them of high rents and usury and oppression. And so they welcomed us when we went to them and said, "We've been sent by the government to help you." We explained that they were victims of the old society and were not guilty for having VD, that it was imposed on them by the old society. "Now we're building a new society and we can't bring into it the ills of the old," we said. "So why not come in for an examination and get your VD treated, if you have it."

"What about prostitution?" the host queried. "How could you keep the prostitutes from spreading venereal disease?"

> That certainly was a major aspect of the question. Prostitution was a very commercial operation in old China, just

like in many other societies. It had a strong economic base which forced the women into prostitution. Some had been sold to the flesh merchants just to keep them alive. To handle prostitution we had to liberate the women, give them economic independence, educate them, so that they had other means of earning a living.

Women don't usually go into prostitution for purely economic reasons, or for the love of the thing. They're forced into it, one way or another, by social pressures. Each society has its own social, cultural and moral background on which you have to build your program to deal with it, in the United States or in any other country.

In China the government is responsible for the health of its people, and it therefore has to provide all the means necessary to make people healthy. But to do that it has to first solve the people's economic problems and educate them. When a person is poverty stricken and destitute, he can't absorb any education that warns him of dangers. His immediate danger is starving to death.

Once the fundamental economic problem was solved, we launched big educational campaigns. We had tried passing all kinds of laws, and they didn't work. For example, we had insisted that you take a serological examination before marriage. But among 800 million peasants then in the countryside there was no mechanism to give that many serological examinations. There weren't enough medical people to do it. What's more, no laws or rules and regulations can intrude into the bedroom and be effective. So the means we used were mainly economic and educational.

We educated the public on VD by providing them with questionnaires listing a number of clues—symptoms really —to the possibility of having the disease, and talked to them about it at public meetings. It wouldn't be easy to do the same sort of thing in the U.S. It is very difficult in a highly individualistic society to get people to think beyond the all-important "me" and be concerned about their community.

In China we feel we are responsible for all our people, and that by taking care of all the people we also take care of the individual. We don't think there's any contradiction between the rights of the people and the rights of the individual. Every country defines what it considers the rights of the people. If you find a proper mix between individual rights and collective rights you can direct efforts much more effectively for the common good.

"Does America have the proper mix?" asked the host. George thought a moment.

It would be difficult here. Take the question of prevention in medicine. A doctor can't collect a fee from an individual for preventing him from getting cancer of the lung. If I followed a woman for fifteen or twenty years, say, during her risk period of getting breast cancer, giving regular examinations, teaching her how to examine herself, and so forth, I've devoted time, I've devoted effort, I've put in knowledge. If after all that I sent in my bill and said, "Now pay me for having prevented you from getting cancer," she'd probably throw me out the door.

Which means that prevention in medicine can't be done on an individual basis. A private practitioner cannot collect fees for preventive medicine. There isn't a system or network or service in America that provides it. In China, a country with a billion people, you can't possibly treat them all. The only solution is to prevent disease. And that has always assumed a very high priority in our medical planning and strategy. We have a whole network that can apply preventive measures. That's why although the average span of life thirty-seven years ago was only about thirty-five years, today it has been raised to sixty-eight something. That's nearly doubled. For women it is doubled, from thirty-five to seventy.

We believe that economic measures are as important as medical measures in preventing disease. Feeding your people is part of preventive medicine. If they're starving, and are dying of beri-beri or any of the nutritional diseases, the only way to prevent it is to give them something to eat.

Another factor is improving the quality of life—education, a chance to go to school, literacy, understanding of more than just the ordinary things, an aim in life. If you want to accomplish something, if you have the willpower to do things, if you're encouraged, and models are set up to emulate—that helps give you better health and a will to live longer.

"Are you saying China has a better chance to cope with

AIDS than the U.S. has?" the host demanded.

"We'd have a pretty good chance of containing it," George responded. "There's no way of treating AIDS. Primarily, it would be a matter of education. You can't prevent it by law. An important factor in our favor is the ethics and morality of the Chinese people. Traditionally, they haven't been as open-minded about sex. The forms and methods, the exotic aspects, are not as common in our society. Our approach is always education. We believe that if you give knowledge to the people about a disease, you have a better chance of fighting it."

Later in the month, he visited a few leprosariums in Louisiana, and he spoke about his impressions on a television show in New Orleans. His interlocutor also quizzed him on China's foreign policy. He wanted to know whether China considered the Soviet Union a "potential enemy"? George's answer was perhaps different from what his questioner hoped to hear.

The Chinese like to see what's happening around them. For example, the Russians have put one and half million troops on our border and have their missiles aimed at our villages and towns. We don't consider that a friendly gesture. But we don't like to use the word "enemy". We don't like to speak in extreme confrontational terms, because we believe that problems can be solved with more and better understanding. China is following an independent policy. It is not involved in alliances of any sort with any other country. This keeps the world situation more stabilized than if you built alliances with this one against that one, and I think this is funsdamental to our approach.

George seemed to be in reasonably good health in 1987. He joined in the celebration of old friend Rewi Alley's sixty years in China at a banquet held in the Great Hall of the People, went swimming as usual at Beidaihe, toured half a dozen Chinese cities, and met Edward Heath when the former British prime minister visited Beijing. George spent a good deal of time with Rewi, whose rugged constitution was finally giving out as he approached his 90th birthday.

Rewi was distressed by increasing signs of an ethical malaise within the Chinese Communist Party and in society in general. He and I had many talks with George about this. We had been encouraged by the "new look" of the Party in 1978 when, at a meeting of the Central Committee, the intention of attaining national modernization by the end of the century was announced, and stress placed upon the restoration of democracy and legality and the correction of errors committed by the leadership during the Cultural Revolution, and before. Reporters interviewed people, asking their reactions. The straightforward remarks of workers in a Lanzhou plant were carried in the *Renmin Ribao*

"Whenever the economy made a little progress, whenever our living conditions improved a bit," said one man, "we were hit by a new 'movement', and they'd go smash."

Another worker expressed the wish that the impracticalities and the wild boasts of the Big Leap Forward would not be repeated. "No matter what, we mustn't run our Four Modernizations program like 1958. This time we must be strictly objective," he said. Though in favor of modernizing China, he cautioned:

> You can't do it without democracy. In the past we didn't encourage democracy very much and we were always getting into trouble. It's not surprising that people couldn't liberate their thinking. Before each "movement" we were told we could speak frankly. But when we did, we were blasted and labelled. We hope this time we'll have real democracy, not some watered-down version, and that people, no matter what their ideas, will be able to say whatever they please. History proves that when the Party Central Committee listens to the voice of the people it makes fewer mistakes.

In this atmosphere of acceptance of criticism by the leadership and outspokenness by the rank and file, enthusiasm and creativity blossomed. The economy, the arts, science and technology, all were moving. There was more of an opening to the outside world. New ideas were welcomed.

Yet less than ten years later China was suffering a serious moral decline. The press in 1987 carried stories daily of cases of graft and corruption—a few in high places, and very widespread on the lower levels. Some officials took advantage of their positions to obtain anything from sexual favors to substantial material gains. Everyone understood that protocol demanded the presentation of "gifts" when dealing with a bureaucrat. Even in the grocery stores and butcher shops you got better service if you "knew someone", or went through the "back door", as popular parlance had it.

Crime figures had soared. Prostitution was an active profession again, and with it a sharp rise in venereal disease. Arranged matches and under-age marriages were again common. Women and children were being kidnapped and sold. Child labor laws in many places were ignored. A drug trade was developing, gambling was prevalent.

But few persons, including local officals, had any concept of legality. Cases rarely came to trial. You brought your problem or quarrel to the local Party secretary. If a matter actually came before a judge, he could reach completely arbitrary decisions. Should a lawyer dare to voice an objection, he risked being clapped into jail.

Superstitious practices were once more rife. Fortune-tellers, astrologists, witch-doctors, fake medicine sellers, were back in business. Weddings and funerals were elaborate and costly. People went into debt over them lest they "lose face" before their neighbors. It was not unsusual for a prominent person in the rural areas, even a local Communist leader, to build himself an expensive tomb while still hale and hearty.

What had happened to the China which had by Herculean labors hauled itself up from the direst poverty and backwardness to a solid foothold in the modern world, which had earned respect in the family of nations, which had been the inspiration of people everywhere seeking a more humane, a more satisfying way of life? What had happened to the Communist Party which had shaped the means and provided the leadership making these accomplishments possible, whose members had sacrificed and fought and died to bring them about, whose slogan had been "serve the people"?

For the first time, in the privacy of Rewi's parlor, George admitted to being worried. He was clearly shaken by the rapid decline of the Party's prestige. This was not a Cultural Revolution period when renegades like the Gang of Four were in control. Top Party leadership seemed still essentially honest. How could things be in such a mess?

Rewi and I complained about the blind, stubborn refusal to introduce a written language using an alphabet or phonetic symbols, although the complexity of Chinese characters was reducing China to a nation of illiterates. The traditionalists maintained that to abandon the old forms would mean a loss of the centuries of valuable material contained in ancient books. In a flabby compromise aimed at retaining the characters, they had simplified them to such an extent that those who managed to learn them could not read the old texts anyhow.

We maintained that China could train scholars who specialized in reading ancient Chinese, just as other countries did to preserve the knowledge in their own dead languages, but this idea had never been given any consideration.

Another objection to change was based on the differences in pronunciation in various parts of the country. An alphabetized written language, said the hard-liners, would create insurmountable difficulties in spelling. Rewi and I and like-minded Chinese educators had pointed out—in articles, in meetings with Chinese linguists, in letters to the press—that speech differences among people in England, Ireland, Scotland and Wales, for example, had not stopped them from all using the same spelling in the same written language.

Moreover, we doubted the sincerity of those who paid lip service to "eventual" alphabetization, once everyone pronounced the same. In the forty years since the establishment of the People's Republic no real effort had been made to unify speech. Most classes were still being taught in local dialect, and that was what you heard on the average provincial radio and television broadcasts.

The traditionalists were now coming forward with a new argument. They claimed that since computers could be programmed to write Chinese characters, there was no longer any need to change the written language. Rewi and I said that while it was true that computers can speed up such functions as type-setting, and electronic communication in Chinese characters, a person still has to learn hundreds of characters first, and know how to convert them into alphabetical symbols, before he can feed them into a computer. And he has to be able to read the characters when they come in on the receiving end. The computers do nothing to eliminate illiteracy. The problem of learning and retaining masses of arbitrary ideographs still remains.

Rewi and I felt the arguments of the die-hards were not only specious but harmful. For they were preventing hundreds of millions of Chinese from learning to read and write books, newspapers, texts, even simple instruction manuals, and therby depriving the country of the knowledge it desperately needed to progress in the modern world.

As an educator, Rewi was particularly exercised by the whole traditional approach to education in China. Original thought was stifled, lessons were memorized, everything was learned by rote. The highest praise you could give a child was to say that he was "obedient". From nursery school through kindergarten, except when they were writing, kids sat in class with their hands behind their backs, "to keep them out of mischief". Students were graded on their ability to duplicate on test papers what their teachers had said or written on the blackboard. A teacher's salary and status were determined by the number of students he or she could successfully get through entrance exams to higher schools.

"Is it any wonder China has fallen behind little places like Hong Kong, Taiwan, Singapore, and even South Korea!" Rewi snorted.

George in general supported Rewi's plaints and mine, but he cautioned, "Resistance to change, tight controls, are traditional in China. You have to look at the matter historically."

Elaborating, he said, "Back in the forties in a piece called *The Foolish Old Man Who Moved the Mountain* Mao said there were two big mountains crushing the Chinese people—imperialism and feudalism."

Well, we got rid of imperialism. We drove out the Japanese, fought the Americans to a standstill in Korea, helped the Vietnamese beat them on our border down there.

And we broke feudalism's economic back with land reform. The landlords and their imperial government structures oppressed and exploited the Chinese people for two thousand years. We drove out the Kuomintang dictatorship. We took the land away from the landlords and gave it to the people. We tore up the old deeds, we burned the usurious debt contracts. Hundreds of millions of poor people were freed, they stood up. This was the biggest and most successful liberation the world had ever seen. And it was the Chinese Communist Party and government under Mao's leadership that did it.

And that wasn't all they did. From little machine shops they built up a modern industry, they created a new type army, settled age-old problems with the ethnic minority folk, brought cleanliness, health care, women's liberation, public schools.... The list is long. These are things we shouldn't forget when we talk about our failings today.

What went wrong? You mention a lot of bad things —dishonesty, greed, corruption—inside the Communist Party as well as in society in general. It's true, these things exist. How come? What brought about the change?

As I see it, it isn't that things changed, but that certain things—very important things—haven't change enough. We got rid of feudalism economically, that was great. But ideologically, a lot of it is still with us. The way people have been thinking for centuries, their concepts of right and wrong, their customs and habits—these things don't change all that easily.

You must remember that feudal societies are autocratic, not democratic. They're paternalistic, male chauvinist. You're supposed to take orders, respect your superiors, don't make any waves. The Chinese Communist Party, the government, are against this sort of thing. The Party's Charter provides for a mass line, for democratic centralism. Civil rights are guaranteed in the Constitution. Everyone recognizes that backward attitudes and practices are a brake on the development of socialism. Yet they persist, and in some places they seem to be getting worse.

I think the reason is that some Party leaders, and a large part of the membership, plus the majority of the public, never fully shunted off their feudal mentality. Mao bears a major share of the responsibility. His political analyses, the guidelines he laid for applying Marxist theory to the realities of China, are masterly. For the most part, when we followed his advice, the country progressed.

But somewhere along the line—I'm talking about after Liberation—he stopped taking his own advice, and began slipping back into feudal, autocratic ways. No one could disagree with him. When a tried and true old comrade like Peng Dehuai urged him to reconsider the rash Big Leap Forward and the communes, Mao dismissed him from office. Sure, a lot of improvements needed to be made, but Mao tried to bulldoze them through and crush any and all disagreement. His anti-Rightist campaign took the heart out of China's intellectuals. His attacks on the supporters of the Malthusian theory, which warned of the dangers of unlimited population growth, has created a population explosion seriously threatening the development of our economy and culture. The Cultural Revolution, which he supported, smashed existing Party and government structures, wronged thousands of good people, stalled the economy, and threw the whole country into chaos.

We still haven't entirely recovered. There's still a lot of confusion in people's minds. Things are better since Deng started the economic reforms and opening more to the outside world. We've emphasised the separation of Party and state functions. We've had a big improvement in agriculture, an increased use of Western technology and management methods in business and industry, and more foreign trade.

But it's also brought us new problems. Decentralization, for instance. It's a good idea. We've had too much control of production from the top. But the moment the lower levels were allowed to run their own show, they hogged all the local raw materials and wouldn't give anything to the national enterprises—which had been making the quality products and had good export connections abroad. They protect local enterprises making poor quality products, and refuse entry to good quality products from other parts of the country. This is typical of the feudal attitude of looking after your own bailiwick and not giving a damn about national interests.

Opening to the outside has brought in a lot more foreign tourists and businessmen, but also a lot more foreign ideas. We're deluged with Western movies and TV shows pushing sex, the money nexus, fame and fortune, abandoning family responsibilities, the "me" syndrome... all things that go completely against the grain of traditional Chinese values.

The Chinese leadership is very upset about this sort of thing, and puts out reams of articles and editorials against it. Some writers call it "bourgeois liberalization", which to my mind is a misleading translation of what the term really means to the Chinese. To the average English-speaking person it recalls the Renaissance when the young bourgeoisie was a democratic force fighting to break the shackles of feudal reaction. "Bourgeois liberalization" was a good thing then. I prefer Deng Xiaoping's definition—"wholesale Westernization". That is what we really oppose. The bad, the foolish, the indiscriminate, non-selective swallowing down whole anything and everything that comes out of the West, regardless of whether it suits China's needs and present state of development.

Some, particularly young people, are so taken by the glitter of the West they want to adopt even its outward trappings—they say if China has a "bicameral legislature" and "political pluralism" all its problems will be solved. Of course, it doesn't matter whether your legislature has two houses or ten. What counts is how effective, how much power they have. "Pluralism" means discarding the leadership of the Communist Party and letting various other parties, in turn or together, lead the country. But there isn't a single party on the horizon that has even a shadow of the prestige and public support China's Communist Party enjoys, in spite of the mistakes it's made.

Others say socialism has failed in China, that we ought to try capitalism. But though we've had troubles before, and we're having some right now, if you compare our situation today with what it was, say, twenty years ago, or even ten years ago, that argument simply doesn't stand up. We're obviously much better off, we have a much higher standard of living.

So that point is clear. There's no reason to change the form of government at this stage, or abandon the ideological leadership of the Party, or drop socialism and embrace capitalism. Most Chinese, even the most critical, agree on that.

In that case why do we have cries for "wholesale Westernization"? Why are people worried and confused? Why is there more crime? Why are so many bad feudal customs and practices coming back? The reason is because some Party leaders are not sticking to Party principles. They've forgotten the Party's fine traditions. They're not teaching and educating and leading by example. They've drifted away from Marxist, Maoist, socialist thinking and ways of doing things and slipped back into feudal thinking and ways of doing things.

The result is China is being bedevilled by feudalism. Bad working style, insufficient democracy within the Party—to say nothing of among the masses, autocratic attitudes... stem directly from feudal paternalism. Prostitution, sale of women and children, preferring boy babies to girl babies, pornography—what else if not feudal male chauvinism? Clinging to the old forms of writing, education by rote, suppression of student initiative and creativity—all typical feudal Confucianism. The revival of superstition, witchcraft, astrology, expensive weddings and burials.... How in the world can we move on with such poisons coursing through the Chinese body?

Having said all that, let me say I believe we can expel these poisons. The Party made mistakes before—terrible mistakes that brought terrible losses. But it always came back, recognized its mistakes, corrected them, and went on to new achievements. We've got a lot of good people in the Party, and in the Party leadership. Our Communist Party has the will and the determination and the ability to come through. We've done it before, and we'll do it again.

With George this was a fairly solid conviction in 1987. With Rewi Alley and me it was more of an earnest prayer.

Rewi celebrated his 90th birthday on December 2, 1987 at home, and was honored by a steady stream of visiting friends and Chinese and foreign dignitaries. Rewi had a rugged constitution. His only lasting ailment was skin cancer, brought on by long exposure to intense sunlight on the highlands of Gansu where Rewi most of the time wore only a pair of shorts. The affliction plagued him for over thirty years, necessitating one operation after another. They would have worn out a lesser man, but Rewi, although complaining grumpily at times, went on with life as usual.

George tended him constantly through these irritants and through the series of heart attacks he suffered in his final years. He knew as a doctor that Rewi was going, but it still was a heavy blow when Rewi died on Decemnber 27, three weeks after his ninetieth birthday. George was with him at the end.

Rewi was one of his last remaining Western links with the Shanghai-Yanan era. All through the years they had been very close.

Rewi's passsing was a a somber reminder that his own days were numbered. George spoke to me several times of his coming demise, calmly and matter-of-factly.

He threw himself into getting as much done for leprosy as was possible in the time that remained. He went abroad, raised money, collected medicines and medical equipment, and saw to it that each province in China received its proper share.

George travelled to New Delhi in January 1988, where he was presented with the Gandhi International Leprosy Award. By spring he had suffered a visible loss of weight and stamina. Examination revealed only a mild diabetes, not serious enough to have caused this condition. Cancer, though suspected, could not be located. He spent the next few months in and out of the hospital.

In July he was invited to Canada to attend the World Congress of International Conference of Physicians for the Prevention of Nuclear War, accompanied by friend Dr. Wu Weiran. He took this opportunity to have another examination at the Roswell Park Memorial Institute in Buffalo. Several specialists participated. They agreed that something was seriously wrong, but could not find the cause.

Cousins Theresa and Martha drove George and Dr. Wu to Roanoke Rapids, N.C., where they stayed with brother Joe's widow Maria and sister Shafia. George could barely walk, and ate very little. Most of the time he lay on a couch and tried to talk with friends who called.

Sam Underwood, Jr. made a special trip from Greenville to see him. They had been close friends during their Greenville High School days. As Sam later recalled:

Shafik went to Chapel Hill and I went to Duke, and after a couple of years I did not run into him any more. I heard he had gone abroad to complete his education. When I came back to Greenville to practice law in 1937 I attempted to get in touch with him. His relatives told me he had gone to China. Ultimately word came that he had gone on an expedition to the central part of the country and had not been heard from any more.

In the 70's we heard that he was still alive and doing well. I got in touch with his brother Joe in Roanoke Rapids to see whether we could get him to return to this country in 1977 for the fiftieth year reunion dinner of our high school class. Though he could not come that year, we arranged a telephone hook up and talked to him at his home during the dinner. It was early in the morning then in China. He was able to come the next year, in 78, and we had another class reunion dinner especially for him. Through the years since I continued to stay in touch with him, and we visited together in Farmville, Greenville and Roanoke Rapids.

Knowing something of his condition, when I found out that he was going to be in Roanoke Rapids in the summer of 1988 I arranged with his sister to visit him ever so briefly and have one last get-together. I remembered that he was the smartest boy in our class at high school, and finagled permission to take a copy of his grades with me, in a sealed envelope. I told him I guessed they were all A's. Sure enough, most of them were. Shafik laughed, and said he was going to take them back to China to show his grandchildren, and ask them to see whether they could match him!

During high school days he lived here in Greenville. We were in the same Boy Scout troop and were very good friends. Even then he was known and recognized as brilliant....

With Theresa and Martha doing the driving, George and Dr. Wu Weiran went by car to Washington, and then flew to Kansas City, Missouri. They spent two days in the home of doctor friend Grey Dimond. He asked Wu privately whether this wasn't a farewell tour. Wu was non-committal.

Their last stop was San Francisco. Friend Nickie Noyes of China Books put them up. Dr. Charles Grossman, another old friend, flew down from Portland and stayed four days with them. As they were leaving, Charlie said: "See you in Beijing in October."

"Maybe," George replied quietly. "Be sure to see Sufei."

By the time George returned to Beijing he could scarcely eat. He insisted on going to Beidaihe that summer in the vain hope that his favorite beach and the sea air would revive his appetite. Against everyone's urgings he decided to sit in on a conference convened in Beidaihe to discuss the utilization of foreign funds and equipment for the treatment of leprosy.

"I'm going if I have to crawl," he said.

He was no longer able even to drink water when Wu Weiran arrived in early August. Dr. Wu brought him home on the next train. Son You Ma carried him in his arms from the station to the waiting car.

"He was very light," said You Ma. "In half a year he had lost 66 pounds."

A few days later George went into PUMC Hospital. The doctors kept him going on intravenous food and medication. He rallied slightly in September. I visited him two or three times a week, and wrote a letter for him to a medical supply house in Hong Kong for special equipment he requested. He couldn't talk much, but he wanted to hear news of China and the world. Many friends and high officials called. Medical people reported to him on the progress of the anti-leprosy campaign.

"Just two more years and I can lick this leprosy thing," he

said to me weakly.

Leprosy was on his mind to the very last. Burning with fever, he handed Sufei a donation his nephew had mailed from North Carolina. "For the leprosy fund," he whispered "Be sure to give it to the Foundation." He knew his life was ending.

With tears in her eyes, Sufei promised. That afternoon he lapsed into a coma and never came out of it.

He died on October 3, 1988 at the age of seventy-eight. An autopsy revealed tiny cancerous lesions, otherwise impossible to detect, widely proliferated.

In accordance with his wishes only a simple funeral service was held. He lay in state, covered by a hammer and sickle emblazoned red flag and surrounded by wreaths of flowers. Mourners filed by to pay their last respects and to offer condolences to the family. He was cremated at the Revolutionary Martyrs Cemetery, outside Beijing. Burial of the ashes and a large memorial meeting were scheduled for June 1989, to allow time for friends from all over China and many parts of the world to arrive.

George was deeply involved in politics all his life, and even after death they wouldn't let him alone. The events at Tian An Men in June 1989, forced a postponement of the memorial meeting until September. Of the more than sixty people who had promised to come from abroad in June, more than half of whom were prominent members of the medical profession, only about twenty were able to attend in September.

But hundreds of Chinese and foreign friends, colleagues, ex-patients... came from every corner of China. Cables and letters of condolence poured in from abroad. George was extolled in the Chinese and foreign press.

His ashes, in keeping with a bequest he made shortly before he died, were divided into three parts.

One third were buried in Beijing in the Revolutionary Martyrs Cemetery.

One third were buried in his birthplace, Buffalo, New York.

The remaining third Sufei and You Ma scattered on the waters of the Yan River flowing through Yanan, the old revolutionary base Ma Haide, Dr. George Hatem, loved so well.

EPILOGUE

One can only speculate on how Ma Haide would have reacted to two major events which occurred after his death—the "Tian An Men Incident" in 1989 and the abandonment of socialism by the Soviet Union and the countries of Eastern Europe in 1991.

College students began staging a demonstration in May of 1989 in the form of a sit-down on the huge square in front of the "Gate of Heavenly Peace"—the main entrance to the old imperial Forbidden City. The square is flanked on the east by the Museum of History and Revolution, and on the west by the Congress of People's Deputies.

They were protesting against official corruption and inefficiency, and demanding more freedom and democracy. Many of the local residents supported them, adding their own demand for a curb to the rising inflation. No one voiced any attack against either the Communist Party or the socialist system. The demonstration was peaceful at first, almost festive. Whole families turned out on Sundays, carrying children or pushing baby carriages, to offer the students words of encouragement. A workers group from the municipal steel mill also joined the protesters.

The government leaders admitted their faults, and promised to rectify them. They had several formal discussions with student deputies, broadcast live over the national television network. The students camped on the square on and off for about six weeks. All during that time the municipal authorities provided them with food, running water, mobile toilets, pup tents, and daily collected their garbage. Teams of doctors and nurses working in shifts attended their medical needs.

But the students kept upping their demands and refused to return to their classrooms. At last it was determined to move them out. Unarmed troops arrived and were driven back. Then

213

came more troops, carrying weapons. Demonstrators attacked them with stones and clubs, and seized some of the weapons. A few soldiers were killed. One or two of their bodies were mutilated. The troops opened fire. It is still not known who gave the order.

Many people were killed, including innocent bystanders. Original Western estimates of "tens of thousands" were later scaled down to "thousands", and then "hundreds". The average Chinese said there shouldn't have been any casualties at all, that there had been an excessive use of force, that shooting was unnecessary, that the thousands of soldiers could easily have subdued any trouble makers and cleared the square. Public reaction was very angry, coupled with a profound sense of shock that the People's Liberation Army should have been used against the people.

The explanation of the leadership seems to have been that they were frightened by the possibility of a return to the chaos of the Cultural Revolution, that above all China needed peace and stability. There was a crack-down on dissent, and some badly needed intellectuals and specialists fled the country.

Even more horror and indignation were expressed outside China. Most of it was genuine, but analyses were often confused, and occasionally distorted. The media tended to pick up the wrong end of the stick, sorrowing that China failed to conduct its society in accordance with the first ten amendments of the U.S. Constitution, instead of probing into the root causes of China's problems.

Today stability has been maintained, inflation is under control, there is relative prosperity in the rural areas, store shelves are well stocked with consumer goods. But the root causes of China's problems remain and are continuing to cause difficulties.

What would Ma Haide have said about this?

The second event which would have deeply disturbed him was the change in the Soviet Union and in Eastern Europe. Like China, these countries had been advocating economic reform and an opening to the outside world. Yet there was a drop in their economies and a deterioration of their social order. They proclaimed socialism a failure, disbanded their Communist parties, and announced that they were switching over to capitalism.

In China this has given rise to four schools of thought:

1) Admit that socialism has failed and also embrace the

capitalist system.

2) Abandon the present economic reform policy and revert to central control of all aspects of the economy and society.

3) Proceed with the reforms, but more cautiously and at a slower pace, with the main emphasis on the ideological remolding of the top leadership, and expunge noxious bourgeois influences from abroad.

4) Recognize the necessity of enhancing the political sensitivity of government and Communist Party leaders, and implement their political education, as indispensible adjuncts to improving China's social and political climate. But under no circumstances use these, or any other activities, as an excuse to oppose, hinder, or downplay the central goals—economic reforms and opening to the outside world.

Advocates of the fourth approach, which is predominant at this time, say opting for capitalism has severely worsened conditions in Eastern Europe and the Soviet Union. There is no indication that socialism has failed in China. On the contrary, since the reforms and opening to the West were introduced in the late seventies there has been a striking improvement in China's economy. In part this is due to a sharing of control between the central and the local governmental bodies, combining both a market and a planned economy, and learning technological and managerial methods from the West—all within the parameters of a socialist economic system. China has been cautious in her handling of the reforms, and has moved ahead slowly, devoting over ten years to the steps taken so far. As she gains experience she may advance a bit more quickly. China certainly should not halt the reforms and opening to the outside, or slow them down.

Proponents of this concept admit that undesireable influences have indeed crept in from the outside, and that some of the high leaders have shown themselves to be sadly deficient in their understanding of Marxism and in the practical application of political principles. But, they say, these failings can be and are being corrected through education. As the economy and the people's well-being continues to improve over the next few decades, they maintain, even the most skeptical will be convinced that Chinese-style socialism is eminently suitable to China.

This is how the debate stands today. It is just the sort of argument Ma Haide would have loved to take part in. What a pity this is not possible. Perhaps by now the reader can guess what his position would have been?

BIBLIOGRAPHY

Alley, Rewi   *Six Americans in China*, International Culture Publishing Corp., Beijing, 1985

Barrett, David   *Monograph,* University of California Press, Berkely, 1970

Carlson, Evans   *Twin Stars of China,* Dodd, Mead & Co., New York City, 1940

Dimond, E. Grey   *Inside China Today,* W.W. Norton & Co., New York City, 1983

Shapiro, Sidney   *An American in China,* New American Library, New York City, 1980

Snow, Edgar   *Red Star Over China*, Grove Press, New York City, 1973

                      Red China Today—The Other Side of The River, Vintage Books, New York City, 1971

                      The Long Revolution, Random House, New York City, 1972

Snow, Lois   *Death With Dignity,* Random House, New York City, 1974

Su Kaiming   *Modern China—A Topical History,* New World Press, Beijing, 1985